Katherine Anne Porter Remembered

AMERICAN WRITERS REMEMBERED
Jackson R. Bryer, Series Editor

Katherine Anne Porter Remembered

Edited by DARLENE HARBOUR UNRUE

DES PLAINES PUBLIC LIBRARY
1501 ELLINWOOD STREET
DES PLAINES, IL 60016

THE UNIVERSITY OF ALABAMA PRESS
Tuscaloosa

Copyright © 2010
The University of Alabama Press
Tuscaloosa, Alabama 35487-0380
All rights reserved
Manufactured in the United States of America

Typeface: AGaramond

∞

The paper on which this book is printed meets the minimum requirements of American
National Standard for Information Sciences-Permanence of Paper for Printed Library
Materials, ANSI Z39.48-1984.

Library of Congress Cataloging-in-Publication Data

Katherine Anne Porter remembered / edited by Darlene Harbour Unrue.
        p.   cm. — (American writers remembered)
    Includes bibliographical references and index.
    ISBN 978-0-8173-1667-9 (cloth: alk. paper); — ISBN 978-0-8173-8458-6 (electronic)
    1. Porter, Katherine Anne, 1890–1980. 2. Porter, Katherine Anne, 1890–1980—Friends and
associates. 3. Authors, American—20th century—Biography. I. Unrue, Darlene Harbour.
    PS3531.O752Z718 2010
    813'.52—dc22
    [B]
                                                                        2009039638

In memory of John Gregory Unrue (1961–2008)

Contents

Illustrations

Acknowledgments

In the course of preparing this volume of reminiscences, I have become indebted to many persons. First, I would like to thank those who set down their memories of Katherine Anne Porter and allowed them to be included in this collection. I am also grateful to those persons I interviewed between 1981 and 2000 who were willing to contribute their recollections to my biography of Porter. Now, transcriptions of those interviews fill in a significant portion of Porter's portrait. I remain ever grateful to Barbara Thompson Davis and Harrison Paul Porter Jr. for their sustained support of my work on Porter in addition to providing essays for the present work.

I appreciate the careful and judicious reading of the manuscript by Jackson R. Bryer, editor of the American Writers Remembered series, whose suggestions greatly improved the shape and content of the collection; and Beth Alvarez, archivist at the University of Maryland, College Park, who made helpful recommendations that strengthened the accuracy of the collection. The assistance of doctoral student Karen Roop at the University of Nevada, Las Vegas, was also particularly valuable.

Finally, I thank my husband, John Unrue, for continuous wise counsel and unflagging love and support.

Chronology

1890   Callie Russell (Katherine Anne) Porter born 15 May, Indian Creek, Texas, fourth child of Harrison Boone Porter (b. 1857) and Mary Alice Jones Porter (b. 1859). Granddaughter of Asbury Duval Porter (1814–79) and Catharine Ann Skaggs Porter (b. 1827) and John Newton Jones (1833–86) and Caroline Lee Jones (b. 1835). Great-great granddaughter of General Andrew Porter (1743–1813) and James Skaggs, both of whom fought in the Revolutionary War; and Rhoda Boone Smith, a descendant of Jonathan Boone, brother to Daniel. Great-great-great granddaughter of famous Kentucky explorer Henry Skaggs. Harrison and Alice Porter's older children: Anna Gay (b. 1885), Harry Ray (b. 1887), and Johnny (1889–90).

1892   Mary Alice (Baby) Porter, Harrison and Alice Porter's fifth and last child, born 25 January; Alice Porter dies 20 March. Callie moves with father, two sisters, and brother to Kyle, Texas, to live with grandmother Catharine Ann Skaggs Porter.

1893–   Educated by governesses grandmother hires. Attends public school in
1901   Kyle. Attempts to write stories. Begins lifetime of extensive reading.

1901–2   Grandmother Catharine Ann Skaggs Porter dies 2 October 1901. Callie spends remainder of 1901–2 school year in Kyle and summer on grandmother's nearby farm. In fall of 1902 sets forth with father, sisters, and brother on several years of vagabondage; sporadically attends schools while visiting relatives in Texas towns.

1903–4   Briefly attends convent school in New Orleans.

1904–5   Informally changes name to "Katherine Porter" when brother Harry Ray changes his name to "(Harrison) Paul." Attends the Thomas School in San Antonio for full academic year. In Victoria, Texas, advertises as "teacher of Elocution, Physical Culture, and English."

1906   Moves with father and two sisters to Lufkin, Texas, when brother joins Navy. Marries John Henry Koontz 20 June in double ceremony with sister Gay, who marries Thomas H. Holloway.

1907–   Continues self-education and apprentice writing during miserable
10   marriage, marked by her husband's physical abuse and infidelity. Lives in Lafayette, Louisiana, and Houston, Texas.

1911   Baptized into Roman Catholic Church. Moves with Koontz to Corpus Christi, Texas. Writes stories and poems and widens reading to include works by James Joyce and Gertrude Stein.

1912   First published work, an amateur poem, is published on the cover of an agricultural trade journal.

1913   Continues to endure physical abuse by Koontz; considers consequences of separation or divorce. Has reunion with childhood friend Erna Schlemmer, who has moved to Corpus Christi with husband, Glover Johns Jr.

1914   Flees to Chicago, works briefly in movies; returns to Texas. Goes to Louisiana and works the lyceum circuit, singing ballads. Moves to Dallas, works at menial jobs to support herself.

1915–   Divorces Koontz; legalizes name to "Katherine Porter," begins to call
17   herself "Katherine *Anne* Porter." Marries and divorces T. Otto Taskett. Marries and divorces Carl Clinton von Pless. Spends months in Texas hospitals with tuberculosis. Writes children's stories and articles for Texas newspapers. Lives in Forth Worth and writes articles for the *Critic.* Does volunteer work for the Red Cross.

1918   In Denver, hospitalized briefly at sanatorium. Works as reporter for the *Rocky Mountain News.* Nearly dies in influenza epidemic.

1919   Grieves over July death of six-year-old niece, Mary Alice Holloway. Moves to New York City in fall; meets radical writers and Mexican artists. Works at agency writing publicity releases for movies.

1920–   Publishes four retold fairy tales. Travels to Mexico; meets Roberto and
21   Thorberg Haberman; writes for the English-language section of *El Heraldo de México.* Becomes acquainted with, among others, archaeologist William Niven, anthropologist and archaeologist Manuel Gamio, newly elected president of Mexico Alvaro Obregón, cabinet members José Vasconcelos, Plutarco Elías Calles, and Antonio I. Villarreal, and labor leader Luis Morones. Becomes disaffected with the Roman Catholic Church. Ghostwrites *My Chinese Marriage.* Edits the only two issues of *Magazine of Mexico.* Has love affair with Salomón de la Selva that ends with abortion. In Fort Worth, Texas, stays with Kitty and Garfield Crawford, works for the *Oil Journal,* writes shopping column for the *Fort Worth Record,* and performs in Little Theater productions. Publishes articles on Mexican politics.

1922   Returns to New York. "Where Presidents Have No Friends" is published. At the request of President Obregón makes second trip to Mexico, to assemble popular arts show and produce accompanying pamphlet (*Outline of Mexican Popular Arts and Crafts*). First original story, "María Concepción," appears in the December issue of the *Century*.

1923   Takes third trip to Mexico, to gather material for the May 1924 issue of *Survey Graphic*. "The Martyr" is published in July issue of the *Century*.

1924   Has love affair with Francisco Aguilera and becomes pregnant; male child stillborn in December. "Virgin Violeta" appears in the December issue of the *Century*.

1925   Continues to support herself with freelance writing, editing, and book reviewing. Becomes close friends with Josephine Herbst, John Herrmann, Malcolm and Peggy Cowley, Dorothy and Delafield Day, Allen Tate, Caroline Gordon, Hart Crane, and Ford Madox Ford.

1926   Spends summer in Connecticut with writers and artists including Herbst, Herrmann, and Englishman Ernest Stock. Contracts gonorrhea from Stock; undergoes surgery for removal of both ovaries.

1927–   In August 1927 protests the Sacco and Vanzetti executions in Boston.
28   Signs contract with Boni and Liveright for biography of Cotton Mather. "He" is published in *New Masses* in October. Researches Mather family in Salem, Massachusetts; begins research into own ancestral history for long autobiographical novel to be called *Many Redeemers*. Takes salaried position as copy editor at Macaulay. Publishes "Rope" and "Magic." Has brief affair with Matthew Josephson.

1929   "The Jilting of Granny Weatherall" appears in the February issue of *transition*. Depends on financial support and friendship of Rebecca and John Crawford. Goes to Bermuda for five months to work on Mather biography. "Theft" is published in *Gyroscope* in November.

1930–   Journeys to Mexico for extended visit; publishes "Flowering Judas" the
31   story and *Flowering Judas* the book, which fixes her place in American literature. Meets Eugene Dove Pressly. Accepts invitation of Russian filmmaker Sergei Eisenstein to visit Hacienda Tetlapayac to watch filming of *Que Viva México*. With Guggenheim Fellowship makes voyage from Veracruz to Bremerhaven, Germany, with Pressly.

1932   Lives briefly in Berlin, Madrid, and Basel; settles in Paris. "The Cracked Looking-Glass" and the essay "Hacienda" are published.

1933   *Katherine Anne Porter's French Song-Book* is published. Marries Pressly. Attends classes at Le Cordon Bleu cooking school.

1934   "That Tree" and the long, fictionalized version of "Hacienda" are published.

1935   "The Witness," "The Last Leaf," "The Grave," "The Circus," and *Flowering Judas and Other Stories* are published.

1936	Returns to the United States; unofficially separates from Pressly. "The Old Order" ("The Journey") is published.
1937	"Noon Wine" and "Old Mortality" are published. Meets Albert Russel Erskine Jr. Begins college speaking and teaching.
1938	Divorces Pressly, marries Erskine; lives in Louisiana. "Pale Horse, Pale Rider" is published. Receives second Guggenheim.
1939	*Pale Horse, Pale Rider: Three Short Novels* and "The Downward Path to Wisdom" are published.
1940	Separates from Erskine; goes to artist colony Yaddo. "A Day's Work" is published.
1941	Buys farm, South Hill, near Yaddo. "The Leaning Tower" and "The Source" are published. Speaks on radio programs. Receives first Gold Medal for Literary Achievement from the Society for Libraries at New York University.
1942	Divorces Erskine. Attends writers' conferences. Father, Harrison Boone Porter, dies. Inducted into the National Institute of Arts and Letters.
1943	Resigns from the National Institute of Arts and Letters in protest of the practice of identifying some candidates as "Negro" (agrees to reinstatement after practice is abolished).
1944	Moves to Washington, DC, to serve as fellow at the Library of Congress. Begins to publish segments of long novel-in-progress now called *No Safe Harbor*. *The Leaning Tower and Other Stories* is published.
1945–47	Works as scriptwriter in Hollywood; sells South Hill.
1948	Tours Midwest universities as lecturer and teacher in writing workshops.
1948–49	Assumes academic appointment at Stanford. Receives Litt.D. from the Women's College of the University of North Carolina, her first of many honorary doctorates. Moves to New York City.
1950–51	Elected one of two vice-presidents of the National Institute of Arts and Letters.
1952	Publishes essay collection *The Days Before*. Attends the International Congress for Cultural Freedom in Paris.
1953	Begins academic year as writer-in-residence at the University of Michigan. Makes appearances at other universities and art centers.
1954	Receives Fulbright Fellowship to Belgium. Reads in London for the BBC; visits Rome for the first time. Protests actions of the U.S. House of Representatives Un-American Activities Committee.
1955	Relinquishes Fulbright after debilitating bronchial illness. Leases house in Southbury, Connecticut. Brother Harrison Paul Porter and

her editor Donald Brace (her primary editor at Harcourt, Brace) die. Leaves Harcourt, Brace for Atlantic-Little, Brown; Seymour Lawrence becomes her editor.

1956 Attends Conference on the Arts and Exchange of Persons, Institute of International Education, New York City. Continues to speak on college campuses.

1957–58 Works on *No Safe Harbor*; publishes nonfiction. Appears on television programs and participates in radio programs.

1958–59 Goes on extensive speaking tour; fulfills semester-long appointments at the University of Virginia and Washington and Lee. With Ford Foundation grant settles in Washington, DC; works on long novel, now titled *Ship of Fools*.

1960 "The Fig Tree" and "Holiday," both written in the 1920s and misplaced, are published. Returns to Mexico to give series of lectures sponsored by the U.S. Department of State.

1961 Speaks at colleges and universities; continues to appear on television programs and participate in radio programs; completes manuscript of *Ship of Fools*.

1962 *Ship of Fools* published; becomes best-seller; film rights sold. Porter sails to Europe for brief visit; returns to Europe in the fall to begin yearlong stay.

1963 Returns to Washington, DC; initiated into the American Academy of Arts and Letters.

1964 Moves to 3601 49th Street NW (Spring Valley) in Washington, DC. Lectures in Mexico City.

1965 *The Collected Stories* published. Moves with Seymour Lawrence to Knopf and then to Delacorte.

1966 *The Collected Stories* wins both the National Book Award and the Pulitzer Prize. Donates papers and other possessions to the University of Maryland, College Park.

1967 First meeting of the Katherine Anne Porter Foundation, established by her to support young writers.

1968 The Katherine Anne Porter Room opens in McKeldin Library at the University of Maryland, College Park (later in Hornbake Library on the same campus).

1969 Moves to a townhouse in College Park. Sister Gay Porter Holloway dies.

1970 *The Collected Essays and Occasional Writings of Katherine Anne Porter* is published. Moves to suite of apartments in College Park. Reconciles with the Roman Catholic Church.

1971	*The Ladies Home Journal* publishes "The Spivvleton Mystery" (written in 1926), which is one of five nominees by the Mystery Writers of America for the best short mystery story of the year.
1972	Receives Brandeis University Creative Arts Award. Receives and returns Emerson-Thoreau Medal to the American Academy of Arts and Sciences to protest Academy's refusal to acknowledge Ezra Pound's contributions to modern literature.
1973	The Katherine Anne Porter Foundation dissolved. Sister Mary Alice (Baby) Porter Hillendahl dies.
1974	Buys wooden coffin from cabinet shop in Montana. Publishes fragments of autobiography.
1975	Receives a rubbing of mother's Indian Creek gravestone from Roger Brooks, president of Howard Payne University in Brownwood, near her birthplace.
1976	Hires retired naval commander William R. Wilkins as personal assistant. Returns to Indian Creek and receives honorary degree at Howard Payne University in nearby Brownwood.
1977	Suffers first of several severe strokes. *The Never-Ending Wrong* is published. Judged incompetent by a psychiatrist; court appoints her nephew Paul Porter her guardian.
1977–79	Health steadily declines; friends visit.
1980	Moves to Carriage Hill Nursing Home, Silver Spring, Maryland, in March. Dies 18 September.
1981	In the spring, Porter's ashes are buried at Indian Creek Cemetery in a grave adjacent to that of her mother. On her tombstone is engraved "IN MY END IS MY BEGINNING."

Katherine Anne Porter Remembered

Introduction

> [. . .] to give a true testimony it is necessary to know and remember what I
> was, what I felt, and what I knew then, and not confuse it with what I know
> or think I know now.
>
> —Katherine Anne Porter, *Collected Essays*

In 1940, when Katherine Anne Porter was fifty years old, Paul Crume published
a review of her *Pale Horse, Pale Rider: Three Short Novels* and remarked on the extraordinary fact that despite Porter's having been named "a new master of American prose" nine years earlier, with the publication of *Flowering Judas* (her first
collection of stories), almost nothing was in print about her. She "remains more
a literary reputation than a person," he wrote.[1] Crume probably knew that three
years after the publication of *Flowering Judas,* Porter had supplied Stanley Kunitz
with a brief autobiographical entry for *Authors Today and Yesterday.* However, it
included only a few factual details (such as the year she received her first Guggenheim Fellowship). Crume probably would not have identified the lie about her
birth year (she added four years) or the half-truth about her relationship to Daniel
Boone (her ancestor was Jonathan Boone, brother to Daniel). But Crume was correct that Katherine Anne Porter the person was not to be found at that time in any
published account of her life. He began what was to be a long process of filling
in details and correcting the record. He looked up persons in Dallas, Fort Worth,
and Arlington who had known Porter as early as 1916 and asked them to recollect
her from those years, their reminiscences to be woven into his review.

For years, Crume's review and the entry in *Authors Today and Yesterday* were the
starting point for biographical studies of Porter.[2] When Donald Stalling was writing a master's thesis on Porter and her work in the early 1950s, he retraced Crume's
ground and added the recollections of other persons who had known the Porter
family still earlier, in Indian Creek and Kyle. George Hendrick in his *Katherine
Anne Porter* (1965), with the help of his wife, Willene, added more to the gradually increasing body of knowledge about Porter, which by then included the Denver research of Kathryn Adams Sexton. Nevertheless, as late as the 1970s there
remained many gaps, especially from 1905 to 1930, despite Porter's offering se-

lected details about herself and correcting some of the errors, including that of her age.

Since Porter's death in 1980, her life has been taking shape publicly. As archives at Yale, Stanford, the University of California, Los Angeles, and the University of Texas at Austin, and especially the massive Porter archive at the University of Maryland, College Park, have been steadily perused and enhanced by the addition of other persons' papers, and as public documents and records have been increasingly accessible, Porter has come more and more into focus. In *Katherine Anne Porter: A Life* (1982), the first full biography of Porter, Joan Givner supplied valuable details about Porter's hospitalization with tuberculosis and her mysterious first marriage. After extensive research for his *Katherine Anne Porter and Mexico: The Illusion of Eden* (1992), Thomas F. Walsh constructed a thorough chronicle of Porter's experiences in Mexico from 1920 to 1931. My own research for *Katherine Anne Porter: The Life of an Artist* (2005) filled in yet more gaps, and I was able also to correct some of the errors in her biographical record that were the result not only of Porter's own dissembling and misdirection but also of hasty or wrong conclusions reached and perpetuated by other scholars and journalists. In some respects, because biographical entries in encyclopedias and literary dictionaries and online continue to recycle old errors, an accurate account of Porter's life has yet to become fixed in the general domain.

Katherine Anne Porter was born on 15 May 1890 in Indian Creek, Texas, a small farming community in Brown County. She was the fourth child of Harrison Boone Porter and Mary Alice Jones Porter, who christened her "Callie Russell" in honor of the twelve-year-old daughter of their neighbors and friends William and Marinda Russell. Harrison and Alice's three older children were Anna Gay, Harry Ray (later "Harrison Paul"), and Johnny, who died at about one year of age. Their fifth child, a daughter, eventually named Mary Alice but always called Baby, was born in January 1892, and Alice Porter died two months later. Harrison then moved with his four children to Hays County, Texas, to live with his widowed mother, Catharine Ann Skaggs Porter. Until 1901 Callie lived in relative security under the dominion of her grandmother. In 1901, however, when her grandmother died, she entered a long period of anxiety and insecurity initiated by a period of vagabondage with her father and extending through bouts of serious illness, five unsuccessful marriages, and many years of struggling to support herself financially.

Porter's formal schooling was modest, comprising erratic education by governesses, a few years in the Kyle public school, sporadic and brief enrollment in convent schools in Texas and Louisiana, and one full year at a private school in San Antonio. But her real education, by means of omnivorous reading that began at an early age, an insatiable curiosity about numerous subjects, and a social talent that drew important and interesting persons to her, lasted until the end of her life. Despite obstacles and setbacks—for some of which she was responsible, while others were tied to the social and economic realities of her time and place—she achieved the greater portion of the artistic success she had "set my heart upon," as she described the visible realization of her goals in a letter to her family at the end of 1920.[3] By 1980, when she died, she had a sterling reputation as an "artist," the label she chose for herself and placed higher than any other human one.

During my research for *Katherine Anne Porter: The Life of an Artist,* I quickly learned the importance of public documents, but I learned also the special value of eyewitness accounts—reminiscences—that add a living, speaking human being to the data. However, as every biographer knows, the vividness and charm of reminiscences can be misleading. Recollections of events that took place many years, even decades, earlier may contain outright inaccuracies or at least impressions tainted by time and intervening experience. And some writers may inject fictional elements into their reminiscences in order to tell better stories, while others may fall prey to the inclination to sanctify a person who was an admired or beloved friend or relative.

Caveats aside, the reminiscences in this collection are raw biography, with unexpectedly rich portraiture. These sixty-three pieces, written by fifty-two authors, include essays, letters, interviews, newspaper and journal articles, transcribed talks at conferences and symposia, government reports, excerpts from autobiographies that interpolate scenes featuring Porter, and poems that compress memories of her into lyrical recollections. Twenty-five of the reminiscences have not been previously published. Many are culled from those I gathered during my research and distilled in my Porter biography to a word, a phrase, a sentence, or a short paragraph. Eight others have been written especially for this volume.

Some of the authors of these reminiscences, aware of the unreliability of memory, have depended on diaries, personal correspondence, notes, and audiotapes of Porter to help them recall her more completely and accurately. Some of the pieces entwine biography and autobiography as memoirists have had to recollect their younger selves and their youthful viewpoints to re-create their relationships with Porter.

The remembrances are told from different degrees of historical perspectives: at one extreme is Marcella Winslow's letters to her mother-in-law written only a few days after the events described; at the other is Robert Plunkett's clear-eyed recollections three-quarters of a century after he registered a child's impression of Porter in 1930. Some of the authors of these pieces did not know Porter personally but reported the recollections of those who did.

A few reminiscences are no more than a long paragraph that provides a vignette or tableau, while others are deeply detailed, substantial essays. The range is extensive. Porter is seen in the hour of her birth and at the moment of her death, with scenes from the intervening years strung like beads "on an unbreakable cord," as she once described her accumulation of experiences.[4] The years from 1905 to 1915 are largely, but not completely, absent from the reminiscences. Porter herself did not want to talk about those years of painful struggle except obliquely, and those persons, such as her sister Gay, who knew the whole truth, mentioned only glancingly that period in Porter's life.

Not all the reminiscences are elegiac. John Prince recounts the stages of the dissolution of his friendship with her, and Breckenridge Porter remembers his and his aunt's mutual disapproval of one another. A bitter M. M. Liberman revisits events that culminated in her unceremoniously dropping him as trustee of her literary estate.

Common threads run through the collection. Almost everyone remembers Porter's extraordinary beauty, and many recall her ability to mesmerize an audience or charm a friend. Her struggle to release (and sustain) her creative flow was apparent to all who knew her well. Her yearning for a home and her delusions about love are as visible as the range of her knowledge and the scope of her reading. Even those who love her acknowledge her sharp tongue and, in the last years, her paranoid renunciation of friends and relatives. Her showy purchase of a wooden coffin morbidly fascinates many persons. Her complexity and contradictions are evident in the many recollected facets of her personality, illustrating the validity of her declaration to Kenneth Burke in 1954 that she felt as if she were "at least two regiments of people inside, always at civil war."[5]

A subject that implicitly binds the pieces together is the names by which Katherine Anne Porter was known. Erna Schlemmer Johns remembers her as "Callie." "Miss Callie," Erna's son and daughter-in-law call her. She is of course "Aunt Katherine" to her nephews Paul and Breckenridge, and "Miss Porter" to polite young persons. Glenway Wescott calls her "Porter," but to most persons she is "Katherine Anne," as she insisted. "It would seem," she told one of her agents, "that I am called by my first name by any one who ever heard of me. I see no harm in it."[6] Elizabeth Hardwick confirmed Porter's assertion: "She was spoken of simply as 'Katherine Anne,' whether one was actually acquainted with her or not."[7]

In selecting the pieces for this collection I considered the contributions each one could make to a composite portrait of Porter. Some I omitted because others covered the same ground more vividly or extensively. For example, my interview with Janet Lewis Winters and Wallace Stegner's unsent letter to Joan Givner were superseded by my interview with Richard Scowcroft, who recounted Porter's Stanford experience with extensive detail absent in the other two. Likewise, the essential points in Paul Porter's discussion of his aunt's sense of humor is present in his "Remembering Aunt Katherine." Some I rejected because the tidbit of recollection was too slight to stand by itself. For example, although Edgar Skidmore, who shared with me a considerable amount of information about the expatriate American community in Mexico in the 1920s, remembered Eugene Pressly clearly, he only vaguely remembered meeting Porter once at the Regis Hotel.

Within the selections in this volume I have excluded material that was taken from published sources about Porter's life or works and was not part of the personal experience of the person reminiscing. I have corrected typographical errors and obvious misspellings in both the published and unpublished sources. I made consistent the italicizing of book titles and the placing of quotation marks around titles of short stories, essays, and works-in-progress.

I have placed my own ellipses in brackets and have left unbracketed those that appear in the original sources. Unless otherwise explained, all bracketed information is mine. It is important to distinguish, however, between ordinary ellipses and Porter's own running series of points, which were intended to create a conversational tone (an eccentricity adopted by some of the persons writing about her). Whether that of Porter or someone else, I standardized the series to five points, in addition to a terminal period. With the exception of the series of points, I left alone direct quotes from Porter's letters with their original, sometimes unconventional, punctuation and spelling. In the transcribing and editing of letters, "TLS" is used to describe a typed letter signed, and "ALS" is used to describe an autograph (written in the author's own hand) letter signed. I organized for coherence the interviews I transcribed from shorthand notes and audiotapes, omitting the questions I asked, but left intact and unedited the words of the person interviewed.

With three exceptions I have arranged the pieces chronologically according to what I determined was each author's first meeting with Porter. Although evidence suggests that Frederic Prokosch met Porter in the late 1940s or early 1950s, I let stand his dating of a 1962 party he says he attended with Porter since one of the main statements he recalls her making had to have been made in 1962. John Prince met Porter in the early 1950s and became better acquainted with her when she rented a house near his and his wife's house in 1959, but his reminiscence focuses almost exclusively on the winter of 1963–64, where I place it in the sequence. Although Jane DeMouy was introduced to Porter in 1978, her reminiscence, which concentrates on Porter's last weeks and final moments, more properly belongs in the 1980 slot. The reminiscences, many of which overlap because they cover a number of years, fall naturally into seven divisions, which are dated and identified by the places Porter lived during the designated years.

1
Texas and Colorado, 1890–1919

Although for many years not much was known publicly about the first three decades of Katherine Anne Porter's life—years of loss, vagabondage, illness, bad marriages, poverty, and struggles to gain an artistic foothold—reminiscences by her sister Gay, neighbors at Indian Creek, and her friend Erna Schlemmer Johns unveil her childhood years. Kitty Barry Crawford pulls back the curtain on Porter's battles with tuberculosis and nearly fatal influenza in 1918. Beniti McElwee and Rosalind Gardner (who shared their recollections with Pauline Naylor), unnamed persons who recalled Porter to Paul Crume, and former *Rocky Mountain News* colleagues who shared their memories with Kathryn Adams Sexton reveal Porter's important writing apprenticeship in Fort Worth, Dallas, and Denver. Insights into Porter's complex personality and sources of some of her most significant stories and short novels are discovered in the process.

1 / Anna Gay Porter Holloway

Anna Gay Porter Holloway (1885–1969) was the first child of Mary Alice Jones Porter (1859–92) and Harrison Boone Porter (1857–1942). Married to Thomas J. Holloway in a double wedding with Katherine Anne and John Henry Koontz in 1906, she lived most of her life in Texas and Louisiana, working as a bookkeeper in later years. Because Gay was the only one of Harrison and Alice's surviving four children who had memories of the family's years at Indian Creek, when Porter began to mine her own early life for her fiction, she pressed Gay for information about their mother and their childhood. Many of Gay's letters over the years contain passages that re-create scenes from the past.

Source: Gay Porter Holloway to Katherine Anne Porter, 14 December 1955, TLS, Papers of Katherine Anne Porter, Special Collections, University of Maryland, College Park, Libraries.

I carry so many pictures, some of them quite beautiful, that the rest of you know nothing of—one is of that place in Indian Creek, which was a place of beauty, as I remember. Between the house (not the one there now—ours was torn down when you were there)[1] and Indian Creek was one of the most beautiful vineyards I ever saw, with great clusters of purple and white grapes. While you were being born, little fat brother[2] and sister Gay were out there filling up on grapes which were just turning, and I remember to this day how deliciously cool and sweet they were. When they called us to come see the new baby (you) we hated to leave the grapes, but we went in—Mother smiled, turned back the cover and said—"Do you want to see my little tad" and there you were, like a new born little black puppy, your little black curls sticking to your head in damp waves and curls.

Source: Gay Porter Holloway to Katherine Anne Porter, 25 July 1954, TLS, Papers of Katherine Anne Porter, Special Collections, University of Maryland, College Park, Libraries.

And I remember you on a little foot stool showing off before Cousin David Porter (the old Baptist minister)[3] singing your little made up songs, and making your little speeches, and all the old Methodists and Baptists and Presbyterians were fully convinced you were possessed of the devil and would come to no good end. And dear Grandmother[4] was so proud of you and always showed you off—and did you love it.

Source: Gay Porter Holloway to Katherine Anne Porter, 3 November 1962, TLS, Papers of Katherine Anne Porter, Special Collections, University of Maryland, College Park, Libraries.

I have always loved you so, never remember being angry with [you] except when you were a little girl you read in a beauty column that if you ate an onion every night, it would make you beautiful; you got it in your curly little black head that it had to be eaten in bed, and as you were my bedfellow, I could have kicked you to Jericho.

Oh, and I was just receiving beaus, you and the baby[5] would walk in boldly and confiscate the box of candy that all young beaus brought when they called, and ate it every bit, sometimes right *there* and I was too self-conscious to say a word.

Oh, Gawd! If looks could have killed!!!!!

Source: Gay Porter Holloway to Katherine Anne Porter, 26 February 1956, TLS, Papers of Katherine Anne Porter, Special Collections, University of Maryland, College Park, Libraries.

One time Daddy took you on a train somewhere, and you had a little new white pull on cap which you thought so much of—and Dad would pull it off to show those beautiful little black curls of which he was so proud, and you would pop your little new cap on and pull it down to your ears, and after a few times of this, you went into one of your famous tantrums. Mary Alice and I went laughing the other day just thinking of them. You would get on your back and spin like a top and kicking like mad, and Miss Babb, our governess,[6] could find no place to spank, the spankable place was gone from there to some other side.[7]

Source: Gay Porter Holloway to Katherine Anne Porter, 18 October 1961, TLS, Papers of Katherine Anne Porter, Special Collections, University of Maryland, College Park, Libraries.

Katherine Anne Porter's sister Anna Gay Porter, 1905, at the end of the year the sisters spent at the Thomas School. Porter inscribed on the back: "one of the most beautiful." Courtesy Papers of Katherine Anne Porter, Special Collections, University of Maryland, College Park, Libraries.

I don't want a letter in response, a card now and then is enough to bring up a little picture of you, perhaps burying a pet chicken or bird when you were a little girl, with songs, prayers, flowers and a little headstone,[8] or perhaps just one of your cussed little grins, when you were putting something particularly diabolic over—as you usually were.

Source: Gay Porter Holloway to Katherine Anne Porter, 22 January 1962, TLS, Papers of Katherine Anne Porter, Special Collections, University of Maryland, College Park, Libraries.

Getting back to the family skeletons—put this in your little pipe. All the outlaws (especially if they were good looking and rode a fine horse), the horse thieves, card sharps, etc. I liked much better than I did those Methodist, Baptist, Presbyterian, and so brothers that came every Sunday and ate all the fried chicken up.[9] (You remember those days, my little gal, when you were a raving beauty with black curls, a skin like peaches and bits of Italian blue sky for eyes with black lashes that laid on your cheeks when you finally condescended to go to sleep, durn you). I can see you yet chewing away on a chicken neck. You were a good grabber though, and may have done a bit better when *we* didn't see you.

2 / Donald Stalling

Donald Langhorne Stalling (1928–89) was born in Garrison, Texas, and received an M.A. from Texas Christian University in 1951 and a Ph.D. from Columbia University in 1959. He later taught at schools in the United States and Japan. While he was writing his master's thesis, he corresponded with and interviewed persons who had known the Porter family in Texas and who recalled Katherine Anne when she was an infant christened "Callie Porter." He also wrote to Porter asking her to provide biographical information. She replied in a long letter, essentially declining his request and warning him against examining her fiction for clues to her life. In 1956 the biographical chapter in his thesis was sent to her by her sister Gay Porter Holloway, who had received it from Cora Posey, an old friend of the Porter family at Indian Creek. Although there were factual errors in the chapter, there also was considerable accurate detail.

Source: Donald L. Stalling, "Katherine Anne Porter: Life and the Literary Mirror," unpublished M.A. thesis, Texas Christian U, 1951, 23, 28–29, 35, 36.

A trip to Indian Creek, Texas, Miss Porter's birthplace, was rewarding in the search for information about Miss Porter's early childhood and family background. Living in Indian Creek are two elderly ladies [Mary McAden and Cora Posey] who have excellent memories, and who were gracious enough to share their personal reminiscences with the present writer. Miss Mary [McAden], whose father was a close friend of Miss Porter's father, lives in the house where the writer's parents came as newlyweds, and in which Miss Porter was born.[10] Miss McAden was a few years older than the oldest Porter child [Gay] and has memories connected with each of the children.

In the Methodist church at Indian Creek the Porters' third [*sic*] child,[11] destined to be known far beyond the boundaries of Brown County, Texas, and even of the United States as a literary artist, was christened Callie Porter. Callie was a beautiful child, but even when she left Indian Creek at the age of four,[12] [according to Miss McAden] she was still a "big baby."

"I wouldn't say she was spoiled, but when she wanted something, she wouldn't give an inch until she got it. And if she wanted something, she would keep working until she got it."

Mrs. J. P. Kercheville relates that on many occasions as she walked past the town house of Aunt Cat, the yard would be full of children watching or participating in a drama directed by the granddaughter Callie. Aunt Cat's bedspreads would be draped over the goods' boxes to serve as properties for one of the earlier experiments in theater in the round. The porch was curtained off, not as a stage, but as a dressing room and cave of emergent wonders. Callie would invite the passers-by to come in and see the show. Once she charged admission and gave the proceeds to charity.[13]

When Miss Posey was a patient in a hospital in San Antonio in 1906, Harrison Porter and his daughters Callie and Mary Alice [Baby] were living in a small apartment in that city.[14] [. . .] Miss Posey had the following to say about Miss Porter's life of that time:

After Mr. Porter's mother's death the family broke up, and to tell the truth, Mr. Porter and the two [three] younger girls lived a gypsy existence, moving from place to place, and never having what could really be called a home. From what my mother and father told me, they also lived in a rather Bohemian manner. In 1906 in San Antonio Calie was a girl in her 'teens who had a great urge to go on the stage. She was studying dramatics in some school there in San Antonio.[15]

3 / Willene Hendrick

Willene Hendrick (1928–) is an independent scholar who earned a B.S. from the University of Colorado at Boulder, and worked as a nurse in Texas, Colorado, and Illinois before beginning a collaboration with her husband, George Hendrick, professor of English at the University of Illinois at Urbana-Champaign, in writing and editing books, including *Katherine Anne Porter* (1988), *Selected Poems of Carl Sandburg* (1996), *Fleeing for Freedom: Stories of the Underground Railroad* (2004), and *Why Not Every Man? African Americans, Civil Disobedience, and the Quest for the Dream* (2005).

Source: Willene Hendrick, "Indian Creek: A Sketch from Memory," *Katherine Anne Porter and Texas: An Uneasy Relationship,* ed. Clinton Machann and William Bedford Clark (College Station: Texas A&M UP, 1990), 3–12.

Late in August, 1962, my husband and I set out from the hamlet of Santo, between Mineral Wells and Stephenville, where we had been visiting, to find the obscure town of Indian Creek, where a certain well-known writer had been born in a log cabin. Indian Creek was not on our road map, but the *Texas Almanac* showed it as a tiny dot south of Brownwood. When we neared Brownwood, we stopped at a truck stop to have some coffee and ask directions. As we paid, we asked the waitress. She thought for a time, then asked a construction worker who was just coming in.

"Let's see now," he said. "Indian Creek. Well, it's off that way," and he pointed to the south. "Best way to get there is to go to that new school up there on top of the hill, turn down that new highway they're puttin' in up there, go two, three mile and then turn right again on a little paved road. You'll see signs from there on."

They looked at us curiously, as if nobody in recent times had asked directions for the Indian Creek settlement. We didn't explain that we were on a literary excursion.

"You can't miss it," he called as we headed for our car.

But we did, easily. The paved farm road forked often. There were no signs. Fi-

nally, we were on a dusty, washed, bumpy road. We took each turn with new un-
certainty, gazing down the dwindling tracks leading through the fenced farm-
land, nowhere.

When the sign came, it was a battered wooden one, home-made-looking, saying "Indian Creek Baptist Church" and pointing to a large peeling white frame
building, which looked like a barn. We took the blind road left and soon found a
red-brick structure, looking like a schoolhouse but saying "Indian Creek Methodist Church" in large concrete letters across the front. We looked around for a
likely house where someone might live who would know something about the
Methodist church records, for we knew Harrison Porter, the author's father, had
been the Methodist Sunday school superintendent,[16] and we thought it likely that
there were still several people around who knew where Katherine Anne was born
and remembered the Porter family. Some years earlier Donald Stalling, working on a master's thesis on Porter at Texas Christian University, had found such
locals.[17]

From the road in front of the Methodist church, we could see a small two-
story frame house, a battered, abandoned general store, a brick and stone gymna-
sium with its roof now gone, a prosperous-looking large frame house, and, down
a side road, a small brick house and a metal shack.

It was in the last building made of tin and iron that we found the church secretary, a lady of about seventy. She had never heard of the Porter family, and she
said that even if any records of births and deaths had been kept seventy years before, they had all been destroyed, because something had happened to the church
before her time: a fire or a storm had destroyed it. She sent us into the country to
see two elderly ladies she thought might remember the Porter family.

Her directions were clear, and within a few minutes we arrived at the McBride
house. We walked across a sandy yard and were met at the front door by Mrs.
McBride's daughter. We explained that my husband was writing a book about
Katherine Anne Porter and that the Methodist church secretary had sent us to see
Mrs. McBride.

"Oh, yes," she replied, "she knew them, the Porters. She's out in the fields now.
Went for a little walk, out to see my husband and take him some water. She ought
to be back any time now. She'll come back for her dinner."

We asked if Mrs. McBride would mind talking about the Porters. No, the
daughter didn't think she'd mind; she did have some papers and things. The
daughter left us to see if she could find those papers, and in a few minutes she returned to the front porch, where we were seated in the swing, not with papers
but with a medium-sized woman whom she introduced as Mrs. McBride. We explained our mission again.

"I didn't really know the Porters too well," Mrs. McBride began. "Mostly I remember when they left here. There was an auction. They sold all their things. I was there. I remember we bought the churn. Somebody bought the high chair. With the baby sitting in it. But it wasn't the baby you wanted to know about. Katherine Anne was a little girl. Pretty little girl, I remember, running around all over everywhere, with little black curls."

"Can you tell us anything about her? Or the Porter family?" we asked.

Mrs. McBride paused to think about the distant past, and her daughter broke in.

"That Miss Porter; she came not long ago, with her father. They were looking for her mother's grave. Went up to the cemetery to see it. Took Mrs. Porter's picture from the tombstone. The picture was sealed in glass and stuck to the stone. I guess they did it. It's gone now." (It was sometime later that we learned that the visit of the Porters characterized as "not long ago" had actually taken place in May 1936.)

Mrs. McBride remembered something in a dresser drawer, went into the house, and returned with a photograph, a picture of the Porter children. We saw immediately that the smallest, the baby sitting on a woman's lap, was Katherine Anne. The eyes were hers, and the mouth, and the defiant look. The mother's face had been omitted by the photographer. Was Mrs. Porter already too ravaged by illness to allow her face to be shown? Or was she removing her face to emphasize the children? Or was there some other reason?

"The picture was with my mother's things. Mrs. Porter must have given it to her," Mrs. McBride said. We gazed at the picture, trying to read its messages. On the front, stamped across the bottom, we read "Cheapest Gallery, Brownwood, Texas."

"You can have it, that picture, if you want it," Mrs. McBride said.

"But wouldn't you like to keep it?" I said, startled by the offer.

"No, I don't want it. I didn't even know them, not really. They moved away when I wasn't any bigger than that oldest girl there," and she pointed to the picture of Annie Gay Porter,[18] then about five or six. "No, I don't want it. They warn't no kin to us. Yes, you take it. Send it to Katherine Anne if you don't want it. I understand she writes books now."

There was a pause. "You are writing a book," she said to my husband. She sounded tired, as if she had nothing more to say to us. "Miss McAden can tell you a whole lot more than I can. She was older when the Porters left."

As we were leaving, we said we would send the picture on to Katherine Anne Porter (and we did). Then we drove down a dusty road to Miss Leola McAden's house. When we arrived, she was just leaving the dinner table. She was a birdlike little woman, and she was glad to have company. She talked to us for over an hour about all she could remember from her childhood about the Porter family.

Baby Callie (*right*), Harry Ray (Paul), and Anna Gay,
c. 1891–92; their mother, Alice Jones Porter, has faded
from the far right side of the photograph, which was
given to Willene Hendrick by an elderly woman who had
known the Porter family when they lived at Indian Creek.
Courtesy Papers of Katherine Anne Porter, Special Collections, University of Maryland, College Park, Libraries.

Yes, she remembered the Porters well, but mostly she remembered her own childhood and family and warned us often to keep her from straying away from what
we wanted to know. She remembered Harrison Porter as a kind and gentle man.
And Katherine Anne, whom the Porters called Callie; Miss McAden called her
Callie too. She thought that was Katherine Anne's christened name, but it was
a long time ago, and she had never seen the Porter family Bible with its lists of
births and deaths. There had been fishing expeditions with Harrison Porter and
the children. She could show us their favorite spot. The Porter house had stood
near the creek; she could take us to the very spot, but it was a mite warm to take
a ramble in the middle of the day, so she pointed it out to us from her porch. The
Porter log house was long gone. The McAdens, like Mrs. McBride's family, had

bought some of the household goods at the auction. They now owned what had been the Porter farm.

"Do you by chance still have anything from the house?" I asked.

"Oh, no," she replied. "It's all worn out long ago."

We talked and talked. She let us go finally, reluctantly, talking all the way out the door, across the yard, and she was still talking as we drove away.[19]

4 / Erna Schlemmer Johns

Erna Schlemmer Johns (1890–1975) was the first child of Nicholas Carl Schlemmer and Wilhelmina Dorothea Wichtrich Schlemmer, a prosperous German immigrant family who lived across the street in Kyle from Catharine Ann Skaggs Porter's house, where Katherine Anne Porter lived from 1892 to 1902. Erna and Katherine Anne (Callie) were best friends, and Erna's well-educated mother introduced Katherine Anne to the works of Russian writers and European painters. Erna, who traveled to Germany with her family, was the inspiration for Charles Upton's friend Kuno in "The Leaning Tower." She married Glover Johns in 1910 and moved with him to Corpus Christi, Texas, where Porter moved in 1911 with her first husband, John Henry Koontz.

Source: Erna Schlemmer Johns, *To Whom It May Concern,* vol. 1, *The Schlemmers* (Austin: Privately printed, 1977), 62–63.

In Kyle, as in most small towns of that day, social life for families centered around church activities. Naturally Mama's life included church work. In England she attended the Church of England so the Episcopal Church was the denomination of her choice and she was the guiding light for the members in Kyle. The little church was across the street from our house facing in the same direction. [. . .]

The Methodist Church was across the street on the other side of our house. Since the Episcopal Church had services only once a month, the other Sundays we attended the Methodist Church and participated right along with the members. I remember as a young child I sang duets there with a friend, Callie Porter. She sang perfect alto and I sang soprano. Because our voices harmonized naturally we rehearsed very little. I can see us now—two small girls in organdy dresses with pink or blue sashes—singing as earnestly as two little angels, and not badly either.

Source: Erna Schlemmer Johns to Katherine Anne Porter, 3 May 1939, ALS, Papers of Katherine Anne Porter, Special Collections, University of Maryland, College Park, Libraries.

My dear,

When your letter came, on top of a pile of Christmas cards, I felt as if I had unexpectedly received a warm, affectionate hug right in the middle of a lot of perfunctory handshakes. If I have been slow to answer, it is indeed not because I haven't thought of you.

Especially lately, of course. I ordered your book [*Pale Horse, Pale Rider: Three Short Novels*] the minute I read the news that it was out. I am as proud of you as if I had hatched you, and it made my heart laugh, as Elise so quaintly says,[20] when I saw what perfectly grand press comments you have received. I have my own standard of what is good and what is indifferent. If it is good I can't forget it: a melody haunts me, a picture remembered is forever vividly fresh,—and your stories won't go out of my mind.

When I read "Old Mortality" little Miranda at once became Callie, that dearest friend of my childhood. I'm afraid I wanted to brush Aunt Amy[21] out of the way and get on with what Miranda did and thought and said. All sorts of memories were aroused in me,—I think I have already spoken of them to you. Our Busy Bee Club. The day we did circus stunts. Trying to decide the great problem as to whether you were to become an actress or a nun. Why you ever loved me I don't know—I was such a pale shadow beside your vivid personality. We were so strictly reared and such an undemonstrative family I think I was secretly rather astonished that you should be fond of me, and I cherished my little notes from "Witch" many a day.[22]

Source: Erna Schlemmer Johns to Katherine Anne Porter, 13 April 1978, ALS, Papers of Katherine Anne Porter, Special Collections, University of Maryland, College Park, Libraries.

As our shadows grow long the past becomes clearer in our thoughts and how you figure in them! I remember well the big old barn we played in, the patient mules we tried to do circus stunts on—once I even rode an indignant white hog who scraped me off his back by running under the barn. And of course there was our little cigarbox attached to the fence next to the privy (!!) in which Witch and Fairy exchanged notes.—How thoroughly delightful to go back in spirit to those old innocent days.

5 / Paul Crume

Paul Crume (1912–75) was an editor and reporter for many years at the *Dallas Morning News,* where his column "Big D" was featured on the front page. He was the author of *A Texan at Bay* (1961). When he reviewed Porter's *Pale Horse, Pale Rider: Three Short Novels* in 1940, in an effort to fill in the blanks in her biographical record, he sought out persons who had known her in Texas in the years between 1915 and 1918 and beyond. Those whose reminiscences he wove into his review included Kitty Barry Crawford, Lon Tinkle (book editor of the *Dallas Morning News*), and Cora Posey, an old friend of the Porter family who was living at the time in Arlington, Texas. Because Porter was still living, all three asked that they not be named. Crume digested and summarized their memories and left the source of direct quotations unidentified.

Paul Crume. Rev. of *Pale Horse, Pale Rider: Three Short Novels,* by Katherine Anne Porter. *Southwest Review* 25 (January 1940): 213–18.

It has been nine years since the reviewers discovered in *Flowering Judas* "a new master of American prose," but Katherine Anne Porter remains more a literary reputation than a person. Almost nothing is in print about her. She seemed to have sprung full-grown as a writer into the nation's literary sight with one book. Actually, she had been writing for a long time, and her work even as a cub reporter on the *Dallas Morning News* in 1915–1916 never was ordinary.[23] Her new book has in it three novelettes, "Old Mortality," "Noon Wine," and "Pale Horse, Pale Rider," all deft and insidiously subtle in their effects, all concerned with the curious human juxtapositions that develop out of the shuffle of time. In it her life begins faintly to show. And one begins to associate the impersonality of our information about her with her own spiritual isolation in the present tense—the tendency to live in and for the moment.

This is ingrained in the temperament of almost all who create. They are cast in the picaresque pattern of character; that is, they are furiously interested in moments and incidents, are impulsively swept along from momentary experience to momentary experience without much attention to the direction of life. This trait is associated with the power to experience deeply, to discriminate and savor the quality of experience, to observe wholly. A person possessed of this naïveté of the senses may find more to marvel at in the wind-bent sweep of a mesquite's branches than the average newspaper reporter finds in the routine murder of the night. The trait is even more deeply associated with the talent for expressing experience, with that power of fusing memories of the past and dreams unrealized into something that intensifies and deepens the present. To a remarkable degree, Miss Porter seems to have been cast in that pattern. "She doesn't wait for death to effect transmigration," one of her friends said recently. "Every now and then she stops being what she is and becomes something else. In some secluded corner of the world, she spins a cocoon, and presently comes out more brilliantly colored, with longer and swifter wings. She leaves her old life there in a tree, dry and forgotten and dead, something she has put forever behind her."[24]

She was born in the little village of Indian Creek near Brownwood. By the time she came to the *News,* she seems to have been much like the Miranda she so beautifully delineates in *Pale Horse, Pale Rider:* a pretty girl, as friends remember her, with a round face and violet eyes and curly dark hair, hard and slim of body from much dancing and swimming, impulsively generous, friendly. A few years later she had moved to a newspaper in Denver and had decided to become a world-roving newspaper correspondent. She had already started saving all the nickels, dimes and odd bills she could spare in an old white-kid evening glove.[25] She was going to New York and take a boat to the new Irish Free State. She had little money, but she had a passionate conviction that Mr. Eamon De Valera was right.[26]

But by the time she reached New York, that moment had passed. There were other things to engage her profound attention. She took over the top floor of an old house in Greenwich Village with Rose Wilder Lane,[27] Ernestine Evans,[28] Gertrude Emerson,[29] and several other young women whom the booksellers have got to know. At first she was press agent for a movie star of that day,[30] but that changed, too. Miss Emerson, then associate editor of *Asia,* had recently taken a formless manuscript from an American girl who had been married to a young Chinaman. He was to have been Ambassador to Mexico from China, but he died on the boat.[31] Miss Emerson wanted the story re-written. She commissioned Miss Porter to do the work. Going to Ann Arbor, where the widow and her three children lived, Miss Porter talked with them; bought a box of oranges, a percolator and several pounds of coffee, and locked herself in a room. Ten days later she came out with a novel-length book, *My Chinese Marriage.* She was off on her first trip to Mexico even before the book eased into the best-seller lists.[32]

Probably the strain of exoticism which critics have noticed in her work developed from her several trips to Mexico. On that first trip, she was to have begun work with the young men who were setting up Mexico's labor government,[33] but the peso wasn't buying much in those days. After a time, she got a job writing Mexican sketches for a Mexico City promotion magazine—sketches which many of her friends now like better than D. H. Lawrence's *Mornings in Mexico*.[34]

That lasted only until she began composing "The Dove of Chapacalco." Then her job meant nothing. She took a train to Fort Worth, turned up one day at the home of a friend. In Fort Worth, she found a quiet attic bedroom in the home of Mrs. Arthur S. Goetz, and there from morning until night she would work, writing a few hundred words a day. She finished "The Dove of Chapacalco" and wrote another story, "Maria Concepción."[35] She began to talk about Europe and a trip there.

One of her Fort Worth friends observed with a smile that "The Dove of Chapacalco" was so good she would never be allowed back in Mexico.[36]

6 / Pauline Naylor

Pauline Naylor (1896–1976) was editor of the pioneer section of the *Fort Worth Star Telegram* from 1936 to 1959. Her papers are included in the James R. Record Collection of West Texas Pioneers at Texas Tech University.

Source: Pauline Naylor, "Katherine Anne Porter's Ft. Worth Days Recalled," *Fort Worth Star-Telegram* 10 April 1966, sec. 5: 16. For this article, Naylor interviewed Beniti McElwee and combined direct quotations with an indirect summary of McElwee's recollections.

"There is a woman—in her raw elemental state."

So spoke Katherine Anne Porter, girl reporter and publicity chairman for many worthy causes, as she watched a ballroom crowded with Fort Worth women, elegantly dressed and richly jeweled, as they gathered for a benefit bridge tournament in 1917 or early 1918.

Miss Beniti McElwee, 2265 Lipscomb, one of Katherine Anne Porter's friends and fellow workers in various service projects in those World War I days in Fort Worth, holds this bridge tournament as probably the best remembered of many occasions of her association with the Texas-born author.

"Her comment as we watched the crowd waiting for the play to start was a witty reflection, not a barb let loose to leave a jagged gash, rather a quick little prick of a slim steel needle; just enough to make one realize that this very pretty girl, with delicate features and particularly beautiful eyes was a truly perceptive person," says the Fort Worth woman who has followed her friend's career with satisfaction through the near half century that has elapsed since Miss Porter wrote in an early Fort Worth newspaper, the *Critic*, of the work of the Social Service Club and the Hospital Visiting Corps.

Of the card tournament Miss McElwee recalls further:

"Katherine Anne had been writing newspaper stories for days about the benefit party and these had helped bring the large crowd of excited, hopeful players. Near the entrance was a long table loaded with the prizes. Merchants and other supporters had been most generous. There were silver candlesticks, brass lamps, a cut crystal punch bowl, lace table cloths, ornate umbrella stands, mammoth baskets of fruit—a real 'promised land' display.

"The ladies as they entered paused to appraise the dazzling and tantalizing display. Tense eager faces were topped by large impressive hats, harmonizing with the elaborate gowns of silk or velvet. The vapor of opulence rose from every table as the players settled to the serious business of the afternoon.

"And at one end of the ballroom, slightly apart, was Katherine Anne, surveying the scene, perceptive, gay, alert and witty, gathering impressions, and analyzing the faces under the elaborate millinery. And she made her pronouncement of 'woman in her raw, elemental state' with a smile and the little chuckle which many interviewers have mentioned."

Beniti McElwee probably is one of the first to start "collecting" Katherine Anne Porter. The first clippings from the *Critic,* a weekly, in the fall, are those about the work of the Social Service Club of which Miss McElwee was president. Later the club organized the Hospital Visiting Corps, "to do cheer-up work at Camp Bowie Base Hospital." [. . .]

Another clipping of the club's "publicity" in the *Critic,* tells that Miss Elba Forbess is now president "and is doing a great deal" and "Miss McElwee is the efficient little captain of this visiting corps—it is so natural to fall into military terms." [. . .]

The two companions in social service work and cheer for Camp Bowie hospital continued their personal contacts for several years after Miss Porter left Fort Worth, with letters and an occasional telephone call.

Source: Pauline Naylor, "Early Porter Tales Written Here," *Fort Worth Star-Telegram* 17 April 1966, sec. 5: 16. Naylor chose to summarize most of Rosalind Gardner's reminiscence about Porter's time spent with the Vagabond Players in Fort Worth, with only an occasional direct quotation.

"A talented, capable person who could act a role, help with direction, stage setting or whatever was required and who handled the publicity admirably."

This was Katherine Anne Porter of the Vagabond Players, of Fort Worth's original Little Theater, according to a newspaper clipping in an old scrapbook.

Unfortunately, the name of newspaper and date are not included in the clipping. But the date of Miss Porter's affiliation with the Fort Worth Little Theater is well established.

She was a member of the first group that initiated the Little Theater in 1921, under direction of Rosalind Gardner, who had returned from Hollywood, where she had worked with the Hollywood Community Theater.

Katherine Anne Porter, Roscoe Carnike, and Hunter Gardner in the Vagabond Players' 1921 production *Poor Old Jim* in Fort Worth, Texas. Courtesy *Fort Worth Star-Telegram* Collection, Special Collections, The University of Texas at Arlington Library, Arlington, Texas.

Katherine Anne Porter had gone to New York and Mexico after the 1917–1918 winter she spent working here on the *Critic,* a weekly newspaper, and taking part in the Social Service Club's projects at Camp Bowie's hospital and other war work.[37]

In 1921 she returned to Fort Worth to work this time for the *National Oil Journal,* published by Garfield Crawford, and to write special features on the colorful figures attracted to the Fort Worth area by the series of oil booms that had started during World War I.

Her friendship with Mrs. Crawford had led Katherine Anne Porter to come to Fort Worth for her first stay and she made her home with the Crawfords on both occasions, in the 1600 block of College Avenue.

The Barn, at 1313 Alston Avenue, where the Little Theater plays were presented that first season, claimed a good share of Miss Porter's time apart from the reporting job and the stint of creative writing based on her experiences in Mexico.

She found herself the traditional garret in which to write—the attic of the Arthur Goetz home, on Pennsylvania Avenue, just off Henderson, where the 1879 Room is now located.

It was here that her first published story, "María Concepción," was written. She was saving her money to go back to Mexico, but after Garfield Crawford read her stories, he urged her to go to New York, where the market was, and to concentrate on finishing the great amount of material she already had written.

Katherine Anne Porter did go to New York, but she didn't remain long, nor did she "recover" from Mexico, as readers with even slight knowledge of her work know quite well.

Her Little Theater career flourished that first season: she was in two of the half-dozen plays Rosalind Gardner directed, and is well and pleasantly remembered by fellow actors and Little Theater aficionados of the day.

The plays were *The Wonder Hat* and *Poor Old Jim*.[38]

During the season she gave Director Gardner her souvenirs of Mexico, photographs of paintings and crayon portraits of natives, and a village street scene. The artist's signature is Winold Reiss.[39] The photographs are by Nickolas Murray, 129 MacDougal Street, New York.

Miss Porter inscribed the name of the genre of each picture on the back. On one "Type from Tepozotlan," she added, "My maid Maria de la Cruz" and signed K.A.P. in an artistic monogram effect.

Director and actress visited once after the Little Theater days. That was in 1923 when both were in New York.

The Little Theater's pioneering girl director, now Mrs. Rosalind Gardner Shelley, 809 Seventh Ave., was with the Fort Worth Safety Council for a number of years.

7 / Kathryn Adams Sexton

Kathryn Adams Sexton (1916–91) earned a B.F.A. and a B.A. from the University of Oklahoma in 1937 and 1938, respectively. For her M.A. thesis at the University of Colorado at Boulder, she drew upon available materials in Denver, conducting interviews with persons who knew Katherine Anne Porter in 1918 and 1919, compiling a list of Porter's articles published in the *Rocky Mountain News,* and using directories and local histories to construct the social climate of Porter's year and a half in Colorado. Later Sexton was an English professor at Panhandle State University in Goodwell, Oklahoma, and in 1979 she published *A Heritage of the Panhandle.*

Source: Kathryn Adams Sexton, "Katherine Anne Porter's Years in Denver," unpublished M.A. thesis, U of Colorado, 1961, 14, 16–21, 24.

Miss Porter came to Denver from Texas sometime during the latter part of the year 1918.[40] [. . .]

While in Denver this young journalist made her home in a rooming house at 1510 York Street. [. . .] In describing Miss Porter as she appeared during her years in Denver, [her co-worker Helen Black . . .] remembers her as a "glamorous figure" whom she "worshipped." She also recalls that Miss Porter was the epitome of Southern femininity, one who was to be looked up to. She always dressed attractively and in good taste, mostly in gray; and because Miss Porter was of small stature, [. . .] she always looked well dressed.

[Margaret] Harvey [another co-worker] remembers the Miss Porter of 1918 as a glamorous and intriguing person, one whom a passerby would stop to take a second glance at, particularly because she constantly talked with her hands and eyes, large blue ones that danced and sparkled as she expressed herself. Miss Harvey, too, remembers the gray which she wore frequently, especially the gray or black hood which covered her glistening black hair. In a short time, however, Miss Porter's hair turned white and came out as a result of an attack of influenza which she had in the latter part of 1918.[41] During this period, according to Miss Harvey, Miss Porter wore the gray or black hood constantly. When her hair came in, it was curly and of a lighter shade. [Thomas Hornsby Ferril, a reporter for the *Denver Times,* the staff of which shared office space with the staff of the *Rocky Mountain News,* had a desk next to Porter's. He remembers her] as a very good-looking young lady—the short, "baby dollish" type.[42]

At the time that this attractive young reporter worked for the *Rocky Mountain News,* the paper was housed in a [once impressive] building at 1720 Welton Street [. . .]. Miss Black says that she remembers the building in 1918 as more like a "barn" than a handsome structure. She says that the floors were constantly strewn with papers, and a bucket of water and a mop were necessary equipment to put out frequent fires. The rooms on the second floor were equipped with old furniture, and in order to reach the editorial room one had to climb steep and narrow steps [. . .]. [I]n addition to the long dangerous climb one also had to cut his way through the smoke that filled the stairway from the editorial room. Miss Harvey, too, comments on the flight of steps, saying that a person had only to climb them a few times to remember them for years. Located near the *News* building was the Greasy Spoon, the reporters' favorite hangout during office hours.

It was in this setting that Miss Porter earned her livelihood while in Denver. Her salary was eighteen dollars a week. For a vivacious young reporter who desired luxuries, [. . .] this salary was inadequate. To supplement the eighteen dollars per week, Miss Porter originated the shopping column "Let's Shop with Suzanne!" and sold ads for the column. The first of these full-page shopping ads appeared in the Dramatic Section of the Sunday paper, June 8, 1919, and continued in the Sunday papers through August 17, 1919, under Miss Porter's management [. . .].

In this setting Miss Porter became a noted journalist. Her co-workers regarded her as a good writer, a reputation which according to Miss Harvey, she established early in her career at the *News.* The deadline on news stories for the Sunday paper was Thursday night, and Miss Harvey says, "Katherine Anne wrote so rapidly; she could actually dash off her column while the rest of us were thinking about ours." Mr. Ferril says that he regarded Miss Porter's writing very highly then and the fact that she had such a large number of signed articles in the *News* substantiated this opinion for him. Miss Black comments on the quality and style of the columns that Miss Porter wrote at this time. She remembers that Miss Porter's writing showed real individuality and might be characterized by its literary flavor; in fact she feels that Miss Porter should have been called a "writer's writer" then, as so many critics have called her in later years.

Miss Porter wrote many news stories while she was the drama critic and sob sister on the *News.* According to Miss Harvey, when Miss Porter began working on the paper, she covered the courts, divorce cases, etc. [. . .]. Possibly she became the drama critic [. . .] when she and [Eva] Chappell, her good friend and reporter on the *News,* were sent to cover an elopement case and failed to get the story, although the rival paper carried it in full.[43] [. . .] As a sob sister, no doubt, she contributed articles which she did not sign. Her signature does appear on nine interviews, seventeen special assignments, and nine articles pertaining to talent, music, and art of Denver.[44] [. . .]

[. . .] Miss Black and Miss Harvey both comment on Miss Porter's manner at the office. They recall that she was always gracious and courteous to all her co-workers; however, occasionally she remained apart from them. During these periods of estrangement, they remember that she never seemed to be one of them.

No doubt Miss Porter's period of detachment from the office force resulted from [. . .] the period of unrest resulting from the war and a strong desire to go to New York to enter the journalistic field.[45] Miss Harvey says that this was the chief desire of all young journalists at this time, and one which was achieved by Eva Chappell, Miss Porter's closest friend at the *News* office, soon after the close of the war. Miss Harvey feels that this was Miss Porter's ambition too [. . .] because she seemed to be rather unhappy and discontented in Denver. Finally in 1919, as reported in a *Denver Post* article [in 1937], this desire to obtain journalistic work in New York came true for Miss Porter.

8 / Kitty Barry Crawford

Kitty Barry Crawford (1887–1982), born on a plantation in Randolph, Georgia, the daughter of Osgood and Eliza Barry, was educated at Kidd-Key College in Sherman, Texas. In 1913 Kitty Barry married Jasper Garfield Crawford (b. 1883), with whom she founded the *Fort Worth Critic*. Many early researchers who had learned of the friendship between Katherine Anne Porter and Kitty Crawford sought her out for her reminiscences. Although she is not identified by name, she supplied a significant amount of information to Paul Crume and Donald Stalling and is likely to have verified some of the information in the articles by Pauline Naylor.

Source: Kitty Barry Crawford to George Hendrick, 13 November 1961, TLS, collection of Darlene Harbour Unrue.

I am able to tell you, if it will help, about K.A.'s life in Denver as a reporter on the *Denver News*,[46] which she told me gave her idea and material for the story ["Pale Horse, Pale Rider"].

At that time, 1917–1919, I happened to be in Denver mending an infected lung.[47] K.A. and I were good friends. During the terrible flu epidemic of 1918, while a patient at Agnes Memorial sanitorium,[48] I received a call from Mr. Stone, a sports reporter on either the *News* or *Post*, both of us knew in Texas. (I cannot recall his Christian name, as every one called him Stony.)[49]

Stony told me that K.A. was seriously ill, at times delirious, with flu. The woman who owned the house where she lived threatened to put her out, afraid the other lodgers would leave if they knew K.A. had flu, and that he, Stony, could not find a hospital bed for K.A. One of the girls who worked at the *News* was trying to care for K.A. but knew that nursing care around the clock was needed. Stony asked me to help him.

I was astonished at his request, but soon found there was something I might do. Dr. Holden, director of Agnes Memorial, knew K.A. and liked her and admired her work very much. Dr. Holden was chairman of the Denver Board of Health.[50]

The telephone call came during the evening, after Dr. Holden had gone to his home nearby. Patients were strictly forbidden to call him or enter his home—his wife and children were not infected with TB.

I remember walking into Dr. Holden's living room without knocking. He looked at me so sternly I burst into hysterics. When Dr. Holden was told of K.A.'s condition, he acted immediately, telephoning the landlady threatening K.A. and doing a bit of threatening himself, to have her arrested for cruel and inhuman treatment. The next day Dr. Holden found a hospital bed for K.A.

For ten days or longer K.A. was seriously, and for a day or two critically, ill. Gay Porter Holloway, her older sister, came up from Texas. She and Stony called me every day. One day Stony happened to mention that he had been trying for several days to find fresh oranges, that K.A. constantly asked for orange juice. Because of the flu epidemic oranges could not be had in Denver. Garfield had sent oranges to me and Dr. Holden took most of them to K.A.

One Sunday afternoon Gay telephoned that the doctors had given up hope for K.A. She asked if I thought prayer and Mass for her might help. I told her I felt sure it would. She had special Mass said, and less than an hour after[ward] K.A.'s temperature dropped. She had passed the pneumonia crisis.

It has been a number of years since I read "Pale Horse, Pale Rider" [. . .]. I am frank to say, however, that K.A. as a person has always interested me more than her writings. She had and perhaps still has qualities of personality which lift her far, far above even highly talented people. Her delicate beauty—lovely black-lashed violet eyes, dark wavy hair, small nose, pertly snubbed—just to look at her was to love her. [. . .]

Sometimes I think that fate decreed that I miss Katherine Anne every time I tried to contact her for many years, so that I would always think of her as that lovely whimsical, instantly attractive young woman.

I located her once in New York, where she had an apartment with [Fola] La Follette,[51] only to discover she had left for a vacation with strict orders for [Fola] to tell no one where she had gone. I pestered Miss La Follette so much that she finally ordered me through a shut door to leave her alone period. [. . .]

She was to receive an award—I think from the Dealey Foundation in Dallas five or six years ago, but was too ill to come to Texas and I missed her again. Once I was to meet her in Los Angeles to view an exhibit of antique and folk art K.A. had collected for the Mexican government. The day I was to start on the trip a letter came from K.A. saying that the exhibit had been sold to a movie company and that she had used months and months of her life really for nothing except modest pay and a lace mantilla once belonging to the Empress Eugenie.[52]

That lace mantilla she entrusted to my care later together with her Greenwich Village apartment, while she went to Mexico for a fortnight on a special writing mission.[53] I tried to live in the apartment and care for the ring-tail monkey in his cage out in the hall,[54] but had to give up both, entrusting them to one of K.A.'s friends who lived in a back room on the same floor as K.A.'s apartment. (After several months I ran out of money and had to go home.) Long after I got home I received a letter from K.A. in Progresso, Mexico (southernmost port) saying she was having a marvelous time and would return soon. At the same time I got a letter from the woman in whose care I had placed the monkey. She said the monkey never had gotten all the dried milk out of his fur, from the milk I had given the monkey to drink but which it used to bathe in.

You see, for Katherine Anne Porter, as she has said on this day, any day, "The Future Is Now."[55] The future for living, she thinks, is always now. [. . .]

Last year I heard K.A. had bought a permanent home in Washington, D.C., where she lives intermittently with antique sofas, desk, lamps, pictures, collected from all over the world.

Curiously this means little if anything to me. She once had a permanent before-the-war mansion at Baton Rouge, La. Later she had another one at Saratoga, New York. And no doubt a pre-Cortez adobe at Cuernavaca.

[. . .] Mostly I hate "I knew them when" people. But K.A. is an exception. Students come every now and then to find out about the way she lived in Fort Worth in my house, acting in the Little Theater and being pursued by handsome young men at every turn. I do not tell them about the would-be lovers, but about how she wrote several of her stories—"María Concepción," "The Fig Tree," while there and supported herself doing a bit of ghost writing and working for Garfield to earn enough money to get to New York, where her real writing career began.

2
New York, Connecticut, and Mexico, 1920–1931

The years from 1920 to 1931 were in many ways the most important of Porter's artistic career. They were also the most adventurous and the most personally demoralizing years of her life. When Porter wrote her family at the end of 1920 that her artistic goals were in sight, she was correct. Her first original story, "María Concepción," published in the *Century* in 1922, was selected by Edward J. O'Brien for *The Best Short Stories of 1923 and the Yearbook of the American Short Story*. For the remainder of the decade she wrote fiction whenever she had the time between the freelance book reviewing and editorial work she took on to support herself. Eight more of her stories appeared by 1930, and six of the nine were included in her first collection, *Flowering Judas,* which was published to such critical acclaim that her position in American letters was firmly established. Mexico, which she visited four times between 1920 and 1931, seemed to release her creative energy. While there, she dabbled in the cultural revolution, became acquainted with the country's most important political leaders and artists, and had several serious affairs, one of which ended with a soul-searing abortion. Other affairs in New York and Connecticut followed, and one of those concluded with a pregnancy that yielded a stillborn son. Two years later she had surgery that ended all her hopes for motherhood. By the time she returned to Mexico in 1930, she was a forty-year-old woman whose personal life was in shambles. But before the end of that year, she was recognized as an important modernist American writer.

9 / W. H. Cowles

William Henry Cowles (1878–1951), a graduate of West Point, veteran of World War I, and colonel in the United States Cavalry, was assigned, when still a major, to the Military Intelligence Division in Mexico City in the 1920s when Porter was there during three successive visits. Because of Porter's association with the revolutionary government of Mexico, she had come to the attention of U.S. officials fearful of the Mexican government's involvement in events that could lead to the eruption of war on the Mexico-Texas border and fearful also that socialists and communists in Mexico could influence similar movements in the United States. Porter was the subject of a flurry of letters among members of the Military Intelligence Division and various persons in the U.S. Department of Justice.

Source: W. H. Cowles, report to W. J. Burns, Chief of the U.S. Bureau of Investigation (Department of Justice), 10 October 1921, Record of U.S. Embassy in Mexico, vol. 12, National Archives, Washington, DC. A copy of the report is in the Papers of Thomas F. Walsh, Special Collections, University of Maryland, College Park, Libraries. The person who supplied the information to Cowles was Colonel Harvey Miller, acting military attaché in Mexico City. Cowles chose to summarize Miller's report with direct quotations inserted strategically.

My dear Mr. Burns:

With reference to your letter of August 2, 1921, initialed JEH-GPH, information has been received from the Military Attaché, Mexico City, dated August 31, 1921, to the following effect:

Miss Porter is personally known to the writer [Colonel Harvey Miller]. She is an attractive, clever and cultured young woman, about 35 years of age, to all appearances a lady, born and bred. She writes for the magazine "Asia," a recent contribution being a series of articles entitled "My Chinese Marriage" published under the nom-de-plume "M.T.F."

Miss Porter has been in Mexico for a number of months and has associated largely with radicals, although, at times, she has appeared at social functions given by the American colony in Mexico City. Among other radicals with whom she associated was a young Russian woman—a Miss Mikowitz, or some similar name—who, it is believed, was expelled some months since.[1]

That Miss Porter has been on intimate terms with "a few of the Mexican officials" cannot be confirmed or denied. It would seem, however, that such is a fair inference. It may be stated, in this connection, that, in the April number of "The Magazine of Mexico," of which Miss Porter is Editor, the frontispiece is a large photograph of Luis Morones, a Mexican Government Official and a well known radical.[2] The first article in this issue entitled: "The Economic Importance of Mexico" is from the pen of Luis Morones. In an introductory insert, undoubtedly written by Miss Porter, the following is the concluding paragraph:

> Mr. Morones is an idealist and is interested in the practical working out of economic theories. Under his leadership a complete reorganization of the government munitions and military supplies factories has been accomplished. The working conditions have been very much improved, approaching in fact the ideal, wages have been increased, hours shortened and, in justification of his methods, the cost of all articles to the government has been very materially decreased.[3]

The inefficiency of the administration of the military manufacturing plants under the direction of this man and the unfortunate conditions existing in said factories, have been fully covered in monograph reports from this office.

An article written by Miss Porter in the April issue, entitled "In a Mexican Patio," is an unusually clever effort.[4]

"The Magazine of Mexico," a splendid effort, has seen two monthly publications—March and April—of the current year. The promoter of this magazine is Mr. G. A. Hole,[5] a capitalist of Seattle—the Editorial and Managing Director is Mr. W. D. Outman of San Antonio,[6] Texas—the Editor is Katherine Anne Porter. Mr. Hole is a quiet, reserved and unassuming gentleman of whom the writer saw much as Mr. Hole and the writer lived in the same club in Mexico City. The writer also knows Mr. Outman. In the endeavor of the above named parties to print their magazine, the publication of which was suspended with the April issue, a subsidy was sought from the Mexican Government. This subsidy was never obtained. This fact is known to the writer at first hand.

Retinger, a friend of Miss Porter's, with whom it is stated she is in love, was in trouble in the United States some time ago and needed a $500 bail bond. He is a Pole and is in Mexico City at the present time. (Note: Apparently this man is Joseph Retinger, who was regarded with suspicion by the French during the war, and who was charged with illegal entry into the United States from Mexico about March 1, 1921.) Miss Porter is temporarily in the United States.

A supplementary report, dated September 3, states that Miss Porter has been discharged as Editor of "The Magazine of Mexico."

Very truly yours,
W. H. Cowles
Major, Cavalry,
Chief, M.I.4.

10 / J. Edgar Hoover

John Edgar Hoover (1885–1972) was special assistant to W. J. Burns, director of the Bureau of Investigation, from 1921 until 1924, when Burns stepped down and Hoover took over as director. In 1935 Hoover founded the Federal Bureau of Investigation, which supplanted the Bureau of Investigation, and continued to serve as director until his death.

Source: J. Edgar Hoover, Memorandum, 2 August 1921, U.S. Department of Justice, Bureau of Investigation, File number 25-230. The source of Hoover's information was Robert (Roberto) Haberman,[7] who was interviewed by Hoover on 26 July 1921 when he was in the United States ostensibly to study schools and universities to help with the establishment of a technical school in Mexico City. In order to avoid deportation or imprisonment, he may have been working as a spy for the U.S. government to undermine radical movements in Mexico while simultaneously encouraging the Mexican government to deport expatriates such as Porter, who collaborated with Haberman on an article for the leftist magazine *The New York Call* and was unaware of Haberman's apparent duplicity.[8] Hoover summarized Haberman's fresh recollections of Porter.

Haberman also reported that a MISS KATHERINE ANNE PORTER, a writer who has been in Mexico for a year and who is stated to have been born in Texas, is on intimate terms with many of the leading radicals in Mexico, as well as a few of the Mexican officials. She is a writer for the magazine "Asia." She is also intimate with one RETINGER who Haberman states is well supplied with funds. Retinger was believed to be in the German secret service during the period of the war and is even now suspected of activities of a similar nature.[9] Miss Porter is also on intimate terms with COLONEL MILLER, the representative of the Military Intelligence Division in Mexico City, and according to Haberman receives a great deal of inside information from Colonel Miller, as that individual is stated to be addicted to strong drink and to give many parties in which the fair sex participates. Haberman further stated that Katayama[10] has been in Mexico City, but

Frayna[11] has not been in Mexico to his knowledge. Katayama was well supplied with funds which were believed to have been received from Moscow. Haberman emphasized the activities of Retinger, particularly, as he believed he should be thoroughly watched.[12]

11 / Josephine Herbst

Josephine Herbst (1892–1969), novelist, essayist, and political activist, met Katherine Anne Porter in Greenwich Village in the early 1920s. She and Porter became fast friends sympathetic to one another's struggles to be self-supporting writers, but their friendship eventually disintegrated over differences of opinion about the relationship between art and politics and about Gertrude Stein, whom Porter attacked in reviews and Herbst defended.[13] In Paris in 1924 Herbst formed a relationship with John Herrmann, another writer and a communist activist, whom she married in the fall of 1926.

Source: Josephine Herbst, "A Year of Disgrace," *Noble Savage* 3 (1961): 128–60; reprinted in her *The Starched Blue Sky of Spain and Other Memoirs* (Boston: Northeastern UP, 1991), 53–98.

In late spring [of 1926] some Connecticut rivers flooded, backed up into inland brooks, and then ebbed, leaving huddles of sticks, old leaves, and the owlish glitter of a tin can. A trickle of young people drifted into the countryside. You could have an abandoned farmhouse for the asking, with little more required than "to fix things up" or to paint a few walls. Some of the land had been taken over by Polish farmers, whose coarse vitality could better cope with the smitten soil than the tremulous hands of an old New England bachelor, now content with collecting wormy apples for a barrel of hard cider. Katherine Anne Porter rattled around in a stone house in a maple grove [. . .].

And often during the summer, when our house opened from two rooms to six and our garden could have fed a huge family,[14] it seemed to me that each of us in the valley called Merry-all relived some personal adventure as it might have been related in fiction. For surrounded by a company devoted to the art of fiction either as writers or as readers, you felt the source of material of one's own existence stir and come to life, be burnished and glisten, if only for the moment when the faces turned toward you ready to laugh or become bemused. You might be encouraged to ribaldry in recounting some old love affair or in an attempt to be "honest" rob yourself of a subtler truth. One narrator might unconsciously distort for the sake of the paradox, while another might painfully try to trace in the most dissimilar adventures the threads that implied an inner harmony. I might remember the Pears Soap of childhood, its color as translucent as clear quince jelly. Katherine Anne could recall being bathed by the nuns and how the long gown considered appropriate for "modesty's sake" floated out on the bathwater like the pad of a water lily. Or the English painter Ernest Stock[15] might spring a quotation:

When antelopes surmount eagles in flight,
And swans be swifter than hawks of the tower,
Then put women in trust and confidence . . .[16]

thus tempting us to take note of a graver wound than the exterior scars of the shrapnel in his leg, earned in the war when he had been shot down in a plane. As he ran around in shorts, we were not sure he was not trying to expose the one scar in token of the other, but he won no more than a comment from a Polish farm-wife, who scoffed, "Look at him now, running around in underpants, showing off them bony knees!"

He might drop on the grass to sketch our corncrib, empty except for a mouse, or come suddenly as night fell, pale as an Orestes pursued down the coast of Calabria by the Furies, to beg to spend the night. [. . .]

It was an interlude of time as clear and uncertain as a drop of water. It hung, trembling and iridescent, like a fresh green grape. To eat it made a fever in the blood. Should the fever be fed or starved? Where were the sources of energy: in work, in love, in the ground itself? We could try them all, reaching into the bin that seemed to have no bottom. Sometimes the hands alone held restorative powers and one wished only to be rid of paper. To get close to the sky, skin, taste. To refurnish with a walk at night, or with a wild Polish dance where the shy country women danced, pinching up their stiff skirts in delicate scarred hands. To get up in the morning when the dew frosted the red cabbage, to pounce upon the cutworms ready to wilt the tender pea stalks: what savage energy could leap out at the discovery of the cannibal soon to end his feast between two flat stones! What a miracle currant jelly was, and how I gloated on the little jeweled array of glasses sitting in the sun. Nathan Asch,[17] his hair dabbed with the yellow paint with which he was renovating the interior of his house, found an old waffle iron, scrubbed off the rust, and invited us to waffle feasts with maple syrup. Daisy and Ted[18] went in for pork roasts studded with garlic. Katherine Anne picked a bushel of dandelions to make delicious wine, as subtly intoxicating as champagne. John and Ernest Stock made little models of a Breton fishing boat and competed on a pond with the pomp of a Bermuda race. [. . .]

Katherine Anne Porter and
Josephine Herbst, in Erwinna,
Pennsylvania, 1929. Courtesy
Papers of Katherine Anne Porter,
Special Collections, University of
Maryland, College Park, Libraries.

The late shimmering of the Queen Anne's lace began to look like frost. Nathan
Asch packed his wife off to Duluth, where her father, a rich banker, might be persuaded to give them a loan for the duration of their wait for his novel to be published.[19] Then he hitched a ride to the railroad with his black cat, Moses, sourly
peeping from a basket. Katherine Anne vanished with the mist one early morning on a milk truck. Ted and Daisy, deep in debt for pork roasts and goodies, fled
anonymously. Ernest Stock washed his hands of Connecticut, where the landscape had never equaled the downs of England anyhow.

We came back to New York with what we called "the loot": manuscripts of two
novels, a basket of currant jelly, and summer tan. [. . .]

[In 1927] Katherine Anne Porter was living on the third floor of a rickety
house on Hudson Street, called by its witty tenants Casa Caligari.[20] Creaking up
the stairs, you half expected to see a skeleton wag from the ceiling, but instead a

door opened on the second landing to a view of a child strapped to a high chair while it gobbled its bowl of bread and milk. It was Dorothy Day's little daughter,[21] a rare sight, for children were few and far between for our generation. When you came to Katherine Anne's room the prospect opened surprisingly to a domestic pavilion with gingham curtains at a window, a flowering primrose, a small cook-stove with a coffeepot sizzling away, a gray cat on a cushion in a child's rocking chair. Her footing was as precarious as the house was shaky, but she could make light of it, wittily tossing the jacket of a book she had reviewed into a wastebasket or pinning up a jacket of Holger Cahill's *Pagan Earth,* with a drawing by John Sloan, in a place of honor.[22] She was promising herself to do a review of the book, but she never got around to it.

Nor did we get around to many of the things we had promised ourselves we would do when, in the country, we had taken a long view of the time to come. Brute necessity gobbled up time and energy. [. . .] In the grip of making ends meet, everyone was compelled to commit follies. Down to ten dollars, I could throw it away on a delectable hat. Katherine Anne Porter invested in a chair with a delicate frame and a striped upholstery of blue-and-lilac-veined satiny material that gouged a hole in her "capital" bigger than what remained.

12 / Matthew Josephson

Matthew Josephson (1899–1978), journalist, biographer, and chronicler of American economics, was a graduate of Columbia University, an associate editor of *Broom,* and a contributing editor of *transition.* He met Porter in the fall of 1928 when he temporarily replaced the book editor at Macaulay and Company, the publisher of his biography of Émile Zola (1928), and she accepted an editorial job there. They had a brief affair in the winter of 1928–29. In his diary, recorded in retrospect, he recalled that Porter "deployed great charm" and "quite carried me away."[23]

Source: Matthew Josephson, *Life among the Surrealists* (New York: Holt, Rinehart and Winston, 1962), 352–54.

One day there appeared in our publishing office a young Southern woman, who had a fine head and very large gray eyes. She was Katherine Anne Porter, and had been recommended to us for some routine copy editing to be done at home. . . .[24] A small woman, she bore herself with great poise, was low-voiced, soft-spoken, and full of old-fashioned airs and graces that made her seem very different from the New Woman one saw in New York at this time, who habitually wore the "dead-pan" expression then in vogue. Katherine Anne also had much wit, and soon won many friends among the members of my own circle. Like some of them, she too had experienced an interesting phase of "exile," though in revolutionary Mexico instead of Europe, and the subject was very much on her mind. At first we enjoyed only oral versions of her stories; they were reminiscences of her early life in Texas and Louisiana and of her years in Mexico. Her way of telling them was fairly "mesmerizing," as Edmund Wilson once remarked; we often expressed the wish that she would write them down. She would begin: "Today is the 105th birthday of my name grandmother. She died when I was ten years old. When I remember that indomitable woman . . ."[25] There would follow an unforgettable portrait of a crusty, humorous, and hard-swearing lady of the Old South.[26]

Soon I was shown fragments or rough drafts of stories Katherine Anne was trying to write, and [was] invited to criticize them unsparingly. She worked over these things and reworked them in a tormented way, as if depending on autohypnosis to call forth language that truly conveyed her emotion. I was astonished at the high quality of her fragmentary sketches or drafts of stories and exhorted her to finish them.[27]

13 / Robert Plunkett

Robert Plunkett (1919–) is the son of Helen Rebecca (Becky) Edelman Crawford and her first husband, Charles Robert Plunkett, a professor at New York University. After his parents divorced when he was very young, Plunkett attended various boarding schools in the area; after serving in the U.S. Army in Europe he entered the Massachusetts Institute of Technology, where he earned a Ph.D. in mechanical engineering in 1948. He worked at General Electric for ten years and taught at Rice University before joining the faculty at the University of Minnesota. At his retirement in 1988 he had authored more than sixty articles and had been elected to the National Academy of Engineering. He lives in Austin, Texas, with his wife, Helen Catherine Bair Plunkett.

Source: Robert Plunkett, telephone interviews with Darlene Harbour Unrue, 11 May 2006 and 13 October 2007.

Katherine Anne Porter was a good friend of my mother, Becky Crawford, and my stepfather, John Crawford.[28] She was a frequent houseguest at their tall, old four-story house at 74 Orange Street in Brooklyn.

My mother was interested in leftist causes, and she was interested in people, especially writers and artists. Most of the people who gathered at the Brooklyn house were pacifists and anarchists, and they all had an interest in art. They also were fearful of deportation because of their politics and ethnicity, since those were the years of the Palmer Raids,[29] carried out by the U.S. Justice and Immigration Departments and targeting Russians (and Russian Jews especially). I assume that Katherine Anne shared the interests and worries of my mother and her other friends, although I wouldn't necessarily have known that during the period from which I remember her, 1927 to 1930, when I was eight to eleven years old.

I was away at boarding school most of the time, but I spent holidays with either my mother and stepfather or my father and stepmother, Louise. My mother and father were friendly, and it wasn't uncommon for all of them to be together, most often at my mother's, on holidays, when there were usually twenty or twenty-five persons gathered.

I remember seeing at my mother's house at one time or other such persons as Emma Goldman,[30] Caroline Gordon,[31] Allen Tate,[32] Dorothy Day, William Sanger (the husband of Margaret), Peggy Guggenheim,[33] Eva Le Gallienne,[34] Hart Crane,[35] Malcolm and Peggy Cowley,[36] Eugene O'Neill,[37] and Richard Wright.[38] Bill Rollins, who had written a book very popular in Russia, I learned later, lived at my mother's house a lot.[39]

Etched in my memory is a particular scene between Bill and Katherine Anne. She was leaning over the railing of the third-floor porch, and Bill was in the yard below. He said, "I'm going to spit in your eye." Katherine Anne, who didn't seem to me to have much of a sense of humor, especially when it was directed at her, said, "Now why would you want to do that?"

In the backyard of the Orange Street house my mother and stepfather and their friends enjoyed drinks during Prohibition. Once when my mother, stepfather, and several other persons were all sitting out there in the backyard drinking, my baby half sister, Mary Jane, threw one of her famous tantrums, holding her breath until she turned blue. My mother and stepfather rushed inside with her, but that didn't stop the party. Katherine Anne and Bill Rollins stayed on and kept on drinking as if there had been no interruption at all.

Katherine Anne and Bill actually were put in charge of both the house and Mary Jane when my mother and stepfather went to Bermuda to get liquor, which despite Prohibition could easily be brought through customs in those days.

I don't remember that Katherine Anne had a particular interest in me or even Mary Jane. And although my mother mentioned that Katherine Anne had been a patient in tuberculosis hospitals, I don't remember her being ill and staying in her room. She seemed to always be in the middle of the socializing. As a child, I didn't have an opinion on her looks. My recollection of her is of a very skinny little sprite with longish white hair.

14 / Elizabeth Anderson

Elizabeth Prall Anderson (1884–1976) attended the University of Michigan and the library school at the New York Public Library. She was a bookstore manager in New York in 1922 when she met Sherwood Anderson, and in 1924 she became his third wife. They separated in 1928 and divorced in 1932.

Source: Elizabeth Anderson with Gerald R. Kelly, *Miss Elizabeth: A Memoir* (Boston: Little, Brown, 1969), 203–5.

I met Katherine Anne Porter [in 1931] through a letter to her that had been written by a young man I knew at Stanford. Katherine Anne had been deeply involved in the [Mexican] Revolution for some years before I met her. Some said she had even been active in it, but I think she simply knew all the people who were fighting in it. They were all friends together, the leaders of the Revolution and many artists and writers. This was at a time when alliances and loyalties were in a state of flux. The influential person who was your friend a week before might no longer be in good standing with the Powers, and if you retained your friendship, your own standing might be suspect. Katherine Anne, of course, had a great many friends who were controversial, and because of that the current Powers did not care for her.[40] No matter. In a month, the situation would be changed.

Katherine Anne was very popular with her friends, however, and she had many of them. She had a dark prettiness and was a strange, complicated girl who could be perfectly charming or perfectly horrible with no apparent reason for either extreme. She lived in a funny old house near the Lagunilla Market and could neither cook nor clean house, but she could write. Her house, it seemed to me, was uncomfortable and almost devoid of furniture, but Katherine Anne did not mind at all sitting on uncarpeted floors. She had a small room in which she wrote, with a window facing a blank wall, and this satisfied her nicely.[41]

I was not introduced to the young man who also lived in the house so I never knew if he was her husband or not, but he was considerably younger than Katherine Anne.[42] I decided there was probably no formal relation between them when he abruptly disappeared, having been summarily ordered out, according to Katherine Anne's friends.

In the evenings, she had a succession of youngish men who admired her and who took her out constantly. I was told by her friends, who told entirely too many stories it seemed to me, that Katherine Anne had once received a prize of five hundred dollars for something she had written. She went to the bank with the money order and was given the money in gold pieces, as was the custom then for American money. It was handed over to her in the regular white canvas bag and she took it with her on her regular round of seeing people and meeting friends. Before the day was over, she had lost the heavy sack and it was never found. In those days, a person could live for months and months on that money.

15 / Winifred Hill

Winifred Hill (1880–c. 1985) was an American expatriate who lived most of her life in Mexico and moved among both expatriates and Mexican artists and political leaders. As a hostess she bridged the gap between disparate groups in Mexico City society in the 1920s and 1930s. Porter's friend Mary Doherty pointed out in 1921 that Porter refused to associate with the American business colony in Mexico City.[43] By 1931 Porter had overcome that aversion and mixed freely with American expatriates of all political interests and occupations.

Source: Winifred Hill, personal interview with Darlene Harbour Unrue, Mexico City, 17 August 1981.

I came to Mexico in 1907 when I was twenty-seven years old. I was going to art school in New York City when my husband, who was fluent in Spanish, was asked to go to Veracruz during the American occupation to help translate the municipal regulations for the American officers, who couldn't read the language. When the troops left Veracruz, we did, too.

We settled in San Angel on the outskirts of Mexico City and became active members of the American community there. I went to work for an American law firm that had a branch office in Mexico City, and it seemed as if my husband and I met everyone in the expatriate community and a good number of Mexican artists. Each Sunday I entertained twenty to twenty-five persons. We started with breakfast alfresco in the garden, after which everyone retired to hammocks. Later, I served tea. It was all very casual, and it wasn't unusual to be serving tea at ten o'clock at night, especially to the Mexican artists who habitually showed up late in the evening.

I knew Katherine Anne Porter best in 1930 and 1931.[44] She occasionally attended my Sunday parties, most often in the company of a group of American expatriates and Mexican artists that included Mary Doherty, Carlton Beals,[45] Tina Modotti,[46] William Spratling,[47] Dr. Atl,[48] Diego Rivera,[49] Natalie Scott,[50] and Adolpho Best-Maugard.[51] At my house this group mingled with business people who were part of the expatriate country-club set.[52]

In 1928 my husband had bought the Blue Bookstore, which had been founded in 1905 and first owned by the American Book Company. We sold fine writing paper, books, stationery, and magazines. It was an old-fashioned store, not self-service, and it never was a meeting place for American artists. Persons such as Katherine Anne dropped in for writing paper and magazines more than anything else.

The last time I heard from Katherine Anne was the summer of 1931, when she was preparing to leave Mexico to go to Europe. She had been living in Mixcoac outside of Mexico City, and she was selling or giving away all her furniture as well as her collection of animals. She called to see whether I was interested in taking her little piano, which she had bought in order to study music with Pablo O'Higgins.[53] I wasn't able to use it, and I understand she sold it to a café in the city.[54] I never heard from her after that, but my memories of her are vivid.

Katherine Anne Porter at dining table in Mixcoac house near Mexico City, 1931. Back inscription in Porter's hand, "Mme. Ennui." Courtesy Papers of Katherine Anne Porter, Special Collections, University of Maryland, College Park, Libraries.

3
Europe, Texas, and Louisiana, 1932–1940

In 1931, when Porter arrived in Europe with Eugene Pressly, whom she married two years later, her life acquired a dimension different from anything she had ever known. At first she wasn't sure she was going to like Europe, for Germany frightened her. After stopping in Paris, however, she wanted to live nowhere else. Paris expatriate society welcomed her, and despite having only a small collection of stories to her name, she was considered an important writer. She reunited with old acquaintances such as Eugene Jolas and made new friendships with Sylvia Beach, Monroe Wheeler, Barbara Harrison, Glenway Wescott, and Toni Willison. Her creative energy was released anew. Although she had almost completely exhausted the Mexican vein of her fiction, she set into motion the Miranda cycle, which would include her most highly acclaimed stories and short novels. By the time she returned to the United States in 1936, she had embarked on a speaking career, and she knew her marriage to Pressly was over. Soon she met Albert Russel Erskine Jr., whom she married after she divorced Pressly. She nourished friendships with longtime southern friends as well as persons introduced to her by Caroline Gordon and Allen Tate. She had two special new interests, however. She had taken up a nephew, her brother's son Paul, and a niece, her sister Gay's daughter Ann, and set about becoming their artistic mother. She was also reaching out to a younger generation of writers she admired, such as Eudora Welty, and offering encouragement and support. Satisfaction in her artistic life helped compensate for the looming failure of her marriage to Erskine, whom she left in 1940 after accepting a residency at the artist colony Yaddo in Saratoga Springs, New York.

16 / Glenway Wescott

Glenway Wescott (1901–87), an important writer in the 1920s and 1930s, was a member of the American expatriate community that included Ernest Hemingway and Gertrude Stein. His highly regarded novel *The Grandmothers* (1927) won the Harper Prize Novel Award. His best-selling novel *Apartment in Athens* (1945) was reviewed by Porter. Close friends with Porter for many years, he fell out of her favor in the last decades of her life.

Source: Glenway Wescott, "Katherine Anne Porter: The Making of a Novel," *Atlantic Monthly* April 1962: 43–49.

Having had the pleasure of a long friendship with Miss Porter, I find it irksome to call her "Miss Porter." It has been mainly a comradeship of the literary life, and on that account perhaps, in conversation and in correspondence, I often address her as "Porter." A host of her fellow writers and others speak of her and to her as "Katherine Anne," with or without a basis of intimacy. Somewhat like Jane Austen, or like Colette,[1] she has an unassuming sort of celebrity that invites or inspires friendliness. [. . .]

Now let me try to describe her: like many women accustomed to being loved, she dreads and disapproves of photographers, although in fact usually she has lent herself well to their techniques, and they have been on her side. I remember one of her diatribes, some years ago, against a photographer and an interviewer, sent by one of the news weeklies, who, she said, had caught her unawares and committed a misrepresentation of her. In the photograph in question, when it appeared, she looked to me like Marie Antoinette young, her hair perfectly coiffed and powdered-looking, playing her typewriter as though it were a spinet. And it amazed me to note how skillfully she had been able to simplify the record of her life for the interviewer, also.

She has a lovely face, of the utmost distinction in the Southern way: moonflower-pale, never sun-burned, perhaps not burnable. She is a small woman with a fine figure still; sometimes very slender, sometimes not. Her eyes are large, dark, and lustrous, and they are apt to give one fond glances, or teasing merry looks, or occasionally great flashes of conviction or indignation. Her voice is sweet, a little velvety or husky. In recent years she has familiarized a great number of appreciative fellow Americans with it, by means of reading and speaking engagements and phonograph recordings.

[. . .] Literary critics and historians have often remarked on the mighty contributions of the female sex to literature. For the most part those who have done the contributing have been spinsters, nuns, courtesans, invalids, a little exempt from the more distracting, exhausting aspects of womanhood as such. Katherine Anne, throughout her youth and middle age, led a maximum life concomitantly with her perfect, even perfectionist story writing. As I have remarked, she seems to like to simplify a part of the record of her existence for any sort of questioner. In fact, except for essentially private matters of love and marriage and ill health and economics, it really has been simple. And therefore I (and other friends), instead of concentrating on ascertaining all the realities, the dates and the names and the locations and so on, have always interested myself in what might be called story material about her, somehow more characteristic than the mere biography.

For example, when she was a girl, somewhere in the South, she had to spend months and months in a sanatorium with a grave pulmonary illness, diagnosed as one of the baffling, uncommon forms of tuberculosis.[2] She was too ill to have visitors. Letters also evidently were overstimulating and exhausting. Even books seemed not good for her; her reading had to be rationed, just a few pages at a time. Then it was discovered that the intense restlessness of her bright eyes, gazing at the ceiling, examining and re-examining the furniture, staring at the solitude, gave her a temperature. Her doctor therefore prescribed that a green baize cloth be placed over her face for an hour or two every morning and every afternoon, as one covers the cage of a canary bird when one doesn't want it to sing. I feel convinced that if anything of the sort were done to me, I should give up the ghost, on account of the autosuggestion and the discouragement. Not Katherine Anne! That was only the beginning of a lifetime of delicate health and indomitable strength.

All this balance of physiology in her case, strong constitution, poor health, has mystified those who care for her. Perhaps the physicians whom she happened on here and there—"the pulse-takers, the stethoscope-wielders, the order-givers," as she has called them—have been mystifiers in some measure. One of them, in upstate New York, told her that her trouble was all a matter of allergies, and when she inquired, "What allergies?," his answer was, "You're allergic to the air you breathe."

Another, in California, she wrote me, "set out to change my chemistry, which made him say tst, tst, after a very thorough going-over, and he aims to supply all my lacks and to suppress all my internal enemies. There is about the whole project something so blithely Californian that I cannot but fall in with it."

Still another, a young one in Connecticut, pleased her by practicing "real materia medica," and not saying anything at all about her state of mind or her nervous condition. She has always objected to having strangers, even specialists, fussing around in her psychology, comparing them to the most disrespectful, disrupting type of cleaning woman. "They mess the place up; they don't know where things belong or what goes with what."

One year at Christmastime, when she had been felled for ten days by some form of influenza and had been taking one of the sulfa drugs, she got up out of bed, though in mortal weakness, took a look at herself—prettily dressed, with "her hair in a curl or two," with an expression on her face which she could not quite make out, "distinctly remote, disengaged, full of mental reservations"—and then, in a longish letter, undertook to make clear to me her whole view of life. But it was unclarifiable, inexplicable, she had to admit, even to herself as she was living it, "because its truth or falseness cannot be known until the end."

Therefore, instead, she concluded that letter with an account of the medicines she had been taking: "a fantastic row of apothecary's powders, pills, and potions, all of them in the most poisonously brilliant colors, amethyst and sapphire and emerald and purple, each with its own mission of soothing or elevating the spirits, calming the heart or stimulating it, loosening the phlegm and tightening the nerves, stopping the cough and lowering the fever.

"As for the sulfa, I have had to take a tablet every four hours for two nights and two days, and never once did my mind fail to wake me at the right hour, on the hour, like a little radio station. Once I slept stubbornly, and was waked by a sharp rapping at my door. It was four in the morning; the whole house was asleep and quiet. I sat up in bed, knowing Who had done it."

It is hard to read this slight incident rightly, with its capitalized Who, suggestive of the commissioning of Mozart's never-finished Requiem by Whoever-that-was, a being never seen again, and of other such myths. But, stop and think, if that rapper at Katherine Anne's door at four in the morning had been Death, He would have stayed his hand and let her sleep and skip the sulfa. That was in 1943; it is pleasant to think that the greater part of *Ship of Fools* was written on time borrowed from Him.

No doubt about it, there are warring forces in Katherine Anne. Is it that her physique wearies of having to house a spirit so strenuous and emotional, and now and then tries to expel it or to snuff it out? Or is it instinctive in her soul to keep punishing her body for not being superhuman, for not being ideal, for not being immortal? Neither has ever prevailed over the other; both have been invincible. Nothing has come of the great dichotomy; or, to be exact, literature has come of it.

"Every force of instinct and every psychic evil in us," she once wrote, "fight the mind as their mortal enemy; but in this as in everything else, I have known from the beginning which side I am on, and I am perfectly willing to abide by my first choice until death; indeed I can't do otherwise. For death it must be in the end, so far as the flesh is concerned; but what lives on afterward can be honorable." To wit, twenty-six works of fiction of different lengths, honorable and, I am sure, durable, and more to come. [. . .]

Now, to turn to another area of the legendry of Katherine Anne's life, one which she has not perpetuated in any of her fiction: it used to be said that at an early age she had been in the movies as a Mack Sennett bathing girl,[3] along with Gloria Swanson and Mabel Normand *et al.*[4] Certainly she was as good-looking as they, whether or not she could have performed as funnily. For some reason I never like to question or cross-question her about things: but I once ventured to do so about this. It was a matter of journalism, she explained, not show business. Commissioned to write an article for some newspaper or magazine, she pretended briefly to be a comedienne for the sake of the realistic detail and local color.[5]

Not so long ago, she had a try at earning her living by script writing. Her first Hollywood assignment was not so much to write as to be attached in an Egeria-like or muselike capacity to a famous producer, now dead.[6] For a while this amused her; at least she sent back to the Eastern seaboard amusing reports of it. "One or the other of us," she reported—the producer had another salaried writer also at his beck and call, perhaps more than one—"tosses a tiny shred of an idea at him. He seizes it out of the air and without stopping for breath constructs a whole scene. He then asks us what we think of it, and as we open our mouths to answer, he says, 'It's a wonderful scene. Now what else have you got in mind?' And the thing is repeated; sometimes we just sit there for two hours." What he had in mind, or perhaps I should say, in the works, was a film about Queen Elizabeth.[7]

Presently she began to feel like "a fox with his leg in a trap," gnawing away at it; and by the end of the thirteen-week stint contracted for in the first place, she had persuaded her famous man that she was not the inspirer he needed. A part of their maladjustment, she sensed, was the fact that he was a Christian Scientist, whereas she had been brought up a Roman Catholic. During the thirteen weeks he had seemed deeply disapproving of the large salary that he or his studio had been paying her; but at the last, suddenly, she wrote, he "began to worry about my future. What on earth was I going to do now? where was I going? did I have any money? I was happy to be able to tell him that I was relatively rich and wasn't going anywhere."

In fact, she was relatively poor; apparently they had been paying her in Confederate money or fool's gold or something.[8] Not seeing any other solution for her practical problems just then, she transferred her talents to another studio, where she was put to work on a film about Madame Sans-Gêne.[9]

All her life, Katherine Anne has been bewitched by the hope of ceasing to be homeless, of settling somewhere and getting her books and manuscripts and notebooks out of storage and within reach, on shelves and in filing cabinets and in ring binders. With the evanescent Western money she bought a small segment of mountain for a building site, but could not keep it. One day, as she sat peacefully writing in a rented ranch cabin in the Mojave Desert, a western wind arose and tore out a window frame over her desk and slightly fractured her skull; as you might say, the furies! But, never forget, the furies sometimes are on the side of the angels. She did not properly belong out West, at least not then.

In subsequent years, at intervals she has had to depend on the universities and colleges for her livelihood. As a rule, at the beginning of her various stints or bouts on campuses, she has been persuaded by the literature-loving educators who have arranged things, or she has persuaded herself, that not much actual pedagogy would be required of her. Usually, however, they seem to have got the harness on her in some way. I remember a letter from a very great university indeed, in the Middle West, specifying her teaching schedule: only five hours a week actually behind the microphone in the classroom (so specified in her contract), and only about eighty term papers to be read and graded. But she also had to examine the manuscripts of the more creative young persons on campus and to advise them in hour-long sessions; about fourteen of these a week. Also, once a week she had to give a spontaneous hour-long lecture to some special class or group or club. I imagine that no trained and experienced professor would find this schedule at all onerous or unfair. To Katherine Anne, as a mature woman of genius in delicate health, perhaps somewhat proud and euphoric, with so much creative work of her own not only in mind but partly on paper and covered by publishers' contracts, it seemed hard; and all too often her university engagements were terminated by illness.

She and I became friends in Paris in 1932 and began our correspondence upon my return to this country in the autumn of 1933, and it has been continuous ever since. I have been rereading all her letters to me and another precious collection lent by a friend of hers and mine;[10] and now that much of the circumstantial detail in them has ceased to be of interest, and therefore the main elements and outlines of her mind and her life appear more impressively, as it were, a range of hills which the autumn has stripped of leaves, I am struck by something about them that may have conditioned her, even benefited her, in her art of fiction.

It is that they are extraordinarily, uniquely subjective—self-judging and explanatory and disciplinary and self-defending, with matchless detail and finesse in all these mirrorings of the heart and the mind, shifting and shining and, in a way hypnotizing—whereas in fiction she has been free from herself. In fiction she has maintained the oddest impersonality, a disengagement from any sort of autobiographical point of view, a distinctness between her own ego, her sensitivenesses and compulsions and illusions, and those of all the alter egos that she writes about, and an abstention from fantasy and lyricism and rhetoric of which most novelists—indeed, many journalists and historians—are incapable.

It is almost startling to compare her with other famous twentieth-century women in this respect: Virginia Woolf; Colette! As for the writing of our more extreme, compendious, sociological novelists, it is a sort of concavity, which almost teases one to deduce what they themselves are, convexly; rather like the shapes of ancient Pompeians in the awful layers of ashes from Vesuvius.

Katherine Anne is not like that at all. The objectivity of her narrative art, if I may apply to her Coleridge's famous formula (only Shakespeare really filled the bill, he thought), is a matter of sending herself out of herself; of thinking herself into "the thoughts and feelings of beings in circumstances wholly and strangely different" from her own: *hic labor, hoc opus.*

I believe that her vast self-expressive and confidential first-person communication to her friends, freshly inspired or provoked each time, swiftly produced on the typewriter and not rewritten, scarcely reread, has served to purify her mind of a good deal of that pride and willfulness and narcissism and excitability by which the lifework of fiction writers has often been beclouded, enfeebled, inflated, blemished. Of course, her letter writing must have shortened her working days and used up incalculable energy, thus reducing the amount of her production of the more public forms of literature. [. . .]

In every type of short work she is a ready writer, given a green light and a little removal from other people and certain facilities in the way of board and keep.

But never a ready novelist! All that time, a third of a lifetime, her struggle with *Ship of Fools* has been going on. With the everlasting problem of her delicate health and the other difficulties and jeopardies that I have tried to describe without making a melodrama and a sentimentality of her life, certainly she has not worked at the novel uninterruptedly; but she has kept up her dedication of herself to it, only it, and staked her reputation and her self-respect on it. "Even when I was a little child," she once said to me, "I knew that youth was not for me"—a sentence wonderfully expressive of her particular lifelong uneasiness, responsive to her fate up ahead, and great patience from start to finish, knowing or sensing that she was going to grow old at the appointed, self-appointed task.

One cannot evaluate the experience of a literary genius unless and until one has perused all that has resulted from it. Obviously, a great deal of heartbreak and travel have been Katherine Anne's lot. But, let us remind ourselves, no fortunate and facile youthful, or even middle-aged, person could have written *Ship of Fools*. It has required the better part of a lifetime of unshrinking participation in life and unshirking endeavor, of hardheadedness and heat of heart and almost fanaticism, and now we have the result; and surely it must seem to her, in her weariness and pride, cheap at the price. [. . .]

It [*Ship of Fools*] is a vast portrait gallery, with portraits of all sizes hung here and there on the wall, high and low; and some of the portrayed ones seem to dance down out of their frames, some tumble out, some fight their way out, with fearful vitality. I can think of only one possible reason for anyone's not liking this book; just at the start the characters are almost too strong, one shrinks from them a little. No, you may say, I do not wish to spend another page with this smug glutton, or this hypochondriac drunkard, or this lachrymose widow; no, not another word out of that girl in the green dress! But presently, having read a certain number of pages, you feel a grudging sympathy with one and all, or a rueful empathy, or at least solidarity, as a fellow human.

I told Katherine Anne this one day on the telephone, and she said, "I promised myself solemnly: in this book I will not load the dice. We all do it, even you have done it; and so have I in my day, as you well know. But this time, I resolved, everyone was to have his say. I would not take sides. I was on everyone's side." [. . .]

Now, to give a recapitulation and a close to this rambling study of my friend's lifework, let me quote another of her letters, somber once more, but blended with some of her malicious spirit; showing also her great virtue of steadfastness. It was written in Liège, Belgium, where she had been given a Fulbright fellowship to teach at the university. In a letter to her I had vexed her with a weak reference of some sort to my age, and she chose to take it personally and struck back with an expression of some pathos and acerbity.

"When you and others younger than I, by I forget how many years, but a good number, complain of getting old, I think with dismay: What must they be thinking of me?

"I have had such a struggle to survive," she wrote, "so many illnesses that nearly crippled me when I was young, so many intimations of mortality before my time; I felt more decrepit at twenty-four than I have since; and now I do not have a proper sense of time. It does not chop itself like stove wood into decades convenient for burning. It is a vast drift in which I float, eddying back and forth,

Katherine Anne Porter, Glenway Wescott, and Monroe Wheeler, Southbury, Connecticut, 14 July 1956. Courtesy Papers of Katherine Anne Porter, Special Collections, University of Maryland, College Park, Libraries.

spinning round now and then, moving always towards no fixed point; which one day will dissolve and drop me into the abyss."

In any case, she went on to say, she could never trust other people's eyes or judgments in the matter. "When I was sixteen, a woman of middle age, when told *my* age, said 'Ha, she'll never see eighteen again!' And when I was twenty-eight, a man not at all malicious, guessed my age to be forty. Oddly enough, when I was fifty, another man who loved me, also thought me forty;[11] and I told him about the other guess, and wondered if I was never to escape from that particular decade."

Why, she asked me, should she worry about her visible years when others were so happy to do that worrying for her? Though she did not blame *me* for my worrisomeness, this sentence struck home.

She then told me her favorite story about age. She was lunching in Hollywood with Charles Brackett, the screenwriter, and two important film directors, and a few tables away saw the then famous child actress, Margaret O'Brien, with her mother, her governess, her director, and someone else. "And the three men at my table looked her over as though she were a pony they were thinking of buying, and one of them said, 'How old is she now?' and another answered, 'Six years old,' and there was a pause, and then Charlie said, 'She looks older than that.' There was a kind of nod-around among them and the moment passed."

The concluding paragraph of this letter is a kind of prose poem:

"It is five o'clock, I am in a dowdy furnished apartment where the keys don't turn, the gas cocks stick, the bathroom gadgets work half way, the neighborhood is *tout-petit bourgeois,* the furnishings are from the Belgian branch of Sears Roebuck, the place is suburban, the wild yellow leaves are flying in a high bitter wind under a smoky sky, and I have come to the world's end, and what was my errand here? There is nothing I wish to say to anyone here; does anybody want to listen? But it does look as if here again, with all the unlikeliness, the place and the time had met for me to sit at this table, three and one half feet square, and write something more of my own." [. . .]

In that same letter of the dark night of her soul in Belgium, or, to be precise, teatime of her soul in Belgium, she declared that the only disturbing thing about the passage of time, for her, was the fact that she had four books all clearly conceived and partly begun and waiting to be finished.[12] Now, three to go! And now perhaps not many of us will care to bet against her.

17 / Toni Willison

Florence (Toni) Hauser Willison (1903–98) met Katherine Anne Porter in Paris in 1934. Working in Greenwich Village in the 1920s as a button painter and dental assistant, Willison was active in leftist political organizations, as she was to be for much of her life. After her first marriage, to Jack Tworkov, ended in divorce, she married George Findlay Willison, a historian, with whom she had a son, Malcolm.

Source: Toni Willison, personal interviews with Darlene Harbour Unrue, 13–14 June 1996, at South Hill, Malta, New York.

In 1934 I was grieving over my father's recent death when a friend asked me to chaperone her two young daughters on a trip to France. My husband, George, encouraged me to go and convinced me that he and our four-year-old son, Malcolm, would get along fine without me for a few weeks.

Shortly after I arrived in Paris in September and turned my wards over to their French hosts, I called Katherine Anne Porter from the cheap hotel in which I was staying. I told her that my former sister-in-law, Janice Biala,[13] had urged me to get in touch with her and her husband, Eugene Pressly. Katherine Anne was very friendly and insisted that I come right over to their Boulevard Montparnasse apartment, which they were subletting from Janice and Ford Madox Ford.[14] I went, intending to stay twenty minutes, and ended up staying much longer. When Katherine Anne's husband, Gene, who worked at the American Embassy, came home, I invited them both out to dinner. Katherine Anne said, "I have a small roast already in the oven, and it would give us great pleasure if you would share it with us."

It was immediately apparent that Katherine Anne loved to entertain, and she was a wonderful cook. But she was an extraordinary conversationalist, too. In fact, she talked all the time. Gene was very gentle and quiet, a necessary trait, I thought, for Katherine Anne's husband. It was a wonderful evening, and I spent the rest of my remaining evenings in Paris with Katherine Anne and Gene. We went to museums and cafés and to a restaurant where everyone sang old French songs.

Katherine Anne and I shared a love for fashionable clothes. Neither of us had money to buy new clothes, but for the trip I had bought some good quality secondhand clothes that Katherine Anne admired, especially a black formal dress and a white suit. When I left Paris I gave them to her. She wore them for years and years and often told me how much pleasure they gave her.

After I left Paris we exchanged a few cards and letters for a while, and then our correspondence lapsed. Ten years later, however, I was in touch with Katherine Anne again. In 1945 she reviewed *Saints and Strangers,* a history of New England Puritans written by my husband.[15] I learned that she was in California, and I wrote to remind her of our 1934 meeting in Paris and to ask whether she knew that the George Willison who had written the book she enthusiastically reviewed was my husband. I mentioned in passing that George and I, who were living in Washington at the time, were weary of city life and political intrigue and hoped we could find a house in a rural community somewhere in the East. She quickly wrote back that she owned a house near Saratoga Springs that she was hoping to sell.[16] She suggested we make a trip there to see the house, which she had named South Hill, and let her know if we were interested in it. After the exchange of several letters, we bought this house that Katherine Anne had lovingly renovated in 1941 but lived in only a year before discovering she could not tolerate the very thing we wanted—isolation. Even though she didn't have much money at the time, she knew that we didn't either. She sold it to us for exactly what she paid for it and allowed us to make interest-free payments directly to her.[17]

We had many happy years here until George's death in 1972. Katherine Anne came here several times to visit us, pleased that friends had bought her house, and we went to see her when she was at Skidmore College to give a talk and receive an honorary degree.[18] I spoke with her on the phone regularly, and my son, Malcolm, took me to see her not long before she died.[19]

We had a lovely visit. She talked and talked, of course, and served us champagne. When we left, she seemed especially sad, as if she knew it would be our last visit. "Remember me! Remember me!" she called as we left.

As if anyone could forget her!

18 / Paul Porter

Harrison Paul Porter Jr. (1921–) was born and reared in Houston, Texas, the second of four children of Constance Eve Ingalls Porter and Harrison Paul Porter Sr., Katherine Anne Porter's brother. Paul Porter Jr. served in the U.S. Army in Europe in World War II and attended the University of California, Los Angeles. He worked as a scriptwriter, as a claims adjuster for the Southern Pacific Railroad, and finally in New York as an executive assistant to David Muss, chairman of the Muss-Tankoos Corporation. Since 1997 he has lived in Houston, Texas.

Source: Paul Porter, "Remembering Aunt Katherine," *Katherine Anne Porter and Texas: An Uneasy Relationship,* ed. Clinton Machann and William Bedford Clark (College Station: Texas A&M UP, 1990), 25–37.

Once upon a time in Hollywood an interviewer asked my cousin Ann what it was like living with Katherine Anne Porter.[20] After some reflection, Ann replied with a shrug, "It's like living with your favorite aunt, that's all."

I want to say a few things about the same aunt, who was my favorite, too. Nothing scandalous, nothing arcane about the symbolism or provenience of her fiction.

My first memory of Katherine Anne Porter is from the time she visited Houston in 1936, when I was a timid sixteen. This meeting took place at a family gathering in the home of her sister Mary Alice, known to me as Aunt Baby. My clearest memory of Aunt Katherine that evening, almost my only memory, is of a small, silver-haired woman, very animated, smoking a great deal, with a fascinating voice and a mysterious accent. She wore a sleeveless white piqué evening gown made from a design by Schiaparelli.[21] No jewelry, *but* . . . . . her earlobes were rouged! Astonished, her sisters and the other ladies made indulgent little jokes about it among themselves. Of course they had rouge on their cheeks, Aunt Baby quite a lot of it, but they thought rouged earlobes were outlandish, unseemly, just the kind of thing you would expect of someone who went off to live in Paris and exposed herself to the well-known wicked habits of the French. If Aunt Katherine was aware of what they were saying, she ignored it; and she rouged her earlobes for the rest of her life.

I believe it was in 1938 when we met again. She had taken rooms, a kind of railroad flat, in a big clapboard house in Houston Heights, not far from where I lived. She had no telephone, so I just walked in on her, intruded, you might say, although she never did. I was totally enchanted. Everything about her seemed different, meaningful, glamorous—a word she hated, by the way. We looked together through a massive book of Audubon's bird paintings; she made my first avocado and bacon sandwich; she had a whale-bristle hairbrush; there were magical piles of books and manuscripts I longed to look at; and she and the whole apartment were redolent of marvelous soaps and powders and perfumes. One day she played a little trick on me. She pretended that she had lost a coin under a tall wardrobe and asked me if I would retrieve it for her. Down on my hands and knees, I found my face only a few inches from the glaring eyes and gaping jaws of a very alive-looking stuffed alligator. She burst into laughter when I fell over backwards, then kissed me when she saw that I was embarrassed, and said that she was sorry. At once it was all right, and we laughed about it together. Another time, a budding young know-it-all, I reared back and said that the music of Chopin was just too simple to be taken seriously. She explained to me that one of the hardest tasks of the artist was to make his hellishly difficult and complicated art appear simple and clear. She promised me that someday we would listen to Chopin together when she had her phonograph records, which were somewhere in a warehouse, as her possessions so often were. I asked if she had *Ravel's Bo*lero. Without wincing at my blunder, or blushing at her lie, she said yes. I thought, Gee! she must have every record in the world. In an offhanded way she then said something, I forget what, about Ra*vel* and his Bo*lero*. I understood immediately that I had been corrected, but so gently that I took it only as a sign that she cared.

After she left Houston to marry Albert Erskine, we were out of touch for a while. I can't say exactly when I wrote her a long letter telling her all that I had been reading, thinking, and doing. She wrote back at once an even longer letter telling me what I *should* have been reading, thinking, and doing.[22] That pretty much set the tone for the next forty years. She began to send me lists of books to read and music to listen to. Boxes of books began to arrive by parcel post. I was snatched a light-year's distance further along in my education and taste. A whole new world was illuminated and revealed. It was my by-then-favorite-aunt who did that for me, and I have never forgotten it.

Eleanor Clark said that Katherine Anne Porter had an intense but limited interest in music. I know exactly what she meant. Aunt Katherine refreshed and elated her soul with the music of Monteverdi,[23] Purcell, Handel, Bach, Gluck, and Mozart, but had just a thin scattered interest in the composers who came after Mozart. More than anything else, she loved the songs and dances of the Middle Ages and the Renaissance. Often she would sing along, in a tuneless whisper, with her recordings of troubadour songs. She detested Wagner, and disliked most of the Romantics.

Naturally, there were exceptions. There are exceptions to just about anything you might say about her. For instance, she would listen to almost anything by anybody, if it was sung by Teyte, Baillie, Ferrier, or Pinza,[24] or played by Hoffman or Lipatti.[25] She knew by heart passages from the libretto for the Marschallin's role in *Der Rosenkavalier,* a character with whom she identified in ways.[26] When we heard Lotte Lehmann's farewell performance in the role, she was disappointed that Lehmann wasn't wearing the golden wig she had worn in Salzburg years before.[27] Nevertheless, she was touched to tears when the Marschallin sang of the passing of time, of growing old, and of the death of love.

But you mustn't think that classical music was the only kind she enjoyed. She would play "Stone Cold Dead in the Market"[28] and "I May Be Crazy But I Ain't No Fool,"[29] laughing her head off every time. She thought Pearl Bailey and Fats Waller deliciously funny. She had recordings of flamenco, gamelan, and mariachi; Russian, Welsh, and Brazilian folk songs; Piaf, Mahalia Jackson, Trenet, and Dietrich.[30] A friend once told her that her music, and I suppose by implication her taste, was like a bucket of water poured out on the floor; it had no shape. Her reaction was one of total astonishment, as if she couldn't believe her ears. Then she said, in an I'm-being-patient-but-watch-your-step tone of voice, "Angel, you are *wrong,* you know. Everything in my collection is *perfect of its kind.*"

Because of her lack of formal education, my aunt has been described in some quarters as uneducated. I don't understand this. Her library was superb. She was a voracious reader all her life, not just in and about world literature, but also history, biography, philosophy, psychology, religion, natural history, politics, art, music—just about everything except detective stories, which she described as the perfect way to kill time, for people who liked their time dead. She subscribed to dozens of magazines of every kind, from obscure literary magazines to *Southern Review* and *Hudson Review* to *Vogue, National Wildlife,* and *Cat Fancy.*

She read constantly, anywhere, at any time, always scribbling in the margins, underlining, and making notes. I remember that a friend called on the telephone, answered by my cousin Ann, and asked if Katherine Anne was busy. "Yes," Ann replied, "she is, she's busy correcting the *Encyclopaedia Britannica.*" She almost always read after retiring, letting the book sink to her breast as she fell asleep. If she awoke during the night, she simply raised the book, and went on reading where she had left off.

She loved poetry above all other forms of literature. I like poetry, but I can read it only in modest amounts. She read mountains of it, yards and yards of it, hours and hours of it, as easily and happily as I would read a favorite short story. She read it not only to herself, but aloud to anyone who would listen, and she read it beautifully, sometimes moving herself and the listener to tears. She read Eliot's *Four Quartets* to me from beginning to end. If I appeared baffled, as I often did, she would stop and we would discuss the passage. Other favorite poets, in no kind of order, were Homer, Dante, Shakespeare, the Goliards,[31] Yeats, Crane,[32] Warren,[33] Marianne Moore,[34] and many others. She also kept up with unknown and barely known young contemporary poets.

More than once she told me that she would make a bonfire of everything she had written if only she could be a truly great poet. She wasn't a good one, even; and of course she knew that.

She liked most animals, but reserved her special love for the felines: cheetahs, lions, tigers, jaguars, domestic cats of every breed and description, some of no known breed and beyond description. If she stayed in one place for any time at all, she always found a cat to coddle. She spoiled them outrageously, feeding them the same dishes she cooked for herself. Allowing them absolute freedom with no discipline whatever. A superb Victorian sofa, the one praised in a poem by Marianne Moore, was sprayed by a gentleman cat named Juniper, bleaching the purple velvet with loops and squiggles like a Pollock painting.[35] She was horrified when I suggested that Juniper be neutered, insisting that I had ruined the life of my poor Missy by having her spayed, no matter that Missy lived a happy eighteen years after the dirty deed. While I was in Texas on a visit, she stayed in my New York apartment to care for poor Missy. I had hardly landed in Houston before she called. Missy wouldn't eat; Missy wouldn't sleep; Missy wouldn't come to her; Missy hid from her; and every time she passed through the room, Missy hissed at her. "My God, darling," she moaned, "I have *never* been spat at by a small animal!" She thought I would have to return to New York at once; the situation was intolerable. The following morning I received a telegram: "DARLING: MISSY EATING LIKE A TRUCK DRIVER SLEEPING LIKE A BABY BEHAVING LIKE AN ANGEL STOP *WORRYING* AUNT KATHERINE."

If she ever owned a dog, she never mentioned it. She did say once that she wanted a bluetick Walker hound and a Tennessee walking horse, but I think that that was just her notion of what any Southern lady would have on the "property," which she also wanted and didn't have.

She was an early riser, I mean *really* early, and couldn't bear to have a visitor lying abed when she wanted his or her company. Around 5:30 A.M. she would call out, "Paul? Paul? Where are you, angel?" Surely she knew where I was; I was in bed. "Here," I would mumble. "*Where?*" in a rising tone. "Here," I would mumble again. "For God's sake, darling, *where! where!* Where *are* you?" In all my years in the Army, no barracks sergeant ever did a better job of routing me out of bed, wide awake and all attention.

It was important for me to be up because the choices for breakfast had to be discussed. At breakfast, lunch was planned. At lunch, dinner was arranged. At dinner, dinners of the past were remembered, and recipes detailed; and since everything reminded her of something else, there were always stories to be told.

Sherwood Anderson's wife, Elizabeth Anderson, visited Aunt Katherine in Mexico in the 1920s and wrote in her autobiography that she was a terrible cook.[36] If that was true, my aunt pulled herself together and did something about it. She became absolutely first-rate in the kitchen, celebrated among friends and visitors for her table. She specialized in the French, Mexican, and Southern cuisines. That reminds me: I found in one of her cookbooks a recipe with which she had quarreled from first ingredient to last, scratching out this, adding that, altering something else. Finally, she scrawled a big *X* over the whole page and wrote in the margin, "No, no. As wrong as can be." I finally figured it out. She had tried, I'll never know why, to transform a recipe for chili con carne into a recipe for *mole poblano*. She almost did it, too, but not quite.

She collected dozens of cookbooks and bales of clipped recipes, and made more bales of notes. I believe she meant one day to write a cookbook, but never did. She was most proud of her Hellfire Sauce, which required seven kinds of hot peppers, and her homemade bread. She considered storebought bread fit only for feeding pigeons, and even that, she said, was cruelty to dumb animals. Until the age of eighty-seven she baked her own loaves and rolls, with every taste and texture imaginable.

She enrolled in the Cordon Bleu Cooking School in Paris, and bragged about her "thesis," an elaborate casserole that took her two days to make. She carried it home to her husband on the Métro, lifting the lid along the way so anyone who cared to could take a whiff. She took delight in imitating the sighs, kissed fingertips, and uprolled eyes of the whiffers.

She loved to cook, but hated the business of getting food from the kitchen onto plates. She quoted her maid in Paris, who remarked, "Madame, you are a cook most *formidable . . . . . mais! las présentation a manqué un peu!*" And certainly the process sometimes was "lacking." It would start with an alarming banging of pots and pans, the hiss and splutter of hot oil and the whoosh of flames, mingled with whoops, curses, and reassurances from Aunt Katherine that all was well. "Oh tweetlings," she would cry, "this is good, just you wait, you're going to like this!" And sure enough, she would emerge from the kitchen unscathed, triumphantly bringing with her some festive, fragrant dish.

I remember a dinner she prepared for Frank O'Connor and a young lady I believe was his wife.[37] The main course was a leg of lamb, cooked according to a recipe given to Aunt Katherine by Ford Madox Ford. After the usual commotion in the kitchen, she brought out the lamb on a carving board and placed it on the table. She wouldn't allow anyone else to carve, and tackled the joint herself, slicing and hacking and talking a blue streak while the carving board tilted and slipped and gravy ran in little rivulets onto the table. We were all aghast, but after a moment realized there was nothing to do but relax and enjoy the skirmish taking place between Aunt Katherine and the lamb. She kept slicing and hacking and talking: "Samuel Johnson said that mutton should be carved in chunks, but I don't agree, do you? Anyway, this isn't mutton, is it, we know that, don't we, this is a"—*wham!*—"tender little lamb." And that tender little lamb, once she had wrestled it into submission, was glorious. All things considered—the savory food, the vintage wines, and the lively talk—I'm sure that no one ever had less than a good time at her table.

Let me tell you just one more thing about Katherine Anne Porter and food. When she was a small girl she was taken back-stage to meet the famous violinist Maud Powell.[38] Little Katherine Anne curtsied and told Powell that she was her idol; she wanted to grow up to be just like her. Powell hugged the child and told her that she must grow up to be like nobody but herself, and she must never have idols, they would only someday disappoint her. "And darling," swore Aunt Katherine, "I have never had an idol from that day to this." Charming, yes, but not quite true. She not only profoundly revered Joan of Arc and Erasmus, among others, but there exists a reference to one person specifically as an idol. "I hope," she wrote, "my idol Sir Thomas More forgives me for reminding us of this great final phrase summing up his life, his being." And what, you ask, does that have to do with food? Just this: I found those words in, of all places, her recipe for, of all things . . . . . egg custard!

It won't come as news to anyone who ever knew or met or just heard about Katherine Anne Porter that she was a great talker. Douglas Dick, then a young Hollywood actor, said that he could *hear* the punctuation when she spoke. I'm afraid, however, that I didn't enjoy her public appearances, least of all when she spoke extemporaneously, and she rarely spoke any other way, perhaps never did. I once asked her what she planned to say in a speech at the Poetry Center in New York. She replied that she hadn't the faintest idea, that she never knew what she was going to say until she heard it herself, and nobody was more surprised than she by what she said. Knowing this gave me such a fit of nerves that I could hardly stay through one of her performances, and I usually sat in the back row so I could slip out if I became embarrassed. Nobody else seemed to feel the way I did. There was always an air of anticipation, enthusiastic applause when she appeared, laughter at the right places, and at the end a standing ovation.

Naturally, I wasn't that apprehensive when she gave what you might call a private performance. One morning at Hay Meadows, the country residence of her old friends Monroe Wheeler and Glenway Wescott, the several house guests, hearing her voice, trooped one by one into her bedroom to say good morning. Her hair was tangled, she wore no makeup, and her eyes were puffy from sleep, or perhaps the lack of it. But she sat in bed propped up on pillows, sipping coffee brought to her by Monroe, a ratty old squirrel-skin cape draped over her shoulders by Glenway, and she talked. And talked. And talked. About Life. About her life. About her work. About friends and enemies. About cats. About coyotes, throwing her head back and imitating their howl. Gossip. Jokes. Poetry. It was dazzling, better than anything she had ever done in public, better than a lot of things I have paid money to see on Broadway. We were spellbound, we scarcely breathed. Nobody said a word. Finally, Monroe said that she must be exhausted, we had to leave, she really had to rest. "Oh my angels," Aunt Katherine cried, "I'm *not* tired, this has been heavenly. You *know* I love good conversation."

Another time we were at a party given by Sidney Kingsley[39] after an opening-night performance by Martha Graham and her dance company. To quote the old Ray Bourbon ditty, "We went to a party, and *everybody* was there!" I remember Helen Hayes, Eudora Welty, Martha Graham of course, famous actors and actresses, famous dancers, famous musicians and composers, famous people in packs and droves. Aunt Katherine made her way through the mob to a sofa and sat down, and in minutes she was surrounded by an audience, some of them literally at her feet. Surrounded, she sat there talking for the rest of the evening. In the cab afterwards, which we shared with Eudora Welty, Aunt Katherine chattered in a gay, excited way about the praise and attention she had received. Suddenly Eudora patted her on the knee and said gently, "Now Katherine Anne, don't be so girlish." My heart stopped. I waited for an explosion, but it never came. Aunt Katherine just laughed. She took Eudora's hand in hers, and said, "You're right, my darling; but it *was* a good party, wasn't it!" I wonder if anybody else in the world could have said what Eudora Welty said to Aunt Katherine and have had such an affectionate response. Perhaps, but I don't know who.

Aunt Katherine had very little sense of humor about herself, and you teased her at the risk of your life, or at least psychic maiming; but she had a great talent for fun. She could be difficult, unreasonable, touchy, often just plain impossible . . . . . but she was always fascinating, and more often than not, a joy to be with. There was the entertaining talk, of course, but also her warmth and her lively interest in just about everything under the sun. She generated a kind of infectious excitement which she imparted to those around her, making life seem more vivid, brighter, more completely *felt* than usual. Whatever she enjoyed, she enjoyed to the *n*th degree. She was reckless and fearless. There is a photograph of her at the age of seventy-something, perfectly coifed and smartly dressed right down to her high-heeled shoes, being hoisted onto a giant army tank by a squad of soldiers, held horizontal in the air above their heads like a rowing shell, a radiant smile on her face, without a flicker of concern about what anyone thought, or worry that she might be dropped on her head.[40] You could almost call it a quintessential scene in the life of Katherine Anne Porter. In Bermuda, in her eighties, she decided that she was bored with wading in the ripples and wanted to go for a real swim, so off she went, headed for deep water, while Mrs. Hubbard, her nurse/housekeeper/companion, stood in the shallows clutching her skirts around her knees and screaming, "Stop her! stop her! stop her!" So a lifeguard promptly jumped into the water and swam out and stopped her. She was humiliated, furious. "That damned fool woman doesn't know how to have fun," she fumed, "and she won't let me have any!"

She loved jokes, bawdy ones included, which she told with great verve unless they called for obscenity. She simply could not say those words. Confronted by the big *F* she would press her lips together and go "mmph." "What?" I would ask, and she would go "mmph" again, and then say helplessly, "Oh angel, *you* know what I mean." She might just as well have taken that joke out behind the barn and shot it between the eyes.

After we saw the Broadway musical *A Funny Thing Happened on the Way to the Forum,* we exchanged silly lines from it for days. "I have terrible news," yelled one comedian. "I hope it is good!" called a second. Aunt Katherine said that the second comedian spoke for her, even after her long life of bitter disappointments, and she didn't suppose she would ever change. She said that on Judgment Day the Angel of Doom would probably thunder at her, "Katherine Anne Porter, I have terrible news!" and she would chirp, "Oh, I *hope* it is good!"

We had our differences, Aunt Katherine and I, but now, remembering her, I find that time has disposed of everything but the memory of her love, and warmth, and the pleasure of her company. Cousin Ann and I were talking on the telephone about Aunt Katherine several years after she died, and Ann suddenly burst out, "Dammit, Paul, I still miss her, I miss her all the time."

And so do I. I miss her more every passing day of my life.

Source: Paul Porter, "A Bouquet for Aunt Katherine," a talk delivered at a conference at the University of Maryland, College Park, 11 May 1991, celebrating the one hundredth birthday of Katherine Anne Porter. Transcribed and published in *The Newsletter of the Katherine Anne Porter Society* 12 (2005): 1, 2, 4.

"I have planted five orchards in three states, and now I see only one tree in bloom." This rueful observation is made by the Grandmother in Katherine Anne Porter's story "The Source"; but it could have been made by Aunt Katherine about herself. I have no idea how many gardens she planted in her ninety years, but I do know that only one was on land she owned, and she was never in one place long enough to achieve the perfect and enduring garden she saw in her mind's eye.

Her choice in flowers reflected her style in prose: graceful, formal, nothing garish, an illusion of simplicity that disguised complexity. Knowing that, you might guess that her least favorite flowers were orchids. About a corsage of cymbidiums pinned on her shoulder at a function in her honor, she told a friend, "It was horrible. All evening the nasty little thing nibbled on my ear like a carnivorous bug."

She loved many flowers, but loved camellias and roses most of all. Her favorite colors were red, pink, and white. She didn't care at all for coral and orange, and she was appalled by efforts to create a black rose. Also high on her list of people she called "monkey-minded" were the breeders who created floral monsters at the expense of fragrance, for she adored the aroma of flowers. Even her perfumes were floral, which moved one Hollywood cab driver to exclaim, "Lady, you smell just like my wife's rose garden!" Delighted, she complimented him on the keenness of his nose—the cologne was White Rose from Caswell-Massey.

She was forever making lists which I found after she died among recipes, between the pages of books, in the back of drawers, everywhere—scraps of paper bearing the names of flowers and trees, fertilizers, mulches, soils, and insecticides; and that was just for starters. With those dirt-plain and sometimes mephitic purchases she coaxed into bloom flowers that were not only beautiful, but sweetly fragrant as well.

On Roxbury Road in the Connecticut countryside she was seized by the notion of planting a field with tulips. She did plant quite a few if not a whole field, and at once entered into grim dispute with a gang of woodchucks over just whose tulip bulbs those were. She loved fauna almost as much as flora, but she wasn't constant in her love. In wintertime she threw the woodchucks carrots and lettuce, but when spring came, she threw rocks. When this failed to frighten them off, she spoke of buying a twenty-two caliber rifle, boasting that she was an expert shot. Not entirely convinced, I kept quiet and hoped to be in the next county when the shootout started. It didn't matter, the gun was never bought, and as far as I know the woodchucks, battening on tulips bulbs, lived happily ever after.

The home she rented in Spring Valley in Washington, D.C., was backed by a steep slope overgrown by a ragged copse. Along the side of the house were plants put in by the owner. Of course it was all wrong, the wrong colors, the wrong shapes, and too many of what she called "those detestable little shrubby things." Even the slope behind the house was wrong, one of God's mistakes she wasn't about to let Him get away with. But no problem! She would uproot the shrubs around the house and replace them with her favorite flowers. Then she would clear the slope and carve it into terraces to be planted with dogwood, redbud, and fruit trees, all flourishing over a groundcover of violets. Needless to say, the owner took a dim, indeed a very dark view of her plans for the property, and she had to content herself with pulling up a little garden at the side of the house and replanting it with her beloved roses. She pampered them into glorious bloom, but as always the day came when she had to move away and leave still another garden to the mercy of strangers.

In 1970, she moved to a fifteenth-floor apartment in College Park, Maryland. In no time at all she had one bedroom of the twelve-room apartment turned into a potting room. Brown and wrinkled bulbs were laid out on the floor like the shrunken trophies of a New Guinea headhunter. The room was stacked with planters, from tiny seedling cups to terra cotta pots as big as washtubs. Sacks of fertilizer and God only knows what else spilled out their contents, and there were so many liquids and powders on so many shelves it might have been a corner of some old apothecary.

She created a blooming jungle on the west balcony and in the sunlit dining room. A real tree, grown from the seed of an avocado, towered to the ceiling. Almost hidden among the leaves and blooms of plants were ceramic animals and a large working fountain, a bronze cupid and dolphin in a great sea shell, a souvenir of Italy. All of this was a substitute for the real thing, of course, and it must have been frustrating for someone who really wanted to get her hands on a large piece of the landscape that was hers alone, to do with as she liked. Still, her jungle was beautiful, it gave her joy, and everyone who saw it was charmed.

In 1977 she was stricken by her long and mortal last illness. The apartment was taken over by shifts of nurses, different ones every week it seemed; and there was no one who knew enough, or cared enough, to give the plants the attention they demanded. The time came when the enormous apartment could no longer be maintained, and Aunt Katherine had to be moved into a nursing home. But by then, her beloved plants were already no more than dry stalks in pots of dust, and even those were soon hauled away. When the building manager and I walked

Katherine Anne Porter's nephew Corporal Harrison Paul Porter Jr., to whom she dedicated *The Leaning Tower and Other Stories* (1944). Courtesy Papers of Katherine Anne Porter, Special Collections, University of Maryland, College Park, Libraries.

through the empty and echoing apartment for a final inspection, I found that the movers had left hanging on a doorknob a large blue bag filled with dried rose petals, saved by Aunt Katherine over many years. I took it with me. It was a poignant reminder of the devoted gardener who all her long life, in so many places, had created so much green and flowering beauty.

19 / Breckenridge Porter

Breckenridge Porter (1914–99) was the son of Katherine Anne Porter's sister Mary Alice (Baby) Porter Townsend Hillendahl. His father, Herbert Townsend, died before his birth, and his uncle, his mother's brother Paul, adopted him and gave him the name "Porter." When his mother married Jules Arnold Hillendahl, Breckenridge went to live with them but kept the name Porter. In 1936 he was appointed Special Texas Ranger by Governor Miriam Amanda (Ma) Ferguson, and in 1937 he married Francis Bishop, with whom he had five children. Active in Houston service organizations, he had a long and distinguished career with the Houston Police Department.

Source: Breckenridge Porter, telephone interview with Darlene Harbour Unrue, 12 April 1997.

Aunt Katherine gave me the name "Breckenridge" when she came to stay with my mother shortly after my birth in 1914. I probably saw her when I was a very small child because I think she dropped in coming from or going to Mexico in the early 1920s, but I don't remember anything about her until she was here [Houston] in 1937 or 1938. She rented a house on Rutland Street three doors down from Aunt Gay's. She came here, she said, to work on a book. She put up a couple of sawhorses with boards across them that she used for a writing desk. Rumors were that she had had a live-in boyfriend in New Orleans, and that scandalized many persons in the family. Some said she was a "rounder."

Aunt Katherine and I didn't exactly get along. In 1937 I was a long-legged southern boy who had just gotten married and joined the River Oaks police force. Aunt Katherine told other members of the family, who told me, that it was a sad situation, that she didn't think she would live to see the day when one of the Porters would be a policeman.

She and I didn't have much interest in each other. I thought she was uppity, a social climber who thought nobody existed in this world except artistic types. Her attitude and mine were not the same. But she was close to other family members, who corresponded with her. I would hear about her over the years from Aunt Gay, my cousin Paul, my cousin Ann, and Grandpa, whom I visited frequently at his farm near the Mexican border, three miles south of Mission, Texas. I guess she really did become an important writer.

20 / Cleanth Brooks

Cleanth Brooks (1906–94), born in Kentucky and reared in Tennessee by devoutly Methodist parents, was educated in private preparatory schools before earning degrees from Vanderbilt, Tulane, and Exeter College, Oxford, which he attended as a Rhodes Scholar. He was professor of English at Louisiana State University (1932–47) and Yale University (1947–75) and during the same years held a number of short-term appointments, including fellow at the Library of Congress and cultural attaché for the American Embassy in London. Recipient of numerous awards and honorary doctorates, he is best known for his contributions to the New Criticism; his founding with Robert Penn Warren of the *Southern Review;* his collaboration with Warren on influential textbooks; and his book *William Faulkner: The Yoknapatawpha Country* (1963). He and his wife, Edith Amy (Tinkum) Blanchard Brooks, remained Katherine Anne Porter's friends until her death.

Source: Cleanth Brooks, "The Woman and Artist I Knew," *Katherine Anne Porter and Texas: An Uneasy Relationship,* ed. Clinton Machann and William Bedford Clark (College Station: Texas A&M UP, 1990), 13–24.

I first met Katherine Anne Porter in 1937, at Allen Tate's.[41] She was soon to be moving to New Orleans, and then to Baton Rouge. My wife and I really became acquainted with her in Baton Rouge. Indeed, soon after she came, she lived in an apartment just across a narrow corridor from the apartment in which we lived. The result is that we saw her literally every day for a year or so. While I was away at the university—I was teaching at the time at the Louisiana State University— she was trading recipes with my wife or exchanging comments about radio programs or the state of the country as World War II was obviously approaching. Indeed, she and my wife soon became fast friends.

Miss Porter at this period was not doing very much writing—hardly any, I should say, save for letters. She was on a great domestic binge in which she was enjoying cooking, taking rides, housekeeping, exchanging recipes, reading a great deal, and so on. As one can tell from her stories, she was a great conversationalist, and we much enjoyed her stories about her earlier life in Mexico when the great revolution in painting was going on there; about her brief encounter with the movies in Chicago, where, I believe, she played some bit parts; about her life in Greenwich Village, Paris, and Berlin.

Among other things, she talked fairly often about her early life in Texas. She was not defensive about it. In fact, she indicated that she thought that she had not grown up in a wholly backward region, that there were books to read and opportunities to see some plays given by touring companies and to become acquainted with music. In short, she was never pointedly hostile toward her native state, nor did she feel that she had grown up in a kind of cultural wasteland. I grant that she usually spoke in rather general terms. I did not take notes—saw no need to take them. I was not intent on writing her biography. But I did form the impression from my talks with her, as well as from reading her stories, that this woman had not come up out of a totally deprived childhood. Her vocabulary was too good; her knowledge of the language, of people, and of social customs and manners just too detailed and intimate for it to have been any other way.

Biographers from outside may very well have the illusion that Southerners not in comfortable circumstances had no cultural advantages. But such people, I think, do not realize the relative lack of class distinctions in the South and how many families who regarded themselves as people of good stock and good breeding had been reduced to what, according to present standards, would be regarded as underprivileged conditions. After all, the Civil War left a devastating economic heritage on the South. As for my own growing up, though I was never particularly conscious of the fact, I can see now that we were reared in what I can only call something like genteel poverty.

This is not the place, however, to debate how circumstantial and detailed in fact Katherine Anne's accounts of her early life—or her later life, for that matter—were. She did like to embellish a story. I think she did it often unconsciously, and she *was* a wonderful storyteller, as her own short stories, themselves obvious fictional accounts, duly testify.

When Katherine Anne's last marriage broke up, as it did fairly shortly, she was to leave Baton Rouge, but she and my wife kept up a correspondence, particularly in the years soon after she left. [. . .][42]

In the years following her departure from Baton Rouge, Katherine Anne Porter lived in a variety of places, in a number of which we visited her in later years [. . .]. The many changes of address I think show something about her. She was perpetually—so it seems to me as I look back on her life—a wanderer, a seeker, a person looking for the bluebird of happiness, and the one happy valley in which she could be truly at home.

On the whole, she kept up a rather buoyant heart and showed an uncomplaining front to the world, but my wife told me of more than one occasion when Katherine Anne confessed to her a deep despondency, in which she felt that her life had come to nothing. Romantic as she was in personality, I suppose that her hopes were really unattainable. Yet she was always undaunted, looking for the happiness that lay just out of sight but which she was sure she would eventually find. Each new house or flat she took possession of was going to prove the perfect one, and I think her change of houses and her incessant movings about the earth in search of the perfect place in which to put down roots reflect her quest for the perfect lover, the husband who would be everything to her, the husband whom, of course, she never found.

In a sense, hers was a rather tragic life, so it seems to me.

One of the reasons that Katherine Anne so cherished success, as indeed she did toward the end of her life—literary success, fame—was the fact that the real happiness she wanted had always eluded her. But no one knew better, I am sure, than Katherine Anne, in her heart of hearts, that the literary fame and the wealth that eventually came to her with her novel *Ship of Fools* could in no way compensate for what she had sought so long and painfully, and had missed.

To her romantic attitude toward life she joined flightiness of judgment. I do not mean that she lacked intelligence or alertness. Such was not her weakness. But her judgment was surely flighty, if I may use an old Southern expression. In spite, however, of both these attributes and her passionately emotional nature, how classical is her art. I do not mean to disparage it by calling it classical. It is anything but cold and lifeless. On the contrary, it is warm and spirited, but classical in the sense that every word counts; that the form is beautifully, though unobtrusively, present; and that her stories have a proper beginning, middle (that is a development), and a satisfying ending. The paradox of romantic heart and classical art remains for me the essential way in which I have to look at this remarkable woman and her equally remarkable work.[43]

21 / Eudora Welty

Eudora Alice Welty (1909–2001), Mississippi-born novelist, short-story writer, and photographer, was educated at the Mississippi State College for Women (now Mississippi University for Women), the University of Wisconsin–Madison, and Columbia University. She worked for the Works Progress Administration as a photographer in the 1930s and in 1936 published her first short story, "Death of a Traveling Salesman." When two of her stories appeared in the *Southern Review,* Porter was so impressed that she wrote Welty offering various kinds of support. During her lifetime Welty published twelve collections of short stories and five novels. Her novel *The Optimist's Daughter* (1972) won the Pulitzer Prize in 1973. She became Porter's lifelong friend.

Source: Eudora Welty, "My Introduction to Katherine Anne Porter," *Georgia Review* 44.1–2 (1990): 13–27.

When in 1937 Robert Penn Warren, Cleanth Brooks, and Albert Erskine, editors of the *Southern Review,* had decided to use two of my stories, the significance was not lost on me. They had thought my work good enough to take a chance on, to encourage. Still I had not been prepared for a letter out of the blue from Katherine Anne Porter after the stories appeared. She was not an editor, but a *writer,* a writer of short stories; she was out in the world, at Baton Rouge:

> 961 America Street
> Baton Rouge, Louisiana
> October 25, 1938

Dear Miss Welty:

Ford Madox Ford has been given control of the fiction department of the Dial Press, and asked me to help him look about for candidates for publication. I thought of you first, with your admirable short stories. It seems to me that if you have no other plans, and have a book length collection of stories, it would be an excellent idea to write to Ford, giving him some notion of your manuscript. He will then no doubt ask to see it.

Also, if you like, I would be glad to name you as candidate for a Guggenheim Fellowship for next year—rather, for application in the fall of 1939 and 1940 Fellowship. I have already named a candidate for this year. This is done by request of the Secretary of the Foundation who looks constantly for likely candidates, and naturally is no sort of engagement or promise. But if you should care to apply, I should at once write a letter about you to Mr. Moe.[44]

I take this liberty because of my admiration for your very fine work.

Katherine Anne Porter

I seized on the belief Miss Porter offered me; she was the writer of short stories I revered. Her letter was an act of faith, and I was able to recognize this. It also foretold something about her lifelong habit of mind: there was no mistaking the seriousness of her meaning; there never must be, with her, as all learned sooner or later about K.A.P. She spoke truth as she saw it about the written word, about the writing of the written word, the act itself.

She was to give encouragement to me from that time on in the ways that always applied to the serious meaning of a young writer's work—and life; as indeed she gave encouragement to many young writers.

Thus I'd sent along my stories to Ford Madox Ford, who turned out to think well enough of them to try to place them in England up until the time of his death not very long afterward. I'd applied for the Guggenheim in 1940 with Katherine Anne's blessing. It wasn't awarded on that first application. But it was the existence of Katherine Anne Porter's hopes for me themselves, successful and unsuccessful alike, that filled me with gratitude.

However I had been able to express this to her, she wrote back:

1050 Government Street
Baton Rouge, Louisiana
March 7, 1940

Dear Eudora:

Please remember that my recommendation of your work costs me nothing; that it gives me pleasure, and is the best proof I can offer of my faith in your talent and hopes for the future. It is no doubt one of the marks of your seriousness of character and intention that you take obligation for any little help offered or received; in this case, let me assure you, a purely imaginary, self-assumed sense of obligation. Try not to remember it; I would much prefer your friendship, in the most unburdensome meaning of that word. And it would really disturb me if you felt in my debt for such a small thing as a word of praise from me.

I am hoping that your luck will be good this year. Enough for the present, for if this year is good, the others can take care of themselves . . . . . .

Katherine Anne

And even if this year turns out *not* so good, that is no sign at all that the coming ones shall be unlucky!

In September 1940, as I was traveling to Vermont, she invited me to stop off at Yaddo, the artists' colony where she was spending time working. She wrote to me afterwards:

Yaddo, Saratoga Springs
New York, September 18
1940

Dear Eudora:

It was simply lovely having you here even for such a little while, and I wish you could come back now, for I'm moved upstairs to a much pleasanter place and there are bedrooms all over the house unoccupied . . .

Diarmuid Russell [Welty's literary agent] wrote me, and I wrote him and he wrote me again and I just answered, so you see we are getting along splendidly. He gave me some advice which I followed and it worked; and he is a most secure admirer of you and your work, so it is delightful to know you are going to be looked after. He is really in earnest about it; says he finds himself mentally shaking his finger at editors about you. I feel serenely conscious that it is all going to end well. Yours will be a war of attrition, as mine was, Eudora. You just go the way you're going and the editors will fall in, in time. And you have all the time in the world, and all the gift you can handle; in fact, you've got a handful, perhaps more than you know.

I have out of a clear sky but not without premeditation, finished two short stories—whales, about eight thousand words each. One to S.R. [*Southern Review*], one to *Harper's Bazaar*, as usual. I think I was working on the first when you were here. Well, there are two now. "Season of Fear" and "The Leaning Tower."[45] That makes enough floating around for a collection, and I'm going to get out another book of short stories, willy-nilly; they can take it or leave it. We have *got* to beat down this conspiracy against collections of short stories . . . . . . It's a long war, but we will win.

Katherine Anne

By 1941, Diarmuid Russell after two years' unremitting work had succeeded in placing all my stories in magazines, which had made them acceptable as a collection to a publisher who would risk a book of short stories. And now, John Woodburn of Doubleday, Doran in New York had by his long and patient work persuaded his house to publish it. The book was given a title, *A Curtain of Green.* To cap this, he had invited and persuaded Katherine Anne Porter to write an Introduction to it. She added to this wonderful news by writing to me:

> February 19, 1941—Olivet
> [Olivet College, Michigan]

Dearest Eudora:

All the news about you is good news and makes me happy for you, and for myself, because nothing is better than to see you getting off so bravely.

I write with pencil because I am in bed with a crick in my neck which seems to be my way of having a cold, and all my paper, pens, etc., are on the other side of this blizzard-swept campus in my office. A splendid letter from Diarmuid full of rejoicing about you and the new baby [Diarmuid and Rose Russell's second child, William]. Please tell him in your next I have his letter and will write when I am better able.

Meantime—Send the collection *with* "The Robber Bridegroom" et al to Yaddo.[46] I will do what I can to have it included—Above all, tell me *when, where* the preface should be sent; deadlines are my snare—But I will make it.

I know well already what I think of your work, but reading all the stories will give pointers.

No more for the moment. Albert Erskine will be delighted with this news.[47] Meantime my love and good wishes, may all your good beginnings bring you to a happy end!

> Katherine Anne

And soon after:

> Yaddo, Saratoga Springs
> New York, May 2, 1941

Dear Eudora:

Elizabeth Ames tells me you have been invited here [Yaddo] for early June, and I hope you like the place and can stay a long time if you want . . . It will be lovely to see you. Mrs. Ames had said something about inviting you before the regular season, but I heard no more of it.

Your letter was useful and I am keeping it with my notes for the preface, just for the tone. We'll talk all that over when you get here . . . . . .

Nothing more just now, I am at the last gasp of that novel, and must finish now before I do anything else. But after, I shall be free; and meantime I scribble down something else about your work as it comes to me, so the notes are piling up nicely against the day . . . . . .

I got the deed to South Farm today. So it is really mine, and the work is beginning on it almost at once . . . . . . The end of the summer should see me in it. But believe me, this novel is the foundation of this whole thing, and it must go soon . . . . . . I've written it so often, really, it is high time to let it go, now!

Waiting to see you, with my love,
Katherine Anne

I showed your collection to Glenway Wescott, and he was pretty well bowled over. I said, "My money is on her nose for the next race," and he said, "Mine, too. She is marvelous." So your audience grows. He is a good friend to have—never will let his friends hear the last of you . . .

I arrived at Saratoga Springs as one in a dream.

Yaddo was in the old, rural, comfortably settled part of New York State west of Albany, near the town of Saratoga Springs. The estate was private and well guarded, though its gardens were, at that innocent time, open to the public. The Mansion faced you head-on as you approached it through forest trees; it was huge, elaborately constructed: it looked made by impulse for eternity, out of the rock on which it stood. The artists came for their summer at Yaddo solely by invitation. Elizabeth Ames gave her life to being its director—a woman of Quaker-like calm and decisiveness; she was beautiful and to some extent deaf. She stood ready for crises.

The artists—painters, composers, writers, sculptors—lived in the reaches of the Mansion, and beyond their rooms they were given studios to suit their particular needs; these stood hidden away among the old forest trees, at various calculated degrees of remoteness. Artists ate their lunch alone; it arrived in a tin box left silently outside their doors at noon.

Katherine Anne and I were enviably installed in the "farmhouse," a small frame building a distance away from the Mansion on its hill across the road. We shared the farmhouse with only two others, congenial both—a Canadian composer and an Armenian-American etcher,[48] who *did* work all day in their respective studios.

Upstairs, across the hall from Katherine Anne's combined bedroom and studio, was my bedroom. My studio was downstairs in the farmhouse kitchen. On the outside of the studio door was a sign tacked up: "SILENCE. WRITER AT WORK WITHIN." My immediate work consisted of reading the proofs on my forthcoming book, and that was over quickly. Already, though, my editor John Woodburn, in New York, had begun to write me little bulletins, instructing me to remind Katherine Anne about the Introduction: "And kid, you keep after her! She promised to write it *now*! Remind her we've got a deadline."

And I knew I couldn't do that.

In the early evening of each long summer's day, Katherine Anne—with her spring-heeled step, catching up her long skirts—and I set out in single file walking the woodland path up to the great stone Mansion for dinner. This was the only hour of the twenty-four when all the guests came out and showed themselves. They had supposedly been solitary all day behind their studio doors, working.

Within the Mansion, the atmosphere, even the hour, seemed changed; it was hushed, moody, and somehow public. The great room we entered spread out like a stage set for a grand opera on which the curtain might at any moment go up. An overture was in the making: an interior fountain close to us was murmuring, and offstage somewhere an organ began to groan; it was possible that one of the resident poets was still at work, thinking something through.

I began to feel apprehensive that we were all expected to *perform* here, that the assigned soloists and the combined chorus were *us*. The great hall was appointed with throne chairs, divans, velvet stools (one also noticed a sleigh), with candelabra, wine glasses, wine.

If I supposed our opera would be one about the arts, or artists, something like *La Bohème*, I wasn't on the right track. This was 1941. The company was in great part European. Elizabeth Ames had come to the aid of many artists who no longer had homes and were seeking refuge and a place to carry on their work. Our evening was indeed operatic, but it wasn't about the arts; it was about politics. Katherine Anne rose to the occasion—her clear voice would enter as if on cue with cries of "*Au contraire!*" One end of the great room gave onto the coming night; the window was a great tall frame holding the Yaddo moon, and I watched it climbing. Out there beyond and below the stone balustrade, the garden descended, with its statues of the Graces rising from the beds like another chorus. I could smell, without seeing it, the summer stock, the nicotiana. They made me think of home. That first night, I knew for certain only what the *garden* was doing.

From New York, John Woodburn, who was my champion, who had staked so much in bringing out this first book by an unknown, young, Southern, female, short-story writer, wrote to me nearly every day. "How far along is she? How's the Introduction coming?" "Keep after her, kid! Tell her one more time about the deadline!" "Get it out of her, baby."

Was she writing it indeed? If I heard from across the hall her little Olivetti typewriter start up, or still more, if I heard it stop, I felt like an eavesdropper. I let myself out of the house and walked down the road to Saratoga Springs.

It was lovely to arrive there, too, in the bright Northern summer morning. Lining either side of the main street, the great hotels stood facing each other under the meeting boughs of lofty elms, the United States Hotel and all its sisterhood: their red faces, their black iron columns across the front, twisted like Venetian barge poles, and the figures of black, turbaned, Oriental slaves mounted at the top of the steps with an arm crooked up to hold branching lamps with clusters of globes made for gaslight.

The length of the street was strung overhead with banners and flags bidding Welcome. Along the sidewalks I moved with a wonderful crowd of perambulators here for the waters, the faces, the sights and parades: invalids, sporting people, sightseers, families stalled in circles on the sidewalk in a chorus of argument over what to do next. I visited the racetrack where the horses were working out, and the busy public halls where the waters were being dispensed.

By the time I walked home to Yaddo, I might be carrying onions, soup bones, maybe a fresh stalk of celery or bunch of carrots to Katherine Anne, who liked to keep the soup pot going on her little stove, as well as her windup gramophone going, and sometimes now her Olivetti going.

I knew it was to be a wonderfully happy and carefree summer for me—if only I didn't have Katherine Anne's awful deadline hanging over my head: the unmentionable.

Outside our farmhouse sat a brand new Studebaker car—it was Katherine Anne's. She had not quite learned to drive it yet. But I could drive it, and she said she had something to show me: we would take the day off from work!

It was a little distance off, in deep country: the house her letter had told me about securing the deed for. She confided that she was actually now in the very process of restoring it. She had christened it "South Hill." She would finish it, make it all her own, move into it, settle down and *write*. It became a part of nearly every day to jump into the Studebaker and drive out to South Hill.

She could count on a Mr. Somebody who came to see to everything. So a yellow-coned cement mixer churned away among the trees, and at times drowned out the birdsong, and the carpenters who stripped the upstairs walls now down to the laths found little feminine slippers that K.A.P. identified as being a hundred years old, and further came on roused-up bees in the walls too, which had been at work storing honey there for, she estimated, the same length of time. K.A.P. and I stretched out on the long sweet meadow grass in another part of the shade. At peace, we puffed on our cigarettes, and I listened to her tell the way she had discovered Joyce for herself: somehow a copy of *Ulysses* had been carried into this country and ended up in a secondhand bookstall in Galveston, Texas; Katherine Anne had walked by and just picked it up.

When the spirit moved us, we would jump into the Studebaker and ride all the way to Albany and there find six wonderful French antique dining-room chairs, or cinch a roll of ruby-red carpeting, perfect for the stairs when they were made ready to climb (at present we were crawling up a plank to reach the upstairs). All were now entrusted to storage. It was the clearest thing to K.A.P. that everything we engaged in all day long was South Hill in the making. There was supporting magic attached to finding treasures that would take their rightful place in it. There popped into my head the lovely little French virginal that Katherine Anne had showed to me, the very first thing, on the day when I'd come on her invitation to see her for the first time; it was in her new house in Baton Rouge. Where was the virginal now? I wondered, but did not ask. It must be in storage somewhere.

We sank into the luxury of talking books as easily as we sank into the long, sweet meadow grass; we had all day and a picnic lunch. We listened to the birdsong and the carpenters at work. Katherine Anne would often be laughing out loud.

But if it was hard for me, being there night and day with my very presence putting Katherine Anne on the spot, did I think of how hard it was for Katherine Anne? I am certain beyond a doubt that *I* could not have written the first line about anybody who was, at the time, staying in the house with me three steps away across the hall. And if that person knew about my purpose, and was waiting on me daily to set down the words on paper? And if at the same time that person had turned out to be a friend? I'm afraid the possibility never occurred to me that I *could* conclude my stay at Yaddo before my invitation was up.

Then the day came when she tapped at my door and came in holding out to me a whole sheaf of typewritten pages. "You may read this," she said, "if you would like." It was what she had been working on, the first seventy-five pages of *No Safe Harbor*—her novel (which of course was to become, in the end, *Ship of Fools*). In allowing me to read it, and at its beginning, she had made me a gift of her clear confidence in me. As far as I was concerned, the Introduction she was going to write for me had been conveyed to me by way of a blessing. If its significance was to relate to her literary trust in me, I had already received it.

The novel was years later on to appear in the finality of print, but what I had been living across the hall from was the immediacy, the presence, and something of the terror, of its pages coming into being one by one. I'd *heard* the living words coming through her fingers and out of her skin. I don't think I was ever again as stirred, and as captivated, to hold a fresh manuscript in my hands and realize what I held.

The summer was deepening, and with it the pleasures of Yaddo. By then, friendships had ripened among the set of artists, informality had caught up with formality, and picnics sneaked into the lazy noons. Katherine Anne made onion soup for her friends. That could take all day, and as we all agreed, it was worth every minute of it. There was music in the evening at the Mansion, but music was *always* to be heard at our farmhouse. The gramophone would be kept wound up and playing. K.A.P. kept stacks of French records, from Piaf back to Gluck, back to madrigals. In the performance of the opera *Orphée,* when the moment arrived that I listened for—Cerberus barking—a live little dog filled the role.

There was everything going on at once those days. Some way or another, the little Olivetti was seizing its chances, too. From across our hall, I heard it very well—its insistencies, its halts, and again its resuming, the long runs as if this runner could not now stop for breath. And we didn't leave out driving nearly every day to visit South Hill—what else was the Studebaker for?

At South Hill Katherine Anne and I sat in the meadow downhill from what was going on, and watched the building slowly come to pass before our eyes. For the plain, century-old house (looking something like an ark) that she was making her own, the elation, the intensity, the triumph, the impatience of her vision of it took hold of her afresh every day. It made me aware that the planner was profoundly a story writer.

As I look back now, I believe she was putting the house together like a story in her head, restoring to it its history—a story that had as much to do with her past as it had to do with her future. It was a work-in-progress she was highly conscious of, and scrupulously attentive to, a self-assignment she was meeting, an autobiographical deadline.

"How far along *is* the Introduction?" wrote John Woodburn to me. How hard this was on John too, and how well I knew it! He adored Katherine Anne. He had traveled up to Yaddo to ask her in person if she would write the Introduction; they'd celebrated the agreement in Saratoga Springs in the grandeur of the United States Hotel; and he was a sensitive man. *He* couldn't ask her a word about it now, either. But I could hear the groan in his words to me: "Get it out of her *now,* kid! Do you want our book *postponed*?"

It was postponed. The day the Introduction was due came and went, and at Yaddo I had never mentioned it to Katherine Anne. But I had *been* there. And I still was there—the live-in visitor from Porlock.[49] I think now, in this long retrospect, that she made a daily brave attempt to forget about the interfering deadline for the moment at hand, and that what I was actually doing there was helping her forget it. At any rate, *this* was a success. And though I would not have known it at the time, this Introduction was undoubtedly only one of the things Katherine Anne was being pressed to do. She was constitutionally a besieged woman.

I'd begun to realize that the summer was of a kind not unexpected by Katherine

Anne. Her whole writing life was one of interruptions, and interruptions of the interruptions. I was to learn that writers do generally live that way, and not entirely without their own collusion. No help ever comes, unless in the form of still another interruption.

The one thing that was uninterrupted in her life was her seriousness of intent. And when I look back, I seem to see her surrounded entirely by papers, by pages or galley sheets, by her work—"Old Mortality," "The Leaning Tower," and, on that blue typewriter paper, stretches of the novel. It seemed then that she was always writing. *Writing*—its conception—was ever-present to her. At Yaddo, at South Hill equally; writing was the future of her house, the *intention* of her house. And writing was—yes, even for her—very hard to do.

To me it came as no shock that writing itself, the act, might always be hard. The better the writer, the harder writing knew how to be. In fact, the harder Katherine Anne's work was for her, the more exhilarated, liberated my own spirits were accordingly. What I felt able to understand for myself was that writing well was for the writer worth whatever it took. The difficulty that accompanies you is less like the dark than like a trusted lantern to see your way by. I hoped proudly for myself that acknowledging and valuing the role of difficulty in writing well would remain always with me. Katherine Anne was helping me to recognize living with difficulty as a form of passion.

Certainly I was slower in learning to know Katherine Anne than I believed I was in the summer at Yaddo. Our friendship had shown me day after day the enchanting brightness she could shed around her, but it was later, through letters she wrote when we were no longer in the same place, laughing, that I became to any degree aware of the dark, its other side, which she lived with on its own terms in equally close commune. I wondered in retrospect if hers hadn't been the sort of exultation that can arise—must arise—out of some equally intense sadness, wondered if, as South Hill was taking shape before her eyes, there wasn't also something else in the course of being left behind. She was combatting unhappiness, even desolation, I now think, through that whole summer and for times longer than that, and bravely.

John Woodburn sent me the last of his bulletins in August, to Jackson, where I'd returned: "Baby: Here is the Introduction, unproof-read, which I finally got out of Katherine Anne by distilling her. There was no other way . . ."

In the end, of course, she had written her magnificent Introduction "very quickly," she told me. And all her generosity, her penetration, serenely informs it, doing everything in her power for the book and for its author, as she'd intended to do all the time.

It is time itself—there was never any use denying—that is forever the enemy. I learned in those early days that K.A.P. would always take on any enemy—and time in particular—with a deep measure of respect. The price of writing that Introduction had to have been the postponement of something else. As well we know, *Ship of Fools* suffered many another postponement to follow this, the one she assumed that summer for introducing *A Curtain of Green.*

Katherine Anne wrote to me:

> Yaddo
> Saratoga Springs, New York
> August 27, 1941

Dear Eudora:

I go on missing you quite steadily, the whole place changed when you went, though the activities kept on. I got to Albany by bus, not too dull, and at good hours, but there was a grim air of business about the trips, no more pleasant escapade in the morning air, no unexpected finding of Hindu wool rugs, no fun, in a word. My eyes managed to give me the worst upset in my nerves of anything I have known in my life. I was almost reduced to a state of pure terror, night and day, for the better part of a week. My efforts to conceal my state made it worse; I wished to collapse, to tell my troubles, to call upon God for help. I cannot be blind, that is the one thing I would make no attempt to face . . .

. . . Far from being part of the pressure, your preface is gone, accepted, perhaps set up in galleys by now. I came home with my goggles on fine afternoons, sat down and batted out that opus in two evenings' very pleasant work, mailed it special delivery and received some very kind and pleasant words of rejoicing from John Broadside;[50] so have that off your mind as it is off ours . . . Now of course I think of some other things I might have said to good effect, I wish I had gone a little more into certain stories, such as A Memory, Old Mr. Marblehall, and so on. But I can do it later when I write about your work again in another place. For certainly I expect to do so.

. . . I am being moved from North Farm to the Mansion for the month of September, since a new set are going to be settled here. This weekend must be spent packing, sending half my things to storage, taking mss. and music with me, and all. But I shall make quick work of it and work there as well as I can. South Hill is going faster, all at once, the plastering is begun. I should think that is a good sign. Every time I see it, I am pleased with it, it really is my house and just the one I wanted. And some day we will cook our supper on a charcoal grill in that terrace fireplace, maybe with snow outside, and the fire shining through the windows on it . . .

. . . To work, to work. It has always been later than I thought, but now it is later than ever . . . . . . still I expect to make the deadline this time, the fourth for the novel . . . it just rolls along, I don't worry about it any more; this is about all that space, it allows such a long line of continuity, and time for cumulative effect; and I always did know what I wanted to say in this book, my mind hasn't changed, and how could I write anything that didn't belong there? I trust myself, at last.

You trust yourself, too, darling. You are as good as there is in your time, and you have a long way to go and to grow, I can't see the end of it, thank God . . .

With my love,
K.A.

I missed her too, and a long life of correspondence started between us, easy-going and as the spirit moved us—about reading, recipes, anxieties and aspirations, garden seeds and gossip. She's never let me thank her for the Guggenheim, or Yaddo, or possibly even the Introduction, in any proper way. But *she* was a born thanker, for any miscellaneous trifle that might come in the mail from me, wanting to make her laugh:

Yaddo, Saratoga Springs, New York
October 7, 1941

Dear Eudora:

The sugar cane arrived in the most mysterious style, fascinating to think about: in one very short piece with the address tag on it, and a long stalk simply accompanying it, with not even a piece of string on it, unaddressed, un-everything, independent, unattached, there was nothing to stop it from going on to some destination it might have liked better, or turning in its tracks and bolting back to Mississippi again. But no, it stuck to its companion, and came in as it were under its own steam. And how good it tastes: I am still occasionally sitting down with a sharp knife and stripping off a section and gnawing away at it. My father told me once that when he was a little boy, strange and new to Texas, he and his slightly older brother ran away to Louisiana because they were so homesick for the sight and taste of sugar cane. I put that in a story once.[51] I know better now just how they felt, though . . .

Katherine Anne

Doubleday was giving a party for *A Curtain of Green* in November, in New York, and of course Katherine Anne's presence was called for. "I take for granted in some strange way that I am to be in New York for your party, it doesn't seem possible that I should miss it," Katherine Anne wrote from Yaddo on October 19. But on November 5, a telegram followed to tell me in New York, where I'd already arrived:

> Dear Eudora, be happy and gay at your coming out party and remember me just enough to console me a little for not being there. All the good luck and reward in the world to you. You deserve everything. I hope to see you there or here before you go home. With my love, Katherine Anne.

She continued to work on restoring South Hill, and finally a letter arrived, dated August 28, 1942, on handsome letter paper only slightly different a shade of blue from her familiar typing paper, imprinted with SOUTH HILL, R.D. 3, Ballston Spa, New York. It reads in part:

Dear Eudora:

This is the very first letter on the very first page of the letter paper, and this is the first day I have been here by myself. You can hardly imagine the confusion of household gear piled up here and there, but this nice south east room upstairs is in a bare and lovely order, with my table set up and the work-lamp ready, and when I look out I see the maples and the front meadow on my left and the corner of the sun room and part of the east meadow on the right.

. . . I must get settled in before the winter closes around us. Now you can think of me as here: Caroline Slade came this morning with a big, flat basket of vegetables from her garden, beautiful as a bouquet, every little carrot and tomato and celery head all washed and polished, and I put the parsley and some celery leaves in a bottle of sauterne vinegar at once, thinking you cannot begin too early with such things.

. . . Here all is weed and unkemptedness, but the rosa regosa and white lilacs I planted in April are flourishing, it was a lucky rainy summer for I had to leave them to their fate almost at once. They didn't mind at all. They will be strong and fine for transplanting in the spring. They started as little dry sticks and are now green full little bushes. And so other things may go as well too . . .

For a few months her letters continued to be full of pleasure and happiness and invitations. But when winter arrived and closed her in, she grew too cold, and her old enemy pneumonia caught up with her and defeated her. South Hill, like some earlier dreams, but a dream completed this time, had to be put behind her.

By December 18, 1946, she was writing to me from Santa Monica, California.

Eudora Welty at Katherine Anne Porter's house South Hill, Ballston Spa, New York, June–July 1941. Courtesy Papers of Katherine Anne Porter, Special Collections, University of Maryland, College Park, Libraries.

"I live within six blocks of the Pacific," she says. "Sometimes at midnight I hear that desperate creature beating its brains out on the beach, but musically. At last I have some of my books and music; this little place is like a birdcage, open and round, and I have sat here on the edge of my chair for a year, thinking any minute I may find a house of my own . . . I bought a little mountain top in the Mojave desert, after selling South Hill to the Willisons—did you read his *Saints and Strangers?* a fine piece of historical writing . . . I feel well. The novel is not finished, but I think now I have my road cleared a little, there is always so much to be done about other things, other people. But it does really seem that maybe I have reached the end of that, too."

John Edward Hardy (1922–), teacher, scholar, and poet, was born in Baton Rouge and received his B.A. from Louisiana State University, where he was a student of Cleanth Brooks and Robert Penn Warren. He received an M.A. from the State University of Iowa and a Ph.D. from Johns Hopkins University. He taught at the universities of Detroit, Yale, Oklahoma, Notre Dame, Colorado, South Alabama, Missouri–St. Louis, Illinois–Chicago, and Munich, Germany, where he was Fulbright Professor of American Literature. His books include a collection of his own poems entitled *Certain Poems* (1958), *Man in the Modern Novel* (1964), *Katherine Anne Porter* (1973), and *The Fiction of Walker Percy* (1987).

Source: John Edward Hardy, "Remembering KAP," unpublished reminiscence, collection of Darlene Harbour Unrue.

The first time I met Katherine Anne Porter, I spilled a glass of icewater in her lap. It was a hot afternoon in Baton Rouge, probably in the late spring of 1940, toward the end of my freshman year at LSU. I was secretary of the newly organized, vaguely *avant garde* "literature and ideas" club, which had somehow managed to book Miss Porter as distinguished guest speaker at one of our meetings. After her talk, two or three other students and I persuaded her to join us for cokes and ice cream at a popular drugstore–soda fountain just off campus on the northeast corner of Highland Road and Chimes Street.

I have forgotten the subject of Miss Porter's talk at the club meeting—and, of course, the names of the other students who were with us at the drugstore. If it had not been for the spilled icewater, perhaps I should have remembered these other things, perhaps not. But I remember that we were sitting opposite each other at a small, round, marble-topped table, and that the little glass, wet with condensation, slipped out of my hand, skidded across the table, stopped at the very edge, and, as I grabbed to retrieve it, tipped neatly, ineluctably over.

Fortunately, we had already been there for a half hour or longer before the disaster. And once past the initial shock—having first stood up to dab ineffectually at her skirt, and then sat down to join the rest of us in something resembling a moment of silent prayer—she managed to escape the scene with her wits about her, and her dignity remarkably intact. As casually as if it had been so far no more than a routinely stressful day on her crowded calendar, she explained that she had a dinner engagement that evening, and would like some time to herself meanwhile, "to rest and change," before going out again.

If the episode only enhanced my admiration for her, by the same token it did nothing to improve my self-esteem: which for any reasonably sensitive college freshman, of course, hardly sure most of the time that he *has* a self, is fragile at best. But our second and last meeting—at the Johns Hopkins faculty club, on Armistice Day, 1953, the place and date confirmed in my inscribed copy of *The Days Before*—went a lot better for both of us.

She was there for a reading, with a reception and dinner in her honor, principally sponsored as I recall by the university's Writing Seminars: a program directed at that time, as all the world knows, by Elliott Coleman.[52] I had a chance to identify myself to Miss Porter, and sit down beside her to talk undisturbed for a few minutes, before most of the other guests arrived. She wondered how long it had been since we last saw each other; expressed surprise, when I told her, that it was only once, and quite so many years in the past, considering all the friends we had in common, etc.; and finally, as I had steeled myself to expect, asked apologetically that I remind her what the occasion of our first meeting had been. So, I told her all that too, and asked in my turn whether she remembered it now.

"Remember it? Of course, I remember the icewater," she said. "How could I ever forget it? But . . . . . so that was *you*!"

And she burst out laughing, and so then did I, and there we most hilariously were when Elliott came charging up, in belated hostly high spirits, saying that he had looked forward to introducing us but was if anything all the more pleased to see that we had already gotten acquainted and to such so evidently gratifying effect . . . . . thus seamlessly on, to one of his inimitable abrupt, ebullient pauses, eyes glistening, and she put in:

"Oh, for heaven's sake, Elliott. This isn't the first time we've met. Didn't he tell you? I've known Mr. Hardy since he was a baby."

"A baby . . . . . a *baby*? Where was that?"

"In Baton Rouge, of course. I was just recalling how he wet a favorite skirt of mine once."

"So, then, you knew his parents well?"

"Oh, yes . . . . . and *their* parents. Wonderful people."

"Well, I'm damned!" Someone was calling him from across the room. Backing away, he raised one leg and slapped it heartily, then the other, turned and was off through the crowd, still marveling, in the kind of formal prance (much like what my old high school track coach called a "high-knee-action" exercise) that he reserved for occasions of strong emotion.

"Do you think he could possibly have fallen for that?" Porter asked me then, looking after him with a little frown. Perhaps it had occurred to her for the first time that she and my mother might well be, after all, about the same age.

"I don't know," I said. "It's possible. Fact is, you almost had me believing it."

"Do you think we should disabuse him, then?"

I thought about it for a moment.

"I wouldn't," I said. "Elliott's a big boy. He'll believe it if he wants to, and is shrewd enough to trap us with the right questions if he doesn't. Either way, he will enjoy it. I wouldn't want to spoil his fun."

"So, then, we won't," she said.

"Good," I said. And I laughed again, and so did she.

And I have thought about it many times since, and every time decided that we were right, to let it ride.

Elliott and I never mentioned the matter to each other again. But I think I was right, that it was fun for him, whether he believed it or not. I think I was right to see in Katherine Anne Porter then something essential, an essentially *benign* creative mischief, a benign compulsion to simple storytelling, that some of her otherwise most competent critics have missed. I cannot deny the evidence that that justifies studies in the "cold beauty" both of Porter herself and of her work. But neither can I deny the evidence of my own personal acquaintance with her, however brief, as well as that of my critical examinations of her fiction. In my experience, she was capable not only of genuine kindness, a solicitude for other people's feelings, but now and again of an outrageously genial *merriment* in her fictionalizing, both for publication and for impromptu performance, that absolutely must not be overlooked in any valid assessment of her darkness, her knowledge of dispossession and despair, of lying and betrayal and casual and studied cruelty, of the depths of human self-loathing.

At the 1953 dinner, I happened to be seated next to Susanne Langer, who was a guest professor in the Hopkins philosophy department that year.[53] I myself had never been formally introduced to Langer, another of the great modern heroines of my intellectual life, but when both Porter and she told me that evening—one before and the other during dinner—that they intensely admired each other's work, and wanted very much to meet but were shy about presenting themselves unaccompanied, I gladly accepted the heady responsibility to bring them together.

They were a study, face to face—about the same height, as I recall, but Langer lean and tanned, wearing a sensible sort of plain professorial brown dress and comfortable brown walking shoes, Porter in long white elbow-length gloves and a sleeveless, low-cut evening gown with one great rose pinned to the waist—and I should have enjoyed hovering about in the hope of overhearing what in the way of observations on the nature of language, perhaps, the creator of Royal Earle Thompson[54] and the foremost modern distinguisher of Sign and Symbol might have had to exchange. (I forget how the subject came up, but at the dinner table the only thing Langer had told me much about was her love of New England winters: how once in Vermont, on a brilliantly moonlit night returning alone from a string-quartet rehearsal, pulling her 'cello behind her on a child's sled, she had stopped on a wooded slope, propped the 'cello against a tree, and spent an hour doing solitary belly-whoppers down the hill.) But having minimally officiated at last in the introductions, and taken their orders and fetched their drinks and handed them over without mishap, I was more than content this time to quit while I was winning.

I never had an opportunity to talk to either of them again, and have no idea whether they ever saw each other after that evening.

4
New York, Washington, DC, and California, 1941–1951

The 1940s were a decade of transition and loss for Porter. In January 1942 her father died, and six months later she divorced Albert Erskine. Struggling to find stability, she bought a charming old farmhouse near Yaddo and began a long and expensive process of renovating it. She published short stories, essays, a third collection of fiction, and excerpts from her long novel-in-progress while continuing to speak at writers' conferences and taking an active role in politics. She fulfilled an appointment as fellow at the Library of Congress and undertook college and university tours—"trouping," as she called it. After the failure of a serious love affair with Charles Shannon, she accepted contracts with movie studios in Hollywood and a yearlong adjunct position at Stanford University. Along the way she made new friends and gathered more disciples.

23 / Marcella Comès Winslow

Marcella Rodange Comès Winslow (1925–2000) was born in Pittsburgh, Pennsylvania, and attended the Carnegie School of Fine Arts before studying painting in Europe. A portrait painter, she settled in Washington, DC, with her two young children during World War II while her husband, Colonel William Randolph Winslow, was stationed in England. Notable persons in addition to Katherine Anne Porter who sat for their portraits and were frequent guests at her Georgetown home on P Street include Robert Penn Warren, Allen Tate, Caroline Gordon, Robert Frost, and Eudora Welty. Porter boarded with her for six months in 1944, when she was serving as Fellow in Regional Literature at the Library of Congress. Winslow's book, *Brushes with the Literary,* is a collection of letters by her and to her from 1943 to 1959. All the letters quoted below were written by Marcella Comès Winslow to her mother-in-law, the writer Anne (Tat) Goodwin Winslow.

Source: Marcella Comès Winslow, *Brushes with the Literary: Letters of a Washington Artist, 1943–1959* (Baton Rouge: Louisiana State UP, 1993), 42–45, 50–55, 56–57, 59–61, 63–64, 66–69, 71–76.

January 21, 1944

Dear Tat,

[. . .] Do you know who will be here for dinner next Saturday and whom you will meet if you come? None other than the great Katherine Anne Porter. She is supposed to be just out of what the Tates call "the nesting period," and all ready for something or someone new. She is taking John Peale Bishop's place at the Library of Congress,[1] as JPB almost died of heart disease and has been away since before Christmas. Do come.

February 12, 1944

[. . .] I have met Katherine Anne. She is more attractive and interesting than I expected—which was a lot. She strikes me first of all as being a very sincere artist, and then a very attractive woman. Rare combination.

I have already gone out to the Tates' to make sketches for the portrait I am going to do of her.[2] They all came over here last Sunday. A most memorable evening. She is pleased with the idea of a portrait and will probably make a good model though, perhaps, a bit difficult to catch for sittings.

KAP has pure white hair, short, curly. She is short, about your height [five feet, 2 inches],[3] thin, and has lovely gray-blue eyes, a youthful unlined face, high forehead, pointed chin. She is animated in a very ladylike way, and fascinating to talk with. No airs or mannerisms, a good sense of humor and the ability to say devastating things in a charming way, like Allen. I will find out more about her while I paint her.

February 22, 1944

[. . .] The very night J got sick,[4] Katherine Anne came down with Pneumonitis. She is recovering rapidly, I hear. That morning I had gone to the Library of Congress to make some sketches of her, taking her a valentine box of the cookies which I had made for the children. [. . .] Did you hear KAP on "Invitation to Learning" last Sunday? This was her 13th time on the program, the only woman so consistently invited.

April 1, 1944

[. . .] By the way, Allen thinks your conversation is far more scintillating than Katherine Anne's. She talks a bit much, and apparently tries them some with her vanity. She is the Prima Donna—but fascinating. Vamps all the young men who come to see Nancy.[5] They just fall for her and ask, "Why isn't she married?" KAP may rent my house this summer with two other women.

No one reckoned with the jealousies that could flare between two southern women writers struggling for recognition in the literary world. A fight erupted between Katherine Anne Porter and Caroline Gordon Tate over some spilled perfume, which I gather was the reason Allen phoned me to ask if Katherine Anne could rent my third-floor room. I was not only glad to have the extra sixty dollars a month she paid for the room and board but flattered that someone whom my mother-in-law had always said she would rather write like than anyone else was willing to share my old bathroom with the clawfoot tub on the second-floor landing—and share my life as well.[6]

April 5, 1944

[. . .] Katherine Anne Porter moved in to take my spare room and had a fever of 101! Nothing to worry about. She seems to get fevers even moving across the street, she says. She is rather frail and given to bronchial trouble, having once had tuberculosis. It is nice to have her and especially the $60 a month for room and board. I have the first check!

April 13, 1944

[. . .] I forgot to tell you that while I was away [. . .] KAP dosed herself so effectively with the medicine the doctor had given her that she passed out cold for a day. No one could rouse her and she has no recollection of about 48 hours! She had a touch of her usual bronchial trouble so when the doctor came to see Mary,[7] she asked him for some sleeping pills and said later they made her feel so good that she kept on taking them every time she woke up.

April 15, 1944

[. . .] The doctor told us the only thing wrong with KAP is exhaustion. It seems the Tate household was too much for her. She simply caved in. Allen is sick with a cold now after returning from John Peale Bishop's funeral in Maine [. . .].

KAP has a tremendous appreciation for Allen's writing. Feels he will be considered the greatest poet of his day after T. S. Eliot. She told me how sorry she was that I didn't ask Harriet Winslow's permission to take her to their last musical, as early chamber music is her all-time favorite. Had I done so, SHE would have been the one in the biggest chair, front row center!

April 23, 1944

[. . .] So much to tell you—now that I have a fascinating "Femme Fatale" in the house. I don't have as much time for letter writing as formerly. I don't, however, find Katherine Anne a Prima Donna—at least, as yet. She wears remarkably well, so far, and is most considerate. She is too popular for her rather frail person, though as the slightest extra exertion knocks her out. She runs fevers for nothing at all and, literally, seems to be a too high-tension person. One has a feeling the fuse will blow. How she managed to keep her feet so firmly on the ground with all the attention, adulation and emotional strain of her tempestuous life I can't imagine, except that she has a tremendous interest in *everything*. I have hardly hit upon a subject that she does not know something about (usually a great deal) from old colonial silver to astrology. She could run for political office as easily as she could get a chef's job at the Ritz.

She tells an amusing story about going to a French cooking school where the Maître Albert asked her loftily if she (naturally) desired to learn to make pastries. She answered, "No, I desire to cook a wild boar." Which she proceeded to do, and if you want the recipe I can supply it.

Today, being Sunday, I am taking a cooking lesson. By the time Randolph returns I will have mastered a few tricks. We are having a chicken in garlic and Worcestershire sauce which we will eat with noodles and sour cream. Next, I shall learn to make an onion pie. She stuffed a capon for our Easter dinner. Superb!

So far, she has given me $52 for board this month. We arrange that she pays me $1.00 for a dinner she eats here, as she goes out often. That helps quite a bit [. . .].

Johnny's case of the mumps was very slight. Mary had it bad enough for everybody. She is getting to be quite a personality. KAP is, fortunately, interested in children, and thinks Mary a tremendously forceful character. [. . .]

Mary takes KA's authorship very much for granted and has said she will write a book herself as soon as she gets a typewriter. She refers to publishing as "Knopfing" the pages. She has decided it will be about death and hell. I think she gets carried away with Katherine Anne's interest in her.

April 30, 1944

[. . .] These summer days which have come on the heels of winter are so lovely. I call them summer, not spring, because we are sweltering already.

No doubt you are eating greens, and more greens. We had our first tender ones yesterday with some ham. I am so glad the points have been taken off because I am going to contribute a ham to Katherine Anne's birthday party on May 15th.

It is going to be a select little group of her choosing—mostly from Mexican days—the painter Federico Castellone, who is at Fort Belvoir; another, a young Alabama painter named Shannon, who has shown in New York and been stationed in the Pacific; several influential South American diplomats; Lincoln Kirstein;[8] and Monroe Wheeler if he can make it from New York. The Tates aren't even being invited—hush-hush—that is another story; anyway, they don't know many of this group. I am being invited because I live here. KAP always makes a lot of her birthday. She is already talking about having chicken liver pâté, which is one of her specialties, and beaten biscuits, and a very special vegetable salad. We will probably overflow into the garden.

I started painting her portrait today. If I can keep the quality I started with, it should be one of my best. [. . .]

KAP's mumps passed so quickly that it is a great question in my mind whether she had them at all. She is very open to suggestion. She had a stiff neck and fever and swollen glands, so, maybe it was a sort of mumps, though she never got puffed out at all the way Mary did.

May 1, 1944

[. . .] Last night KA and I went to the opening of an exhibit at a new little gallery, saw a few friends (one of whom, she informed me today, she was madly in love with once and, literally, almost murdered—a South American),[9] among whom was the young Bart Barber who is getting KA to talk on his radio program. [. . .]

KAP is in "your" bedroom on the third floor next to the studio. That is the only reason I can capture her for sittings. She adores the idea of a portrait, but is hard to catch. Her social life is demanding and her health is frail. She seems always in a state of exhaustion. That doesn't stop her from wanting to experiment with gourmet dishes. Nor does it stop her from entertaining anyone willing to sit at her feet and listen to her stories about her colorful past; her loves, won or lost; her tales, true or false; her writing success ("I could publish my laundry list") and her inability to find time for her writing. I am willingly one of the feet-sitters. I drink in every word and believe every one of them.

May 20, 1944

[. . .] Katherine Anne so far has been very reliable about money. She keeps up to date on payments and remembers meals she has had here and pays me promptly. [. . .]

KAP's party was a delicious treat—I particularly liked the salad (after the ham of course) which was a combination of French-style beans, asparagus, celery, with sour cream and mayonnaise. Lincoln Kirstein, one of the directors of the Museum of Modern Art, who is a private at Fort Belvoir (and worth $40 million, I hear), was the best known of the guests, but so rude that his goose is cooked with me. He walked out after dinner and never returned. Not a word was said to either of us.

June 11, 1944

[. . .] The Tates are leaving July 1st and I will miss them. KAP and I had a mint julep party for them. We got bourbon through one of the Senators and Allen made the juleps Kentucky style.

June 15, 1944

[. . .] Katherine Anne was very pleased that you liked THE LEANING TOWER. [. . .] Her job at the Library goes until September 1st. And then she does not know what she will do. She can't write holding down a job, or being unsettled, yet she has to have one to live. It is a vicious circle. [. . .]

Mary and Johnny call Katherine Anne "Miss Pota" with a southern accent. They used to chant: "Miss Pota has the grippe. Miss Pota has the grippe," which changed to "Miss Pota has the mumps. Miss Pota has the mumps." On her birthday, May 15th, they drew a large paper cat for her, under which they printed in large letters: "To Miss Pota. We aire glad you aint got no more grippe and no more mumps. Mary and Johnny."

June 22, 1944

[. . .] Since you liked Katherine Anne's letter so much, I am sending you another. You can tell how nice she is. And that is not just her letters. She is a really sweet person. However, she is restless and dissatisfied and put off by so many worthless things—as well as people. She likes people but they distract her. She lets them distract her and then she worries because she can't write. Allen says she does everything she can to prevent herself from writing—it is almost as though she is afraid to tackle it. Usually she writes in a blaze of inspiration from numerous notes. Practically never has to write anything over. Just gets stuck and then waits for the proper mood—but tires herself out with distractions, so the mood gets waylaid. She never could write at Yaddo, or places where she is expected to write.

She is a genius. Unpredictable and undisciplined about her life and work—not her manners. Strangely enough, she cannot bear to be late for an appointment, and is usually prompt somehow, some way, for interviews and parties—yet, if I had not picked her up, bag and baggage, and dumped her in my car, she never would have made the train to New York for a radio program recently.

She is a LADY, and one never forgets it for an instant. She was educated by the nuns in New Orleans, and still bears the imprint of their training— little feet crossed under her when she sits down, modest in her dress and ways. She told me she wanted to be a nun, but her father squelched the idea, giving her anti-Catholic literature to read. Now she is hoping to return to the church. She sent away for a huge silver Mexican rosary which she has hung over her bedpost, perhaps expecting that to do the trick. She adores beautiful things. Likes just to hold a piece of old silver in her hands to feel its beauty. The most sensitive person I have ever met—so much so that one wants to do things for her and remove some of the worry—but she can't bear to be under obligation. That is torture to her. Considering how she can't find her way about on buses and streetcars, one wonders how she

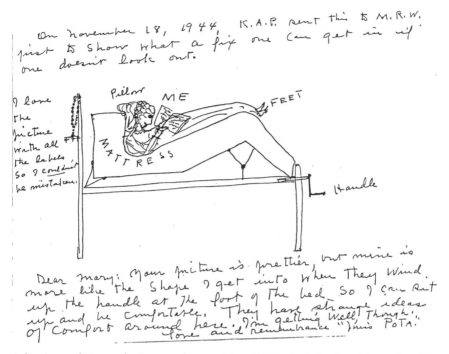

On november 18, 1944, K.A.P. sent this to M.R.W.
just to show what a fix one can get in if
one doesn't look out.

I love the picture with all the labels so I couldn't be mistaken.

Pillow   ME   FEET

MATTRESS

Handle

Dear mary: Your picture is prettier, but mine is
more like the shape I get into when they wind
up the handle at the foot of the bed so I can sit
up and be comfortable. They have strange ideas
of comfort around here. I'm getting well, though.
love and remembrance "Miss Pota."

A drawing made in 1944 by Porter and sent to Marcella Winslow's daughter, Mary, who with her brother, Johnny, was fascinated with "Miss Pota." Courtesy Papers of Katherine Anne Porter, Special Collections, University of Maryland, College Park, Libraries.

has found her way through these 50 years of her life doing absolutely everything and experiencing extreme poverty as well.

Katherine Anne's life is unbelievable. I'll tell you about it some day.

August 7, 1944[10]

[. . .] I dropped into P Street to see Katherine Anne and found her in a state of dishabille and bad shape. She was so distraught over the departure of her most recent love (Charles Shannon, years younger, the painter who is doing his military here), and the discovery that he was married as well, that she completely forgot she had invited the Edgar Ansel Mowrers to dinner. I was sitting by the window and explained: "Katherine Anne, there are two people in evening dress coming up the steps!" She didn't even have makeup on and became panicky. She explained: "My God, this is the second time I have done this to them!" But they had to be admitted and the conversation was strained to say the least. E. A. Mowrer is a distinguished journalist and his wife, who is English, also writes. She knew them in her Paris days. I don't know how KA lives these things down but maybe they happen so often she takes them in her stride. Her typewriter had to be repaired but she can't remember where it went and how she will get it back. I doubt she had occasion to use it much this summer with Shannon in the house.

September 1, 1944

[. . .] Katherine Anne plans to return to Yaddo after she goes to New York for a party to be given by her publishers. She will try to finish her novel which even she, herself, says is good. Allen thinks it is remarkable as far as it goes. KA writes that "it seems as if things were only beginning and that, here it is, the end of something and the beginning of something else." It is the end of something interesting for me—living with her—genius, beauty, prima donna, femme fatale, fascinating person. I have enjoyed all of it.

24 / Eleanor Clark

Eleanor Phelps Clark (1913–96) earned a B.A. from Vassar College in 1934, and throughout the 1930s and 1940s she supported leftist political causes while working as a freelance writer and an editor for German refugee scholars. In 1952 she married Robert Penn Warren, to whom Porter introduced her in 1944, and with whom she had two children: Rosanna (who was Porter's goddaughter), and Gabriel. She published three novels, including *Baldur's Gate* (1970), and three works of nonfiction: *Rome and a Villa* (1952), *Eyes, etc.* (1977), and *The Oysters of Locmariaquer* (1964; it won the National Book Award in 1965).

Source: Eleanor Clark, "The Friendships of a Lifetime," *Washington Post Book World* 26 July 1981: 1–2, 9–10, a review of Enrique Hank Lopez's *Conversations with Katherine Anne Porter: Refugee from Indian Creek* (Boston: Little, Brown, 1981). Although much of the essay is a catalog of Lopez's errors of fact and judgment in his book, Clark amplifies her criticism with reminiscence of her long friendship with Porter.

[. . . Porter's] life was by some lights madly unconventional, which is to say, according to Hoyle, for arts circles in her time and most others; in the light of present mores it looks positively stuffy. It quite lacked the extremity of dissolution and crack-up dear to the trade, and was on the whole more grim and lonely than in any way glamorous, though lightened by fine gifts of friendship and the mark of the phoenix on the brow. Down and out, though she was often close to it, Katherine Anne Porter simply did not know how to be.

[. . .] She took a long time dying, a matter of several years when strokes had left her bedridden, partly paralyzed and with her beautiful head tormented by nightmarish, if oddly selective, animosities. These indignities came to a stop in September, 1980, four months after her 90th birthday. Luckily her last domicile, in a nursing home outside Washington, was as brief as many others that will reward or elude the fact-diggers.

It was there in June last year, that my husband Robert Penn Warren and I last heard her voice. We had known and cherished her separately first for a good many years and together for many more, on dozens of those other perches that used to serve her as home for a while. She had always frowned on suicide, but the words that came through most clearly on that last visit were, "Oh God . . . . . oh God . . . . . let me die." She had lately turned, or returned—this being one of the more debatable points in her biography and one not mentioned here—to the Roman Catholic Church, but the priest who had been visiting her regularly in the next-to-last shelter, the last with her own precious belongings around her, was himself recuperating from a heart attack just then, so she was without whatever comfort he might have brought.

[. . .] As [Lopez's] book proceeds, [. . .] we are pummeled [. . .] with long ill-digested parts of treatises by two or three psychologists who probably never heard of her, to explain her marital fiascos, "writer's block," and "mistrust of people."

[. . .] My own unscientific opinion, based on a devotion of 44 years, is that barring some preliminary cause for huff or hatred she was as trustful as a well-treated puppy, and this was part, though only part, of her romantic and some other foul-ups. As everything in a life relates to everything else in it, this overreadiness to trust people, especially handsome younger men as she grew older, no doubt did relate, as the opposite trait would if it had existed, to her mother's very early death and that of her remarkable grandmother not many years later. [. . .]

Lopez writes that she didn't always tell the same version of a story. That is so. A mutual friend has remarked, "I would never say that Katherine Anne *lied*. She fantasized." Not about everything, far from it, though she did in fact lie about her age for quite a while in her middle years, which [Lopez] calls "justified" by her continuing "youthful appearance." It has been suggested elsewhere, in a published piece of a biography yet to come,[11] that she ascribed a false affluence to her childhood home in Texas, but she never spoke of it in any such way to me or to any other friend who has happened to mention it in my hearing. On this the Lopez account is I think fairly reliable.

The same cannot be said in regard to her rather brief marriages. The little more than an overnight fling described here as her first marriage was in fact the second legal one. She told me about it one evening when we were having dinner alone together; there was no incentive to fabrication and nothing in her tone to raise any thought of it. The real first, which she liked to speak of as an elopement from the Ursuline convent that she and her sister attended in New Orleans some time after her grandmother's death, appears not to have been the scapegrace, demeaning alliance of some accounts but one to a quite proper young man of some social status, who evidently presented the only handy out at the moment and whom she came to regard as both boring and stingy.[12] I have heard her tell more than once, with no discrepancy in the versions, about the day she up and left him, stopping to charge some very expensive lingerie to his account at a fancy store, before hopping on the next train out, I believe, to Chicago. I assume he was the father of the two stillborn babies she mentioned to me several times, since she said that both births occurred before she was 21.[13] Give or take a year or two of age, that would still make husband number one the progenitor. Fast work for a marriage of one or two days, especially one described as probably unconsummated. [. . .]

There is no malice that I can see in all this. On the contrary, one blushes for the poor man in his relaying of her comments on "the parasitic kind of adorers" around famous writers and "the peculiar race of people who live by a reflected glory." She had had café glimpses of the phenomenon around James Joyce and Ezra Pound in Paris and of course knew it as a staple of literary lore, as in connection with Rilke and D. H. Lawrence. One might add that the line between adorers and exploiters can be tenuous indeed. Lopez's misjudgments of his subject, conveyed mostly by flavor and innuendo, tend not to the derogatory but in the direction of unwarranted compliments, in the end more damaging as they give an impression of her pretending to accomplishments she neither had nor claimed. He has her, for example, "as fluent in French as in Spanish." I never heard her say more than a few words in Spanish, always little popular drinking toasts, and have no idea how she went about her one long translation from it.[14] But her French was close to nil; for translations for her songbook she had to rely on friends.[15] She could not have carried on a conversation in that language and I doubt if she ever had to try, as her life in Paris with Pressly seems to have been singularly hermetic, with no exposure, that I ever heard any trace of, either to French writers of the time or to any other indigenous circle.

France for her was a blank, a dud; perhaps she was too low in spirits then to care. But the language would have eluded her anyway. She was a born non-linguist, and I think the fact may well have compounded her alienation in 1931–2 in Germany, where she did care to look under the surface. Not that anybody is supposed to love the rise of Hitlerism but an extraneous factor, conceivably of isolation due to language, seems at work in the scorching hatred that makes *The Leaning Tower* the least satisfactory of her short novels, or long stories. In comparison with *The Berlin Stories,* set in about the same time, by Christopher Isherwood who evidently spoke German very well, that one of her creations suffers badly, which of course says nothing about the status of their respective life works.

Space is lacking here to discuss her forthright, occasionally skittish literary judgments—what motives entered or didn't into her famous put-down of Gertrude Stein ("The Wooden Umbrella")[16] or her praise of Dame Edith Sitwell, and so forth. Instead let us just affectionately recall, as with different terms of reference she would do for us, that she was a pretty bad dancer, a complete non-

Katherine Anne Porter and goddaughter Rosanna Warren, c. 1957, at the Warren home in Fairfield, Connecticut. Courtesy Robert Penn Warren Papers, Special Collections, The Kentucky Library, Western Kentucky University, Bowling Green, Kentucky.

athlete, a music-lover of genuine intensity but quite limited range, ditto for poetry, and that given her fierce need for isolation, in order to move into the depths that she must write from or die, it seems safe to assume that she would have been a very poor mother. As Lopez pictures it, her marital break-ups were always by her choice, as if the other party mightn't have had grounds for impatience too, especially as her splendid company cooking implies nothing about endurance of a daily kitchen grind, or any other daily interruption. In short, like plenty of other artists great and small, she must have been hell to live with very long. Yet her affections and loyalties were many and for the most part long-lasting, and her sometimes conspicuous share of female vanity didn't keep her from knocking herself out for other writers she admired; several of them, including this writer, were much younger women.

So much for vanity. It was harmless, except perhaps at times to herself, as witness several discomforting portrait photographs, by George Platt Lynes and others,[17] reproduced in [Lopez's] volume. She would speak, and is reported as doing so here, of "those dreadful posey pictures that George likes to take," but she did pose for them, dressed up to the nines and with her fine profile at its most advantageous tilt, and wasn't averse to giving copies of them to friends.

In any case the snapshots also printed in the book are a lot nicer, as are several in our possession. In one of those she is in borrowed winter garb on a toboggan with our children, jaw bravely set for the start downhill; another shows her radiantly smiling at a little girl, our daughter and her goddaughter, at a 2-year-old birthday party; in a third she is in a three-way hug with the same child, a few years later, and the co-godmother, Tinkum Brooks. The godmothers have their proper wrinkles, the little girl is clearly crazy about them both, and all three are really and truly laughing.

This is the Katherine Anne we too were crazy about, and now so sadly miss. The aloof lady of the portraits we never knew.

25 / William Goyen

Charles William Goyen (1915–83) was a Texas-born writer and editor. After teaching for one year at the University of Houston, he left to serve in the U.S. Navy during World War II. When he returned, he set about becoming a writer by working hard at his craft and making the acquaintance of sympathetic writers he admired, such as Katherine Anne Porter. His published works include the novels *The House of Breath* (1950), *Ghost and Flesh* (1952), *In a Farther Country* (1955), and *Come, the Restorer* (1974).

Source: William Goyen, "Katherine Anne Porter: An Appreciation," *Dallas Morning News* 28 September 1980: G1.

She lived in a four story brownstone house on East 65th Street (the house is now destroyed) when I first met her. It was in 1950, in the summer, and she'd invited me to come have a drink on the occasion of the recent publication of my first novel, *The House of Breath*. In fact she'd just written a fine and serious review of the book for *The New York Times*.[18]

I was scared to death, and found a tiny, fragile, beautiful woman bubbling with life and laughing, though I soon learned, she had little cause. Even then she was ill and as long as I knew her—or later when I didn't keep track of her much I heard from others or read it—she was periodically ill and frail. Yet just two days ago she died at the age of ninety. Who would have guessed she'd endure that long. At any rate there she was in isolation, indeed separation, in the hot middle of a great city—a woman of accomplishment and renown whose phone rarely rang and if it did she rarely answered it.

She had very little money ("there's never been a living in it," she said of her work) and let out the first two floors, one of which, I remember, housed a boa constrictor or some such great snake and a young man, its keeper, from Texas. Here she lived on the upper two floors, the top one from which she—as the months passed and we got to be friends—would daily let down a basket with a book or a note for me and into which I would put her mail and sometimes milk and bread; for at times she found it tiring to come down the flights of stairs to the street. We named me and the basket "Miss Porter's P.O."

In those early days I learned, again, how much alone the gifted can be. But here in this elegant New York town house she lived among beautiful things, Eighteenth Century furniture, exquisite glass, and plate silver. And, even then, I saw on her fingers a precious ring. Later I remember she very much wanted a vaunted string of pearls, and there was an emerald—ring or brooch—which haunted her and which, I believe, she finally got. Yet possessions came and went in her life.

She owned, she once told me, two houses which she'd never lived in.[19] In both cases she suddenly went in another direction, she said. But she was basically homeless, an oddly possessing and surrendering person, holding on and letting go. Her work, slow and long-seasoning ("I'm a late bloomer and a slow ripener," she said) was the stable center of shifting households, as it was of her vagrant life, and its reality. Many days, months, she did not write but her work was visible, tangible. Once, when I called on her in a house in Santa Monica,[20] where she'd been brought by a studio to work on a motion picture but they never called her, week after week, until she finally left,[21] we sat and talked around a coffee table heaping with the manuscript of *Ship of Fools,* still, after many years, in progress. Slapping her palm down on the pile, she said, "Well, there it is, honey."[22]

It was her total dedication to literature and to writing that drew me to her, and her sense of making something good no matter how long it takes. In these days of throwaway "product" her longlasting achievement is even more precious to me.

On that first [*sic*] meeting with Katherine Anne Porter she told me that she'd been watching all day a man in a room across the street polishing a table. All day with slow, even, patient strokes he had been polishing, on and on. She wondered what the table was for that such a thorough job should be done on it. But then, she said, she realized that he was no doubt doing a good job just so that it would be good, a good piece of work.

The man's work rose symbolically before me as she spoke of it. But what drew me as much was the woman's watching the man at his good work, on and on. She sat at her window and watched and he did his work, and, she told me, twilight came. I saw this as an aspect of the artist—who has enough time. And I remembered the last line of *Pale Horse, Pale Rider:* "Now there would be time for everything."

The artist, the true maker, has time enough, no matter what, or better have. Hastily made things, held briefly together, half-baked concoctions, heartless assemblies of shiny machines that break apart though "guaranteed"—these are the structures we live with almost without question; we have learned to accept short-term existence; limited performance; half-life; the book of the month; literary machines that run down half-way along and won't start up again—our shelves are graveyards of stalled engines on the way; the momentary popular, and the modish, the slick and the quick.

When I first read the stories and novellas of Katherine Anne Porter, sitting in a frame house on a gravelled street in Houston, my first feelings were of soundness in clean fresh writing. I wanted to do that! It was unadorned, serene, complete, what I read. Little did I know of the travail, the long labor, the disappointment, threatening bitterness at failure, the waiting that brought art into being—if it did. As I went on, through the years, to read more of her work and to hear her speak about the making of literature, I saw more and more how she held to the pure, abhorred the counterfeit, the eccentric, the fastidious, the obscure, the self-concerned. She spoke somewhere of being on the side of the "living green and the sunlight" and detesting the dark and the decadent.

And so she achieved in her style a kind of sublimity through preciseness and fully felt, fully formed feeling. And she came to defend the organic language of Shakespeare and Milton and the pure Elizabethan speech that was the ground of the singing speech of East Texas—she wanted to keep that—and she wrote some harsh pieces that riled critics and writers who were using the lingo of the streets as the language of fiction in the Fifties. She made enemies. She lashed out. She would choose Thomas Hardy over Proust, Hawthorne over Hemingway; there was not a surrealist bone in her body; she was not an ecstatic, not a rhapsodist, not a mystic, not "poetic," not "experimental"; she took Sarah Orne Jewett over Thomas Wolfe,[23] Willa Cather over Anais Nin;[24] she loved Colette and the Brontës, hated Gertrude Stein.

She made something good. She held it back, kept it until it was right. In a handful of books she put down what others have written through half a shelf to try to get. In a world of oversize, of multiplicity, of power through accumulation, she stands for simplicity. She reminds us that there is time enough, that art has its own time and holds to it, in the face of death and ugliness wrought by a self-poisoning race of men and women of ignorance and greed. From such a civilization she has now departed and left a small and perfect testament to beauty, orderliness, shape, meaning, and it is endangered. While the world was brewing its own poison—and burying it under its own gardens—in order to produce manifold billions of plastics, acrylics, styrofoam, she was polishing her table over and over slowly and thoroughly, as though there were time enough. She's among those, through the years, who've kept me heartened to do the same.

Farewell, Katherine Anne, and be welcomed.

Los Angeles

September 22, 1980

26 / Richard Scowcroft

Richard P. Scowcroft (1916–2001) was an influential member of the Creative Writing faculty in the program founded by Wallace Stegner at Stanford University. After earning a B.A. from the University of Utah and a Ph.D. from Harvard, Scowcroft published the novels *First Family* (1950), *A View of the Bay* (1955), *Wherever She Goes* (1966), *The Ordeal of Dudley Dean* (1969), and *Back to Fire Mountain* (1973). The youngest member of the Stanford English Department in 1948, Scowcroft and his wife, Anne Kendall Scowcroft, enjoyed entertaining Stanford's visiting writers.

Source: Richard Scowcroft, telephone interview with Darlene Harbour Unrue, 9 July 1995.

I'm not sure that anyone really came to know Katherine Anne Porter well during the academic year she was at Stanford. In the spring of 1947 she had come to Stanford to give a talk that was part of a college lecture tour. In her fifties, she was charming and very beautiful, and for her talk she wore a dramatic black cape. She talked about a book she was writing and could finish if she had two or three weeks of freedom.[25]

At a party in her honor afterwards, she dazzled the old fogies in the department, many of whom were from Texas, including the department chairman, R. F. Jones, and they began to talk about how wonderful it would be to have her at Stanford for a year. Eventually, with some creative financing and money from an outside source, Jones and Wallace Stegner, the director of the Creative Writing Program, worked out a year for her that included minimum teaching with significant time for her own writing. Although she accepted the position for 1948–49, she was offended that the course she taught carried no credit, and she blamed Jones, to whom she wouldn't speak during the time she was here, although she was friendly with his wife.

I doubt that she got any writing done during the year. Although my wife, Anne, and I offered to help her find a suitable place to live, she impulsively rented a mountain cabin in La Honda that a student had told her about. The primitive cabin didn't have heat, and it took her four hours on a sequence of buses to get to campus. She told me she was going to have a nervous breakdown. She finally found a cottage in back of a professor's house. It was charming and private, but she didn't like it. She called it a cave and a black hole.

Frustration with her living accommodations wasn't the only reason she failed to find the solitude and peace of mind necessary for her writing. She was so friendly with students that they felt welcome to drop in anytime they wanted. Neither could she say no to any social invitation, whether it was a cocktail party at a faculty member's home or a tea held by a group of Texas women.

Anne and I, who were young and recently married, had her to our house several times for dinner. She talked and talked, mostly about her earlier life, especially her childhood. We got the impression of an impoverished but elegant old home with a great library. There was no money, but there were former slaves around.

She was very witty. Once Truman Capote's name came up in the conversation, and she said she had known him at Yaddo and had seen him in Hollywood a few years earlier. Suddenly she stood up and did a very funny, albeit ungracious, imitation of him.

In the spring of 1948, Katherine Anne vanished from the Stanford campus for a month or so. I went by her cottage and left messages, but I had no word from her for several weeks. She had gone to North Carolina to accept an honorary degree and hadn't told anyone she was going.[26] When she returned, she had an academic robe and mortarboard and seemed cheerful and happy. She asked Janet Winters, the wife of Yvor Winters, who was also on the Stanford faculty, where she could wear her "costume." Janet told her, "At Commencement."

She showed up in her academic regalia at the spring commencement. Jones was surprised to see her in the procession in front of him. Since she continued to hold him responsible for the no-credit status of her class, she still refused to speak to him.

She left the campus quietly in the summer. I heard that she considered the Stanford experience one of the worst she had had. Anne and I had a card or two from her, but we never saw her again.

27 / Isabel Bayley

Isabel Bayley (1911–93) met Katherine Anne Porter at a University of Kansas writing workshop Porter conducted in 1948. Bayley, who became Porter's devoted friend, corresponded with her and made visits to her as long as Porter lived. In 1983 Bayley assumed the trusteeship of Porter's literary estate, which passed to Barbara Thompson Davis upon Bayley's death. Bayley edited *Letters of Katherine Anne Porter* (Boston: Atlantic Monthly Press, 1990).

Source: Isabel Bayley, "Forever May," unpublished fragments of reminiscence, Papers of Isabel Bayley, Special Collections, University of Maryland, College Park; fragments selected, organized, and edited by Darlene Harbour Unrue.

I had seen her in 1951, just about the time she made that recording of "Noon Wine," now kindly sent to me by Calvin Skaggs, who had just finished making a film on Katherine Anne Porter for the *American Masters* television series that would include enacted scenes from some of her stories.[27] He had wanted to hear her voice before he began work dramatizing "The Circus," "The Grave," and "The Witness," and I told him that she had recorded "Noon Wine" but that I had never heard it.

Now in 1986, listening to her recording of "Noon Wine" on that day full of sunshine at the house I shared with my husband, Hewlitt (Hew) Bayley, above the lake in Canada, I could see her as she had sat in the taxi with us on our way to dinner at Pierre's to celebrate her sixty-first birthday that May of 1951. She weighed just over a hundred pounds at the time—exquisite in her white wool dress and short cape and black pumps—talking happily in the voice I was hearing more than three decades later, and six years after her death.

We had osso buco there in the pleasant little restaurant on 53rd Street, a mere dozen blocks south from where she was living then in New York, and she asked my nautical husband about the use of "Under Weigh," which she was considering calling her novel (eventually called *Ship of Fools*). Nobody seemed to understand the sense in which she meant it, a sort of limbo, she said, smiling across the table to us and clinking glasses. We ordered marrons with ice cream and talked for hours in the little restaurant that hurried no one. We talked for another few hours after we took her home to her house on 65th Street. Concerned about her frail health and not wanting to exhaust her, we tried several times to leave. "Why do you think of going? Because I cough a little?" And she would urge us to stay. At last she waved goodbye to us, with affectionate small bendings of the fingers behind the grillwork in the glass doorway, with the red velvet portières behind her. How exquisite she looked—a fragile figure in white. Would we ever see her again?

So I had asked myself every time we kissed goodbye, and I breathed again that sweet Molinard perfume she loved—Toutes les Herbes de Provence: at the University of Kansas, where we first met three years before; at Cornell in 1952; again in New York before she went to Ann Arbor in 1953 and rented us her garden apartment at Gramercy Park; and the next month when I drove my little English car, a Hillman Minx, to Ann Arbor to leave it for her to enjoy during her academic year at the University of Michigan. Almost every time she spoke at the Poetry Center on 92nd Street in New York, I sat before her in the little theater. What a festive occasion she made of it for those of us applauding as she strode on stage in her long dress and long gloves. One year she read her "Defense of Circe," another year, an excerpt from what had started out as a short story and had become, after all the people in it had "tangled like a basket of snakes on a hot stove," a novel. Oh what blessed reunions and reunions and birthdays there were—among them, the great party her publishers gave for her at the 21 Club when the novel came out and her own *French Song-Book* party at the University of Maryland to honor Barbara Harrison Wescott and Monroe Wheeler, who had published the book in Paris on her forty-third birthday, 15 May 1933. She sat straight and attentive between Barbara and Monroe in her green taffeta dress from her Pakistani god-child,[28] her white coat flung over her shoulder, as the musicians played and sang the songs she had collected for the song book. After the concert she kissed each of the musicians and singers before my husband and Barrett Prettyman, her lawyer and friend, escorted her out to the car. She tossed kisses to those of us who stayed for more talk and wine than she had strength for, and a grand-nephew[29] ran up to her with yet another orchid to pin to her green dress. We wondered whether she would be exhausted the next day. Would we see her again?

The first time I saw her she was wearing a spruce green cape with an immense circular sweep reading her "Old Mortality" to a group of us in a writers workshop at the University of Kansas. Why did it seem hard to believe that this striking woman was the writer whose work I had discovered for myself in little magazines and read hungrily though discontentedly, for I could not buy the book some of the stories were in. I had a library book copy, one I had bought from the library by pretending to have lost it. She inscribed it, "For Isabel, Wishing her well, June 28, 1948."

The next morning when we sat together, she and I, in a little courtyard going over some stories of mine that she was critiquing, I remember my surprise at her seeing my characters more alive than anyone we had just passed while we carried our tray of coffee to the courtyard. "Put this down, will you?" she said. "This came to me this morning. I thought sacrifice, real sacrifice, in which somebody gives something which he needs for his own use to someone else who may or may not make good use of it—that is senseless, and it corrupts both of them. Yet it corrupts the one who makes the sacrifice even more than the one who is willing to accept under such circumstances." As I jotted this down, I found myself feeling close to her, natural with her, even inexplicably protective, so that next day when she did not come to the seminar because she had a cold, I went to her with a gardenia. We stood together at the door of the "barracks," as she called the quarters where the staff lived, looking out at my shiny little "buggy." She admired it, and we talked of driving it to Kansas City to hear Josephine Baker[30] if she recovered from her cold in time.

When I asked her, in the letter I sent with the notes I had taken of her lectures, who it was she had said that called Lady Mary Wortley Montagu[31] a dreary rattle (my husband, a "master" in eighteenth century letters, could not forgive me for missing this), she wrote back to say that the words were those of Edith Sitwell. "Tell your husband," she said, "that I found a danger in my early absorption in the eighteenth century: it leads to the seventeenth, and so on until I found myself up to the eyebrows in the late-medieval history of Europe, that is to say the world, and finally took for my territory the period from the reign of Charles VI of France to the death of Erasmus. But if we want to understand better what is happening today, there is the place to look for its beginnings and development. It hasn't been at all illogical, given the premises."

"Knock three times and ask for Joe," she joked, when I telephoned her in New York in August of 1950 to ask about stopping to see her on my way home from a trip abroad. She welcomed me when I arrived at her house on 65th Street, and we talked for three blessed hours. She had picked up a piece of paper, and with that easy grace of marking the moment she scribbled something for me: "I am no more what once I was / And what I was no more shall be, / My jolly summer and my spring / Have taken thieves' farewell of me." She finished the other stanza of the Clément Marot poem, signed it "Translated by Katherine Anne Porter—for Isabel—30 August, 1950, New York."

It was not long after I came back from another European trip that she wrote me she would be at Cornell, and there I sat, the spring of 1952, hearing her say to the university community at Ithaca as a way of introducing her talk, "The ancient Hebrews had a prayer against the hardening of the heart."

Always welcoming and generous, she took me to a dinner party given for her after the lecture. She stroked the head of the baby of our hosts in a way that astonished me—vigorously, as though expecting the baby to withstand just about anything. There was no tenderness in the hand that went up and down, yet a kind of affection from creature to creature.

I sent her notes I took on what she had said to the Cornell students, and, on her way to Paris to attend the Congress for Cultural Freedom she wrote, "Your notes will provide the spine for my Paris speech, on May 15, my birthday." When she returned, I visited her, and we sat in the spring sunshine side by side, on a green velvet canapé with long stalks of apple blossoms standing in a crystal vase at her feet, in the apartment friends had found for her on 17th Street while she was in Paris telling those at the Congress about the sinister aspects of getting together to celebrate freedom of speech and thought in the arts and in government: "If they were not in danger, we would not cross seas and far countries to gather here in this citadel of liberty to celebrate them, to boast of what is left of our freedom."[32]

She had greeted me in a white terry cloth robe tied around the middle with a red narrow scarf. She had obviously just had time to put on a little lipstick between my telephone call and my arrival, but she kissed me as though my visit had been long anticipated, and as though she had all the time in the world. The light from the window showed all the beauty of her startlingly blue eyes and her translucent skin. We sat long at her Italian monastery table and talked over wine served in her Bohemian blue glasses. We talked of Cotton Mather and how she was able to make a case for everyone but him and had not yet finished writing his biography.

In September 1953, before the academic year began in Ann Arbor, I drove from New York to see her and deliver the Minx. When I appeared at her door, she was groggy, not yet dressed for the day. I sat in the sunshine at her big open window while she took a morning bath and dressed in a grey skirt and darker grey cashmere sweater, pulling on sheer, nylon stockings and stepping into black suede pumps. Soon we were driving in the Minx between swarms of college students and cars to the liquor store, then to the closest small country road we could find for her driving lesson. With her hand on mine to get the feel, I slowly shifted the four gears. "I have it now," she said, and after a little while, "and don't think I'll forget it." It was hot by the time we got to the smorgasbord for dinner. We piled our plates with herring and hard-boiled eggs, little red beets, macaroni, chopped carrots, and kidney beans. In my room, where we had left glasses to cool in a sinkful of water, we drank Jack Daniels bourbon while she talked of astrology, the occult, mysticism. "However suspect much of it is," she said, "you get someone like Yeats, and he makes great poetry of it."

In July 1954 Hew and I drove to Ann Arbor to pick up the Minx, which sported a new grille after "someone," as she said, "bashed in the old one." She was weary of lecturing and grading papers, and she had been ill off and on during the year. She seemed to be looking forward to a year in Belgium with a Fulbright Fellowship.

I next saw her in New York City on St. Patrick's Day in 1957 at the Poetry Center, where she read her essay on Circe. I watched her walk onto the stage and peer out at the audience in the darkened theater (she had learned this from Wanda Landowska,[33] she told me). In the same theater Hew and I had heard Dylan Thomas read "Under Milkwood" a few days before his death. My memory of his haunted, dark eyes roaming over us from the podium were a counterpoint to Katherine Anne's merry blue eyes looking out at us as we laughed at what she said of her goddess. She wanted such evenings to be a celebration, for which she had put on a long dress of black lace over white silk and long white gloves. Her skilled pacing and bursts of energy kept us on the edges of our seats, had us standing and clapping our hands when she stepped forward and curtseyed in a charming, old-country style. She ended her reading as usual with the recitation of the seventeenth-century poem "As Life What Is So Sweet," which she had found in a book of poems in Sylvia Beach's bookstore in Paris in the early 1930s.

Everyone seemed to come to the party her publishers gave April 2, 1962, at the 21 Club in New York to celebrate the publication of *Ship of Fools*. John Malcolm Brinnin, Russell Lynes, Oscar Williams, Frances Steloff, Cyrilly Abels,[34] Monroe Wheeler, Glenway Wescott, Jack McGiffert of CBS who produced *Camera Three*, on which Katherine Anne appeared, and many other family members, friends, publishers, and publicists were there. When I came into the Jack Room, Katherine Anne was sitting in black silk and pearls chattering, posing for photographers, and reading telegrams, one from Hew, who was unable to make the trip. She had been working since six that morning, good-naturedly doing all the barbaric things expected of a writer to sell the book, including interviews and television shows. She was so exhausted she could hardly hold her food, and she kept leaving us to rest. "Are you meeting people?" she had the energy and kindness to ask, as she seated me beside Barbara Wescott, to whom the novel was dedicated. "Come see me in Washington!" Katherine Anne called over her shoulder as she left.

I saw her off in November of 1962 for her yearlong visit in Europe. She appeared at the top of the gangplank and descended to the lower deck of the *Leonardo da Vinci* with the bearing of a queen in her little black velvet beaded crown of a hat. She was flanked by her niece Ann, Ann's husband, Walter, and Ann's two little sons, who carried pots of gay flowers. I had heard her read a week earlier at the Poetry Center when she looked incandescent, her skin white and smooth as the oleanders I used to tuck in my letters to her. Now she was saying, "This trip will have to be a rest cure." She took charge of the cabin. "Oh, it is not as big as I expected! Do you know, this is the first cabin I've had all to myself?" She seated the children—"Donald, you here; David, you here"—and picked up the pile of telegrams. She started reading a wordy, long, solemn one: "We have read your book, we feel privileged . . . . ." "Their privileges stop right there," she said, and handed the boring message to Paul, her nephew. Soon she stood up in the midst of flowers (Seymour Lawrence [her editor at Atlantic-Little, Brown who guided *Ship of Fools* to completion] had come carrying a long box of roses; a dark-haired waiter had come with a tray of glasses). She held her champagne glass at the very tip of the base ("This is the medieval way," she said, holding it steady). With clinking and happy laughter we all said, "Bon Viaggio!" and drank. Cyrilly Abels said that the fools on this ship don't know what they are in for.

We corresponded while she was away that year, and Hew and I rejoiced with her in the financial and critical success of *Ship of Fools*. When she returned, she and I continued to write one another and talk on the phone. But the distance between Washington, DC, where she had settled, and our home on the lake near Toronto, made visits difficult. I did not see her again until 1968, when I went to her seventy-eighth birthday celebration that was planned to coincide with the opening of the Katherine Anne Porter Room in the McKeldin Library at the University of Maryland, to which she had given a mammoth collection of her books, papers, and other possessions.

The next day I was in Washington driving past Embassy Row and into 49th Street, and up the drive to her large brick and stucco Tudor house, with its mass of periwinkle and tall irises in bloom. Inside, the mail was piled up on a table under a Greek bas-relief of Orpheus and Euridice that she had bought in Europe. One of the envelopes contained President Lyndon Johnson's congratulations on her birthday and an invitation to lunch at the White House.

It was here in this house six months later on Twelfth Night that she gathered her friends to burn the pine boughs, the little ritual she enjoyed each year. Eleanor Clark, Robert Penn Warren, Barrett Prettyman, Peter Taylor, William Humphrey, William Jay Smith,[35] Cleanth and Tinkum Brooks—each had delighted in the sound of her voice on the phone, as Hew and I had, when she said, "We will have juicy smoked turkey from Vermont and ham from Virginia; we will sit at little tables and talk." At my little table sat Red Warren and Bill and Dorothy Humphrey. Katherine Anne in her black satin tunic and trousers with diamonds and emeralds moved about with more sparkle than her jewels. A great silver bowl held cognac to be flamed over a long spiral of orange peel and lumps of sugar. We moved into the library and sat before the fireplace and watched the crackling pine wreaths flame high. Red Warren said to Hew, "I fear this is the last party, and I'm pretty cut up about it."

Warren was happily proved wrong. In 1969 her friends, Hew and I among them, were celebrating her seventy-ninth birthday with a party at the Katherine Anne Porter Room in McKeldin Library. The party included a book signing, at which an elderly man with a copy of her *Collected Stories* under his arm told her, "I used to be afraid of growing old. But you seem to be having a ball."

It was at a party in the spring of 1970 for the publication of her *Collected Essays* that we next saw her. When we arrived at the F Club, where the party, hosted by Barrett Prettyman, to whom the *Collected Essays* was dedicated, was held, Katherine Anne was already there, resplendent in her white *peau de soi* dress, with her white coat thrown over the back of the large arm chair in front of the fire. She introduced us to Sonja Smith, wife of William Jay Smith, poet at the Library of Congress, and Pat Collins, wife of astronaut Mike Collins. At dinner Katherine Anne said to Barrett, "I had stage fright this afternoon; I was afraid I wouldn't be the belle of the ball."

Barrett was on his feet. "This is a double celebration," he said. "We celebrate the publication of Katherine Anne's *Collected Essays,* and we celebrate Katherine Anne in her eightieth year." He talked about the hours he had spent with her "purporting to be full of handling her legal affairs," not one moment of which had been dull. He presented her with Henry James's copy of George Eliot's *Adam Bede* that James had inscribed to Rhoda Broughton.

When Barrett asked her to say a few words, she got up, asking, "How much do you want me to say? I could talk all night." Then she said it was because she was always so lonely writing that she enjoyed having friends around and kept talking to keep them from going away. As she spoke, lines on her face went away; she became translucent and transformed and young—and was, of course, "the belle of the ball."

In the next ten years, the final decade of Katherine Anne's life, I kept up a steady correspondence with her and talked with her frequently on the telephone. Our numerous plans for her to visit us in Canada always collapsed, usually because she was ill or had fallen and broken bones or was undergoing various medical procedures such as cataract surgery. We managed to visit with her several times after she moved to College Park, and I attended her birthday parties in 1971, 1978, 1979, and 1980.

In 1978 she and I celebrated her birthday quietly with a nurse in attendance. In the past year and a half she had suffered several strokes, two of them severe, and she had been left with alternating moods and undependable clarity of mind as well as periodic slurred speech. As we sat together comfortably on this day, she seemed to be talking to something, as though she held in her right hand a little crushed bird. Indeed it was to her right hand that she was talking tenderly. "You must think I'm crazy," she said to me, holding up the poor paralyzed thing whose nails had been beautifully manicured. "But I wrote with that hand; I did everything with it."

I promised her that I would come to all her remaining birthday parties. For her eighty-ninth birthday in 1979 I was met at the Washington airport by Clark Dobson, who had baked the chocolate birthday cake I held on my lap in the drive to College Park, and Jack Horner, Katherine Anne's kind Hermes. We arrived at her sprawling apartment and hurried to refrigerate the cake with the rich, buttery icing with red and yellow flowers and green leaves and its message HAPPY BIRTHDAY KATHERINE ANNE. At four o'clock she was wheeled into the dining room and seated at the oval table with a pink cloth spread on it. She was dressed in a white Pakistani dress given to her by Barbara Thompson. There were six gilt-bamboo-backed chairs around the table, set with gold Tiffany forks, sandwich glass plates, and champagne glasses. Father Joseph Gallagher, a big, bespectacled man, sportily dressed except for his black shirt and white priest's collar, was there with a camera, which I motioned him to point at Katherine Anne's left side, rather than her right, where her cheek sags. The left profile was still lovely, the beautiful straight nose handsome in the contours of eyes and cheek. Katherine Anne rounded her lips above the pink and green and yellow candles and blew them out. As we toasted her for her eighty-ninth birthday, she drank with her usual delight in her favorite wine. I reminded her how we had toasted her twenty-five years before at her Fiesole table on 17th Street in New York, when Geraldine Page and Alexander Schneider[36] had come for dinner and lifted her own Bohemian blue glasses to her.

In the evening after the others had left we sat by ourselves in her room over steak, and she handed me big, juicy strawberries between birthday telephone calls. We talked of people we liked: of Eudora Welty, whom we heard say to Dick Cavett,[37] "All those people walking down the street in New York and nobody looking at anybody." Katherine Anne swiftly remarked, "Now, do you see what kind of mind she has?" We told each other little stories. I told her about Wanda Landowska and the musician with whom she was rehearsing in Toronto who came walking across the stage during a break in rehearsal carrying a glass of water to her. "I thought you might want a drink of water," he said to Landowska. Replied Landowska, "Au contraire!" and headed for the Ladies' Room. Katherine Anne, bursting with laughter, exclaimed, "To think I never heard that Landowska story!" And then she said, "I was an admirer of hers, but never a worshipper."

When I called Katherine Anne to say I was coming to her ninetieth birthday

Isabel Bayley, Katherine Anne Porter's devoted friend and
trustee of her literary estate, sitting on the Hillman Minx
she and her husband lent Porter to use while she fulfilled her
appointment at the University of Michigan, Ann Arbor, in
1953–54. Courtesy Papers of Katherine Anne Porter, Special
Collections, University of Maryland, College Park, Libraries.

party, I heard the gratitude in her voice. She was soon to be a resident of Carriage
Hill Nursing Home, where she would receive the round-the-clock care she now
needed. "I am leaving here," she said. "In two days I am going to move to a perfectly lovely place." Between the time of my phone call at the end of April and her
birthday, May 15, a great change had taken place. Alas, the Great Good Place was
hardly that. A cluster of friends were there to celebrate with her. Clark Dobson
wheeled in the cake. Ted Wojtasik brought balloons bobbing gaily about on their
tether. Jane DeMouy brought flowers. Jack Horner filled our glasses with champagne. I gave her a little picture Hew had taken to amuse her. In it I held her *Ship*

of Fools open beside Erasmus's *In Praise of Folly,* Mandeville's *The Fable of the Bees,* and Sebastian Brant's *Ship of Fools.*[38] I read her a little jingle I had written beneath the photograph:

> Erasmus, Mandeville and Brant
> Try to do what others can't;
> Try to look at us as fools,
> Instruments, mere Evil's tool.
> Katherine Anne cleared the confusion:
> Good and Evil's in collusion!
> Her we thank for light of day
> Four score and ten today, today!

Although she smiled in appreciation of all the gifts, her heart was no longer in the celebration. Someone put the white roses Hew sent at her elbow, and someone else brought ice cream to her. She had no appetite for the birthday food, and she sketched an arc with her good arm to take in this room in which we found her. She was telling us, I thought, that she didn't care to cling to this diminished life.

I thought of how, in years of talk between us, one always felt, no matter the occasion, the disappointment, the delight, that in her presence it was almost sinful not to celebrate life. She had written me from Liège, "Everybody's end no matter what, is a part of the purifying ceremony for heart and mind." I thought of her valiance, her gaiety of heart; alongside her knowingness, her seeing life as tragedy, her pristine quality, her delicacy, her freshness, her resilience. She was forever May.

28 / John Malcolm Brinnin

John Malcolm Brinnin (1916–99), poet, critic, and teacher, was born in Halifax, Nova Scotia, to American parents, who moved to Detroit, Michigan, during his childhood. Brinnin earned a B.A. from the University of Michigan and attended graduate school at Harvard. From 1949 to 1956 he was director of the Young Men's–Young Women's Hebrew Association Poetry Center in New York City, earning national attention with the high quality of his programs, which several times featured Katherine Anne Porter. Brinnin published six volumes of poetry, three travelogues, and scholarly works on T. S. Eliot, Gertrude Stein, Truman Capote, and William Carlos Williams in addition to Dylan Thomas. Brinnin was Porter's close friend whom her editor Seymour Lawrence entrusted to look out for her when he sequestered her at a remote inn in Pigeon Cove, Massachusetts, in 1961 to allow her the necessary solitude to finish *Ship of Fools.*

When Brinnin became director of the Poetry Center in 1949, his first official act was to invite Dylan Thomas, whose poetry he had long admired, to come to the United States. Thomas accepted enthusiastically, and Brinnin became a reluctant chaperone to the eccentric and hard-drinking Thomas, who gave a series of readings and lectures and accepted a number of social invitations. The occasion on which Thomas and Porter met was a welcoming party for Thomas hosted by Ann and Harvey Breit,[39] who had interviewed the poet for an essay in the *New York Times Book Review.* Brinnin and Thomas attended a cocktail party given by area academics before heading to the Breit apartment in the East 50s.

Source: John Malcolm Brinnin, *Dylan Thomas in America: An Intimate Journal* (Boston: Atlantic–Little, Brown, 1955), 18–20.

As we floundered uptown in my car through piled-up snow and ice, [Thomas] began to fall asleep. He had drunk too fast and too much and while by now I needed no further evidence of his incredible capacity, I could see that he was feeling the effects of this evening's bout more sharply than those of any other since he had arrived. His chin fell onto his chest as we plowed along, and he slept until his cigarette burned his fingers, jerking him awake. Since he had had no more than three or four hours in bed since he had stepped from the plane two days before, I suggested that we give up the party and return to the hotel. But he would not hear of this. Muttering that he would be all right in a moment, he slumped back into sleep. [. . .]

Oblivious to pelting hail and the sloshing of traffic, Dylan slept on. Then, bolt upright, he came awake all at once in the way which I soon came to know as characteristic. He was all for the party now: what were we doing just sitting here? We went up into a room buzzing with writers and editors, some of whom were old friends of mine. Wysten Auden was there, James Agee, Louis Kronenberger and the Trillings, Lionel and Diana, and James and Tania Stern and Charles Rolo,[40] Katherine Anne Porter and many others. As Dylan, by a loud and awkward entrance, seemed to demand considerably more attention than the party was disposed to grant him, becoming again the very figure of the wine-soaked poet, I looked at Auden and winced inwardly. [. . .]

When Katherine Anne Porter, toward whom Dylan had made mumbling, fumbling and gently rebuffed overtures through the course of the party, was about to leave, he approached her again, to suggest that they make a date for a drink on the following day, and to announce that he was going to accompany her home right then. As she was politely refusing both of his notions, Dylan held her hands in his, and, in his most engaging baby-owl manner, told her how glad he was to have met her; then suddenly, as if she had no more weight than a doll, lifted her in her coat and gloves until her head was within an inch of the ceiling, and kept her there. Indecision left me at this point; through a little group of half-amused, half-appalled witnesses, I stepped forward to indicate to Dylan that the party was over. In greater composure than any of us, in spite of her unexpected elevation, Katherine Anne was able to say a final good night to Dylan, though not until he had followed her halfway down the stairs. When I helped him into his coat, he was all at once the most docile of literary lions and quite willing to be led away.[41]

29 / Elizabeth Spencer

Elizabeth Spencer (1921–), a native Mississippian, earned an M.A. from Vanderbilt, worked as a reporter at the *Nashville Tennessean,* and taught at the University of Mississippi in Oxford. Recipient of numerous awards, she lived in Italy and for many years in Canada before moving to Chapel Hill, North Carolina. Her works include the novels *Fire in the Morning* (1948), *Knights and Dragons* (1965), and *The Night Travellers* (1991); and the short-story collections *The Stories of Elizabeth Spencer* (1981), *Jack of Diamonds and Other Stories* (1988), *The Southern Woman* (2001), and *The Light in the Piazza and Other Italian Tales* (1996; its title story was adapted for the screen in 1962 and made into an award-winning Broadway musical in 2005).

In 1951 Porter had undertaken a college tour in the south, beginning in Jackson, Mississippi, where she had given an address at Millsaps College and stayed with Eudora Welty. After a talk in Columbus, Mississippi, at the Mississippi State College for Women, she had made a detour to New Orleans to see friends Andrew Lytle and Peter Taylor before swinging back to Jackson to take a drive along the Mississippi coast with Welty.

Source: Elizabeth Spencer, *Landscapes of the Heart: A Memoir* (New York: Random House, 1998), 236–37.

The summer of 1951 had started well enough. I had come to make a new start in writing, but how I wrote anything I don't really understand, for it was a time of many visits.

Not the least were two blessed descents of Eudora Welty from Jackson, bringing with her each time a friend she wanted me to meet. The first was Katherine Anne Porter [the second was Elizabeth Bowen], who had given a lecture in Jackson as part of a series featuring Southern writers. (I had myself been asked to participate, but was unbearably shy on the platform in those days and had declined.) Miss Porter was, as so often described, beautiful, with snow-white hair. Her small figure seemed delicate without being fragile. Her features were remarkable for showing no trace of slack skin; I was reminded of the trim, spare, expressive faces that Florentine sculptors knew so well how to mold.

I had the two of them over to my little apartment one evening. We sat and sipped drinks and talked. I will always be glad that Katherine Anne (as she insisted I call her) talked so much about herself. She felt like doing this, and she did it. Where else could I have heard her precise but soft voice say, "I would have been able to do much more, except for the many interruptions—by that I mean the time I've given to men." I think this is reasonably exact. It was honest and certainly not coy; she was anything but that. Another observation I recall: "I don't understand people who complain about art for art's sake. If we don't love her for her own sake, why else do we love her?"

She and Eudora were staying at the Miramar Hotel, just west of Pass Christian. It was a comfortable rundown old place; I used a made-up version of it in my novel *The Salt Line*. My feeling was that people who had made a habit of coming to the coast through the year had grown used to staying there and nowhere else. I remember sitting on the floor of a large room Katherine Anne had—I think she was propped up on pillows and trying to nurse away a cold or a headache—and listening to her and Eudora talk.

5
New York, Europe, Michigan, Virginia, and Washington, DC, 1952–1961

At the Congress for Cultural Freedom in Paris in 1952, Porter spoke at the opening session on behalf of the U.S. delegation. She spent her remaining time in France renewing old acquaintances, making new friends (such as Elizabeth Hardwick), and escaping to Brittany to work on the foreword to her first collection of essays, *The Days Before*, which was published soon after her return to the United States. In demand more than ever as a speaker and college teacher, she continued to make appearances at such schools as the University of Wichita, and she assumed writer-in-residence positions at the University of Michigan, where she met David Locher and Jeanne Rockwell; the University of Virginia; and Washington and Lee, where she met Rita Johns. The Fulbright Fellowship she accepted after her year at Michigan was cut short because of illness at the beginning of 1955, the year in which she left Harcourt, Brace, after the death of Donald Brace, and joined forces with Atlantic–Little, Brown and her new editor, Seymour Lawrence, who guided *Ship of Fools* to completion. She became friends with Flannery O'Connor and formed a lasting friendship with the young writer Barbara Thompson.

30 / Elizabeth Hardwick

Elizabeth Hardwick (1916–2007) was one of eleven children born to Eugene and Mary Ramsey Hardwick in Kentucky. After earning B.A. and M.A. degrees at the University of Kentucky, she moved to New York City, where she began her literary career by writing for such magazines as the *Partisan Review, New Yorker,* and *Sewanee Review.* Best known as a critic and essayist and as one of the founders of the *New York Review of Books,* Hardwick also published the novels *The Ghostly Lover* (1945), *The Simple Truth* (1955), and *Sleepless Nights* (1979), the last a critical success. Hardwick was married to poet Robert Lowell from 1949 to 1972, and he introduced her to Katherine Anne Porter in Paris in 1952 at the Congress for Cultural Freedom. Porter liked Hardwick instantly and imagined an ancestral connection in their common Kentucky roots.

Source: Elizabeth Hardwick, "Katherine Anne," *Vanity Fair* March 1984: 81–85.

She was spoken of simply as "Katherine Anne," whether one was actually acquainted with her or not. But this should not be seen to indicate any folksiness in her image. Quite the contrary was true of this fastidious writer. From the time of the appearance of her very first stories, she occupied a high place in our literature. Everyone who cared about writing knew and admired her work. In the years before paperback publishing, I can remember searching the secondhand stalls for *Flowering Judas,* her first collection, and seeing it as a prize equal to a copy of *Doctor Martino and Other Stories,* by Faulkner, and *In Our Time,* by Hemingway.

    She was first and last a short story writer and even in that form not one to flood the market with this and that. Short stories, as a practical matter, are, along with poetry, a small business, and as such they are the object of a certain sentimental honor—a little like the honor a big and prosperous dress designer may accord the coat-lining and button manufacturers who hold on in the back streets of the enterprise. It is not felt one can really survive this way. And, in addition, most of Katherine Anne's stories appeared in small literary magazines, among them *Hound and Horn, The Virginia Quarterly Review,* and *The Southern Review.* Indeed, *The Southern Review* was the main publisher of her work, right up through the stories in her third collection, *The Leaning Tower.*[1]

Faulkner and Fitzgerald could put their financial, if not their artistic, hopes in the possibility of acceptance by a mass magazine such as *The Saturday Evening Post.* Of course, a lot of aggressive tinkering went on in those offices, and there the serious writer had to face a most puzzling question: Who reads the story after it's finally in print? Everyone who counted read *The Southern Review,* and if at the height of her fame and for her longest story, "The Leaning Tower," Miss Porter came out with $300—well, that was her career.

During these years her publishers, Harcourt, Brace, helped her along because it was decided she should write a novel. That was it. And this became a sort of comedy, a comedy with a very long run. The novel, *Ship of Fools,* was published when its author was seventy-two years old, and by that time Mr. Harcourt and Mr. Brace had gone on to their reward and a subsequent publisher had had some years of worry about his investment. But in the end, Katherine Anne got hers—a million dollars. Late, no doubt about that, but quite a lot of fun nevertheless.

Katherine Anne Porter was born in 1890 and lived until 1980—that is, she lived to be ninety years old. The attainment of this great age still does not seem quite suitable to this beautiful, blown-about woman who was unsettled the whole time, not hardy and not self-preserving in the matter of health. She smoked for as long as her breath held out, drank when she felt like it, and when she could afford it planned to live, as they say in Texas, "high on the hog." She practiced all her life the main diversions thought of as feminine: clothes, cooking, spendthrift sprees, pretty houses, four marriages,[2] more lovers, and certain airs of the flirt.

All of this was a sort of improvisation. She did not have the lucky, sedentary fortitude of Colette or, on the other hand, the cascading nervous energy of Virginia Woolf. Yet she was an *artist,* a word I remember her using often. I think it meant a kind of waiting, not properly, or at least not always, to be understood in her case as procrastination. The perfection of her stories, the extraordinary simplicity and freshness, was hard work, but I am not sure she had the idea of summoning them by hard work. They were, for the most part, begun, put aside; and when they were taken up again, I imagine she felt a surprise that there was something already there, and so in a rush of inspiration each was finished.

For the rest, for the day-to-day, there was the charm of her blue-gray eyes and her striking white hair. There was her somewhat overdressed fluffiness and the almost hallucinated attraction she felt for the *expensive.* It was like a gambler's compulsion. I remember 1952 in Paris, at the conferences and performances arranged by the Congress for Cultural Freedom. In her hotel room she showed me a purse—or rather a "pocketbook," as both of us spoke of it—that had cost hundreds of dollars, hundreds of the old dollars. She said: Do you like it? And I said:

For *that* much, no. She said: Would you like it if it were cheaper? And I said yes. Then she said: But you see I wouldn't. Then I'd have to think twice.

Also at that time we sat together for a performance in a concert hall. Just across form us was a very old lady, a well-known American expatriate, who was a fright to behold.[3] Katherine Anne looked at her and said: If I looked like that, I'd kill myself. She herself was then past sixty, and I did not feel she meant any soulless contempt for the unsightly old woman. Horribly, I believed she was stating a plain truth.

None of this struck me as unworthy of the greatly gifted writer, no more unworthy than jogging or playing squash to keep in trim. It was her idea of the preservation of the flesh. And little could be held against her since nothing worked: not the husbands, not the lovers, not the often disappointing houses. I cannot think of anyone more truly independent. If there was egotism involved, independence is no less real for being something you're left with after you've sloughed off every protection.

There was never anyone except herself. When husbands got in the way, she ran off, ran off literally. Her life, for all her passion for the Vermont marble dining table and at last the greatly longed-for emerald ring itself, by way of the success of *Ship of Fools,* was one risk after another. Always on the frontier; always, it seemed to me, very American, an American traveler with a wide range of experience. Not one of her stories is provincial. She was from the first unaccountably sophisticated. The hardscrabble hill of her youth did not leave its mark on the line, on the paragraph, or on the purity and fineness of intention. [. . .]

Katherine Anne's great age, achieved as it was after a youth of tuberculosis and a life of bronchial troubles, astonished all of us. But live on she did and live to find time for follies, indiscretions, and misbegotten chatterings. Her first two marriages seemed to have gone by like the wind, but she did not suggest that the winds had been useful and it is hard to believe they were. She brushed them away, a bit of ruffling on her coat sleeve. Allen Tate used to say: "Who knows, there might have been yet another husband dropped off somewhere."[4] And this was a kind of admiration, and certainly fascination.

Still, still she never lost her inclination to romance or showed hesitation about fanciful enthusiasms for younger writers, assistants, and companions. In this she brings to mind an ancient *belle époque* figure who, when asked at what age a woman was finished with love, replied, "Ask someone older than I am."

As I look back over the late attachments I knew about from gossip or otherwise, I see in them a conscious and careful make-believe. And certainly a rich and confusing mixture of intentions. Katherine Anne knew the impossible when she met it; and if she was a rather beseeching nest builder, it would have been a naïve, foolhardy person, imagining himself at an advantage by age or other perquisites, who thought she was ready in fact to offer a snug accommodation. Thus there was a noticeable resilience after an amorous failure, if failure is the proper word. Someone always turned up.

Her stories are not large in number, but there are quite enough of them to honor her just reputation. A confidence of structure, an unpretentious, unstrained gift for language combined in her talent with a worldly eye for the shape of things rural, native, and foreign. As a fiction writer she gained from going here and there and never quite wanting to stay. Her superb stories are the happy legacy of a hard life that spanned almost the whole of the century.

31 / Seymour Lawrence

Seymour Lawrence (1926–94), a graduate of Harvard University, became an influential publisher of such writers as Kurt Vonnegut, J. P. Donleavy, Richard Brautigan, and Tim O'Brien in addition to Katherine Anne Porter. After having signed Porter to Atlantic–Little, Brown, he took her with him to Alfred A. Knopf, where he assumed a senior position. She went with him yet again when he left Knopf to start his personal imprint, Seymour Lawrence, with the co-publisher Dell/Delacorte, which published Porter's *Collected Essays and Occasional Writings* (1970). From 1952 to 1984 he was married to Merloyd Ludington Lawrence, with whom he had a son and a daughter, Macy, who was Porter's goddaughter. Through skillful psychological management, he was responsible more than anyone else for bringing Porter's *Ship of Fools* to completion after more than thirty years' gestation.

Source: Seymour Lawrence, letter to Darlene Harbour Unrue, 9 December 1992.[5]

In 1954 I was 28 and served as Special Assistant to Edward Weeks, Editor of *The Atlantic,* and as Associate Editor of the Atlantic Monthly Press, the book publishing division of the company. I became director of the Press in 1955.

[. . .] After we had exchanged several letters in 1954 and 1955 regarding the Zarzuela section,[6] and a visit to her apartment on East 17th Street in NYC she invited me to lunch at Southbury, Conn. where her agent Cyrilly Abels was present (Cyrilly was either editor or fiction editor of *Mademoiselle* and had published *A Christmas Story*.)[7] After a delicious lunch of broiled lamb chops, fresh garden vegetables, brown bread which KAP had baked that morning, and a vintage wine (KAP was a connoisseur of wine from her years in Paris) she gave me a portion of the Zarzuela section. As I was about to drive back to Boston we were standing in her driveway when KAP asked, "Mr. Lawrence, my dear friend and publisher Donald Brace died this year and there is no one else at Harcourt Brace I know or trust. Can you recommend a good publisher?" Without a moment's hesitation I replied, "Miss Porter, I wear two hats: I'm an editor of *The Atlantic* but I've also been recently appointed Director of the Atlantic Monthly Press. Our books are published under the joint imprint of Atlantic–Little, Brown and we would be honored to be your publisher." KAP replied, "Why, Mr. Lawrence, I believe that's a proposal and I accept." Then came the business of extricating her from the Harcourt Brace contracts, repaying the advances she owed, and setting up a new contract with monthly payments to enable her to finish the novel.

[. . .] I was more her publisher than her editor. KAP did not tolerate "editing" except minor copyediting.

[. . .] I never cared for the title *No Safe Harbor* which was too vague and its negative first word disturbed me. One day I asked her if she had ever thought of another title. She replied that *No Safe Harbor* was Harcourt Brace's title, not hers, and her original title was *Ship of Fools* based on *Das Narrenschiff,* which she had read in Zurich or Basel. From that day forward the title was *Ship of Fools.*

[. . .] Prior to the Yankee Clipper Inn at Pigeon Cove,[8] we would find obscure New England inns for her to work in, under an assumed name, where she would not be distracted by friends or visitors. A quiet inn at Southborough, Mass., proved to be a clandestine weekend hideaway for Boston businessmen and their girl friends—and we soon moved her to another inn.

At Pigeon Cove I asked one of our authors, the poet and biographer John Malcolm Brinnin, who lived nearby in Gloucester with his companion Bill Read, to keep an eye out for her. They dined together nearly every night and they had jolly evenings together with KAP presiding, telling stories accompanied by much laughter and good wine.

[. . .] We celebrated the publication of *Ship of Fools* with a gala party at the "21" Club in NYC where KAP had to push away a drunken professor who kept pestering her.[9] She finally succeeded in warding him off and as he departed he was heard to mutter "Thank you, Mrs. Treadwell."[10]

Ship of Fools led the bestseller lists for months and was successful in many languages throughout the world. Reprint rights were sold to New American Library for a record sum of $250,000 [. . .]. Movie rights were sold [. . .] for $400,000 [. . .]. KAP became a millionaire and one day when we were discussing the book's success she turned to me and said, "Angel, nothing quite fails like success."

32 / David Locher

David Anthony Locher (1924–), poet and librarian, was born in Dubuque, Iowa, and educated in his youth at private parochial schools. He earned a B.A. at Loras College in 1947 and a master's degree in Library Science at the University of Michigan, Ann Arbor, in 1955, after working in a shipyard in Sausalito, California, briefly attending St. Paul Seminary (in St. Paul, Minnesota), and doing missionary work in the Bahamas. During his professional career he was librarian at the Gleeson Library at San Francisco University and head librarian at Loras College.

In the first selection, Locher traces the history of his friendship with Porter. Locher wrote several poems about Katherine Anne Porter in which he tried to capture his most vivid memories of her. "Summer Straw & Blue," the second selection below, was written twenty-three years after their meeting.

Source: David Locher, "Katherine Anne Porter," unpublished reminiscence, collection of Darlene Harbour Unrue.

I met Katherine Anne Porter December 3, 1954, on what she called in an inscription in a book of mine, "a dark day in hospital but not an unhappy one." I was a graduate student in library science and worked at the switchboard of St. Joseph Mercy Hospital thirty-two hours a week, sometimes forty hours a week, on the afternoon-evening shift. One day I found out that KAP was in hospital. I had heard of her but had never read one of her stories. She was suffering from nervous exhaustion and was allowed no visitors; so I asked Father Jacyna, the chaplain, to check to see whether I could come up to her room and have her autograph a book. I rushed out and bought one.

Next day Father Jacyna told me KAP had said I should come to her room during my supper break and she would sign the book for me. Father told me also that he had talked with her and that everything was all right with KAP and the Church (and I don't think that ever after that was she really outside the fold, as they say).

I went up intending to stay a few minutes and stayed a half hour despite the

NO VISITORS sign on her door. She was sitting up in bed in a kind of kimono, surrounded by books and magazines. We talked, and I was in awe, as I always would be in her presence. I asked whether I could be in her Recent American Writers class the coming semester, when she was back teaching, and she said yes, I should come to see her in her office, which I did later on, and she signed the slip giving me permission to enter her class.

The class met at 1:00, and I was there most of the time. One day along about late April or early May, I was absent from the class when KAP was taken ill again. A friend of mine told me later that I had missed a terrible scene, that KAP was talking to the class when suddenly she put her head down on her hands on her desk and said over and over again, "Oh, I am so sorry, I am so sorry." Jackie Greenhut, an English Department secretary, came to her aid, rushed out and got help, and that time KAP was taken to University Hospital, where a few days later I went to visit her. I made her a silver and blue moonstone rosary, which I took to her.

In this class there was another library science student, Suzanne Peplinski from Green Bay, Wisconsin, and since she and I knew each other we always sat together in the front row. Sue and I had one big thing in common, movies, and we always managed to see one on Thursday, when the picture changed in the local movie theater. However, in order to see a special movie one Friday, we skipped KAP's class. The movie started at one o'clock, and at 12:30 we stopped by a small drug store that had a diner in it. Who should be sitting at a table in the corner having lunch but KAP. I was startled, but when she saw Sue and me she invited us to sit down with her. We did, and we told her we were not going to class because of "another engagement." It was all right with her, she said, because she was not going either; she simply couldn't face a class that day.

In the summer I took the Creative Writing course KAP taught. Around the sixth of August the semester ended, and I went over to the Michigan Union, where she stayed, to say goodbye since I was leaving on the midnight train for Chicago. It was early afternoon, and KAP was unable to receive me, not being dressed yet, but the major-domo put me on the phone to her. I had another book for autographing, which the man took up in the elevator and then brought down to me. So, KAP and I said goodbye over the phone. I felt so bad. I thought it was THE END (and it was the end of formal school classes for me), and I said I might never see her again. I can still hear her voice on the phone: "David, honey, life has few separations that are really complete and entire, and we will meet again."

Another time, long afterwards, she told me that when it comes to people, those who want to stick with us do so of their own accord, and if they don't want to, nothing we can do can bring them along with us.

Although we corresponded regularly, it was six years before I saw Katherine

Anne again. The last week in August 1960 I had a chance to go with a friend of mine to New York City and Pittsburgh and decided it would be a good chance to visit KAP if she were receiving visitors—which she was. On 23 August I took a morning Eastern Airlines flight from La Guardia to National Airport in Washington, took a bus to the Mayflower Hotel, from which I phoned KAP, and she told me to come out at once, that she was expecting me. I took a cab out to her house on Q Street. I arrived there just before noon.

It was a jumbled day, and I was to stay there overnight in the back bedroom upstairs, which her nephew used when he came down from New York—I think she was expecting him the following weekend. I was to leave the next morning for Pittsburgh (which I did).

Katherine Anne greeted me royally and called me *honey* and *darling,* which she always did over the years when we were talking on the phone long distance. During this visit, she said she wanted me to have two memorable meals with her, but I had promised my cousin and his family, who lived in another part of Georgetown, that I would dine with them that evening. So KAP decided she would fix a nice lunch. We talked and talked, and when she finally decided we should have lunch it was one o'clock in the afternoon. She fixed a salad of lettuce and tomatoes and tuna maybe—I can still see her dramatically shaking salt and pepper from big shakers, holding them high in the air over her kitchen table.

She showed me, from her back porch, the nice garden behind the house and the Judas tree that grew there. She autographed *A Defense of Circe* for me. She played some of her favorite old records for me, some of the old French 78's she had. She told me that Pete Seeger had recorded a song from her *French Song-Book,* but she did not have the record. She told me of her admiration for Joan of Arc, which is why she had written an essay on Joan for *The Re-Trial of Joan of Arc,* but only half of the essay had been used as a foreword to the book.[11]

I asked her if she had any old pieces of manuscript that I could have, and she immediately wanted to know just what reasons I had for wanting any manuscript. I told her just to have and to remember her by. She showed me two large filing cases filled with folders of unfinished work. In one drawer were, as I recall, eleven chapters of a work on Cotton Mather, and she took out one chapter to give me and then said, "No, I had better keep this." Then she opened a bottom drawer and took out a folder which contained a partly finished essay on T. S. Eliot, some of it in note form, and different sizes of paper. This she gave me, saying if she ever wanted to work on it again, I could give it back to her as a loan (this I did several years later, and she was going to return the essay to me just as it was, but she never did, although time and again she would tell me on the phone that the essay was mine and she had it in her study, wrapped and ready for sending to me—soon).

She also showed me two large baskets that I took to be Mexican, something like bushel baskets, in one of which she had articles written about her, and in the other were articles and stories of her own, in the magazines in which they had first appeared.

We talked of so many things that I cannot remember it all. She said she had to get *Ship of Fools* finished, time was running out, and the publisher was getting nasty. We talked most of the time in her parlor, but she showed me the room I would have upstairs with the old-fashioned adjoining bathroom; she showed me her treasured pieces of furniture, the old table that was part Italian and very old; something Spanish, a sideboard or armoire.

We did a lot of literary talking and reminiscing about Ann Arbor. I recall asking her about Hart Crane, if he were really a very good poet, and she told me about him with tears in her eyes, said he would have been great in her opinion if he could have controlled his life, and not have given way to the vices of alcohol and sex. She said she had done everything she could to help him when they were friends in Mexico, and he had behaved so terribly to her she could barely talk about it. She would do what she could to keep him sober and out of jail, but in no time he would find a boy for sex and go off the deep end. She said that things finally got so bad she just could not have Hart around any more; he was tearing her apart, and later, when she heard of his death, she felt only relief that so much unhappiness was gone and that he would not be hurting himself anymore.

When we were playing records she suddenly said when I asked her if there were a recording of "Flowering Judas," "Oh yes, there is, and I have it right here." She showed me a special album from Columbia of ten American and British writers reading their works.[12] This album, which sold for $100, had been sent her by the record company, and she said I could have it. She autographed the accompanying booklet for me and then wondered what I would do with the album. I told her I would listen to the record, but I have to admit that I never listened to them all.

Late in the afternoon she asked if I would like a drink. She said she fixed wonderful daiquiris, and I said all right (I had never tasted a daiquiri). She gave me a lesson in how to pronounce the work *daiquiri* as though it were dáh-queer-ee, not dakkeree.

So she fixed the drinks, and we had a few, which she poured from a pitcher. Wow! We lost track of time, afternoon turned to evening, and we kept on talking. I knew I had to get over to my cousin's house (I had never met his wife). It was past 7:30 p.m. when I arrived at his house, and he was a little put out with me. We had a pleasant evening, however, and I was back at KAP's house by cab shortly after 10:30. The house was dark, but she had given me a key to the front door. I went directly to bed because I had to leave for the airport by nine the next morning.

Sometime that afternoon KAP mentioned the young man who rented the basement apartment, but I never met him. I guess I had asked her if there were someone living downstairs. She said yes and had shown me the stairway going down and the outside entrance.

Next morning I was up and shaving at 7:30 when KAP knocked at the bathroom door. I was appalled when I saw her. On her left temple was a long cut, not bleeding but wide open, and her cheek was black and blue. She said, "I am all right, but I should know better than to drink anything when I am taking medication to help me sleep. I don't know how this happened, but I must have fallen in the bathroom during the night." I had heard nothing during the night since KAP had a separate big bathroom next to her bedroom, which faced Q Street, in the front of the narrow house. She dressed, I called a cab for 9 a.m., and KAP called a cab to take her to Georgetown University Medical Center, where a doctor stitched her cut.

I called as soon as I could, and she assured me she was fine. But from then on, she frequently mentioned regretfully the time I came to visit and she hadn't given me anything to eat.

Source: David Locher, "Summer Straw & Blue (Ann Arbor, July 1954)," *America* 16–23 July 1977: 23.

Summer Straw & Blue
(Ann Arbor, July 1954)

early July it had to be
the blue & green time of year
coloring afternoon space
with grass smell & grace—

& there is Katherine Anne Porter
stepping lightly
over the greensward square
under the oaks
beyond the elms—

& there am I watching
her approach—my teacher
dressed in summer straw
& summer blue
pale linen catching cool wind

& just touching her head
the tan coolie hat
time's parasol
tilting the sun downhill

our greeting was small, smiling,
I bowed over her hand, awed,
because she, as artist,
had sketched my own mortality
(strange how memory can live,
so very long,
& always be the moment that is)

she bought me a book that day,
my choice, at author's discount
& ever since, Judas flowering
can blossom only
with the sound of her voice.

33 / Jeanne Rockwell

Jeanne Rockwell (1920–) was a graduate of Bucknell University. She worked on newspapers in New York, Virginia, and Ann Arbor, Michigan, and published essays in *Harper's Bazaar, Mademoiselle, Vogue, American Girl,* and *True Confessions* as well as the *Michigan Quarterly Review.* Her books include *My Way of Hunting: The Adventurous Life of a Taxidermist* (1956), written with her father, Robert H. Rockwell, and the anthology *Good Company: Poets at Michigan* (1977).

Source: Jeanne Rockwell, "The Magic Cloak: On Meeting Katherine Anne Porter," *Michigan Quarterly Review* 5 (1966): 283–84.

It was a cold rainy spring or a cold rainy fall. In Michigan it doesn't make much difference. I found myself too chilled and tired to stand any longer on a wind-swept street-corner waiting for my husband to pick me up.

Deciding to toss the canary another seed, I turned into a dingy campus eating place run by a candy chain. I would squander a dime on a coke, and if that didn't pull me up from the depths of fatigue and depression, perhaps I'd shoot the works and buy some crackers.

Giggling, whey-faced couples filled the varnished pine booths, but nearest the tea and coffee urns, alone at a long empty counter, sat a white-haired lady, eating a sandwich in small bites, sipping tea. With lemon, I believe. Some distance away, a roundish stolid Negro waitress lounged like a slow handmaiden of the Fates. It was a dismal time, the day at an end, the floor unswept, the impatient kitchen staff flicking the harsh lights and pointing to the clock.

"Okay if I sit here?"

The woman in the dark purple velveteen cloak shrugged and nodded. Then, like a knife-point pricking the ear drum, it occurred to me that she might be Katherine Anne Porter. I'd read her work, back in college, but I'd never seen a picture of her and, intent on a newspaper career, had other idols to follow. Down in the busy city room where I worked, we'd heard vague rumors that Miss Porter was living in town, or was on campus for some lectures, but I'd paid them no mind.

In any case, as I stood there hesitating, not wanting to miss my ride home,

Miss Porter smiled, waved her hand towards a stool, and I sat down about a yard away, suddenly weak and famished.

"That's a beautiful cloak," I ventured softly after I'd ordered and waited a long time, glancing sideways at the delicately drawn jaw, aristocratic nose, noble line of brow. A pleasant nod and smile answered my pleasantry. She went on eating, nibbling a chicken sandwich, and all at once I couldn't bear the suspense. "You're not Katherine Anne Porter, by any chance?" It was still a mere guess, for Ann Arbor is a haven of aristocratic ladies with silver-white hair. But, somehow, she seemed totally different, a stranger. An interesting one.

The flashing eyes raked me appraisingly. She nodded then, and turned back to sip from her cup, held in both hands, as if to warm cold fingers. I munched my crackers, swallowed hard, and wondered what to say, what to do. I could hardly blurt out "I write too." How inane—that would be the end of it. Perhaps I should just leave. Then I managed to mumble, "I'm a reporter."

"Student newspaper?" The voice was low, the words beautifully articulated, the manner of mild amusement.

"No!" Raw New York contempt for being stranded in the hinterlands edged my words. "Local daily, Booth chain. Before that, INS . . . no matter." There was a companionable silence as we both ate.

"I'm thinking of quitting."

I had also been thinking of jumping out a window, desperate with the dead end of a job where I'd gone as far as I wanted to go. It was time for a change, and somehow the idea lighted like a bird in my head that this proud, straight, successful woman might give me some clue to which I could cling. In her dark beautiful cloak she seemed a mythic figure, the Hera of another world, surrounded by flights of birds, able to divine the nature of auguries. Somewhere inside, I wept invisible tears wishing she'd tell me what to do.

"Married?"

I nodded, head down, turning the plain gold wedding band I'd bought myself. "Yes. Husband's gotta teaching job."

"University?"

"No. Junior high school. He coaches. Teaches P.E."

"Football? Basketball?" The words were rapped out. Miss Porter seemed interested.

"Yeah. And track. He ran in Madison Square Garden. Tall guy. Thin. Quiet. Likes history."

"He drink?"

"Noooooo. Well, you know, nothing to speak of. A small glass now and again for sociability."

"He's not a drunkard then. Not an alcoholic?"

"Oh no! He's a wonderful guy!" I swung toward her on the stool.

"Children?"

I grinned, and felt almost equally filled with pride and exasperation. Miss Porter smiled faintly, eyes sympathetic. I wondered fleetingly if she had children.

"One son." I replied. "Red headed. About so tall!" I measured the air at shoulder-level. Then I shook my head, returned to a despondent slump, trying to think, looking past her and out into the dim windy street along which our decrepit car would come.

I swung around on the backless stool and started to get up again, anxious not to take her time yet reluctant to leave. I hadn't asked her a single significant question, hadn't pulled out a pencil to record a word, but that didn't bother me, my paper would have to let this story go, if it was a story. At the same time, I knew that something was badly amiss in my life, and perhaps even in hers. So, naïvely I blurted out, "That boy of ours. Playing hookey from school! Can you imagine that? In the THIRD grade!"

I felt foolish, and managed a wry grin.

"You spank him?" she said, with an odd understanding smile.

"Sometimes. Not often." I hesitated. "Red heads are stubborn, don't you think? He's inclined to be wild you know. But sweet."

"I was red-headed myself once." I can't be sure she said that. The sentence only comes unbidden, from that unconscious well where all writing comes from.

"You've a son. You'll write; you'll . . . . . DO." The words had an odd ring of command. Miss Porter nodded briskly, smiling at me, her entire person an encouragement to go on living. She patted her lips firmly with a paper napkin, crumpled it into a ball, swept some accumulated crumbs from the counter into her hand and dropped both crumbs and napkin neatly onto the thick crockery plate. Her serene face was now turned away so that she too looked for a moment, steadily, out into the gathering dusk.

Standing up now, feeling lightened, almost happy, I took a step away, then turned back hastily as if she might have disappeared in the interval. "Miss Porter, I want to thank you." I ducked my head in gratitude, troubled somehow for her lonely mien.

"Not at all," she murmured, shaking her head just once.

"No, I mean it. You've saved my life."

She smiled then, enigmatically, and raised her hand with the long white fingers together in a gallant and somehow gay gesture combining absolution and farewell.

Barbara Thompson Davis (1933–2009) met Katherine Anne Porter while working for the *Washington Post* the fall after her graduation from Wellesley College. Porter was drawn to the young woman, and for the rest of her life enjoyed the friendship that bloomed from their first meeting. It was because of that friendship that Davis agreed to accept the trusteeship of Porter's literary estate upon the death of Isabel Bayley. Barbara Davis has published fiction, book reviews, and interviews, and twice has won the Pushcart Prize.

Source: Barbara Thompson Davis, untitled reminiscence. This essay, written specifically for this volume, appears here for the first time.

I met Katherine Anne because no one else in the city room of the *Washington Post* that autumn of 1956 made a peep when the Editor shouted, "Anybody here ever heard of Katherine Anne Porter?"

I was a copy girl in the Women's Section, as lowly a position as the editorial floor of the place possessed, but this was one of those moments an English major could be turned to profit. Katherine Anne was to be my debut as an interviewer, and I reread all her stories and, armed with the standard green steno pad, marched into the Jefferson Hotel with the heavily beating heart and the untested confidence of a mostly A-student.

Katherine Anne almost foxed me: she was waiting in the lobby with a cheery, firm, "Let's take a walk." And as we wandered the empty streets of a darkening Sunday afternoon, she chattered on at high speed in a distinctive vocabulary that I labored to note. I remember the word "pawky" because I didn't have the least idea of its meaning. My piece was going to be as good as my memory and improvisational skills would support.

We were almost immediately lost. I had been in the city for about three weeks and knew perfectly the way from my friends' house off Dupont Circle to the *Post* building on L street, but nothing at all about the way we walked in the vague direction of the Capitol. Neither did she. When it grew perilously dim, a red-and-tan taxi came along and got us back to the Jefferson. She was tired; I extracted from her only a few precise quotes and the dates of her Washington appearances, the most significant at the Library of Congress. The five hundred words or so took me at least ten hours to write, mostly because I was reaching for a style as precise as hers and I didn't have it in me.

That day I saw only the persona she had created: an important writer (I thought "great") and a beautiful woman with a compact, shapely body in a well-cut suit, perfectly careless white hair, who moved with marvelously quick grace. I knew she was at least a decade older than my mother, whom I thought lovely but indisputably marred by time; Katherine Anne seemed not so much young as ageless.

I certainly didn't see then how consciously she had invented herself, or how many childhood models she had chosen to emulate. If I thought about artifice at all I would have thought it was an outgrowth of her gift, that she had assumed a manner and appearance to match the vocation she had chosen, rather the way a novice will change her habit, her carapace, when she takes her final vows. Now I think she began choosing ways of being in early childhood, to carve for herself a special place in spite of being the second daughter with a baby sister whose birth had cost their mother her life and their father any focused attention to his children.

I covered two or three of her readings in the next year, but at a far remove, hovering in the back of the room in my all-purpose black cocktail dress. Katherine Anne would arrive almost late, once sweeping down the aisle in a long cloak—velvet maybe, or satin—that trailed after her like a train. And there was the night she stepped out from backstage all in black but her white kid opera gloves, which she proceeded to discard without haste, smoothing and draping them over the black podium before she began to speak. The well-mannered audience was dead still. I titled that piece "Mistress of the Grand Gesture."[13]

In September of '58, I went to Charlottesville, where Katherine Anne—still decidedly "Miss Porter" to me—had followed Faulkner as the second writer-in-residence at the University of Virginia. I probably could have done the interview by phone (I can't believe the *Post* was offering to pay travel expenses), but I had a new beau—in Katherine Anne's lingo—who had just acquired a car and a driver's license and was keen to practice on the open road.

It was a glorious fall day; I found Katherine Anne in her office, welcoming but cautious. She did not want to talk about her novel-in-progress, perhaps because it wasn't, in fact, in progress. Instead she talked about her friends, about the writers of the books in the pile next to her desk. She had just read Agnes Bolton's memoir of her years as the wife of Eugene O'Neill, *Part of a Long Story*, which drew her back to her own Greenwich Village days, peopled by many of the same characters. As I was leaving she gave me the Bolton biography, inscribing it with the date and the place and the notation, "Hoping your story will be very different!" With it was a photograph taken by a university photographer of her seated at her desk holding a glossy 8 by 10 of Faulkner, no doubt in the same place. The photographer must have been a novice because he had angled the shot in such a way as to make her look portly and dowdy and utterly uninteresting. I still have that glossy; I was afraid the *Post* would publish it.

It was a year before I thought of asking her if she'd be willing to be interviewed for the Writers at Work series in the *Paris Review*. (It never occurred to me to ask the *Paris Review*.) She was by then settled in a house on Q Street in Georgetown, her furniture collected from years of different storage places. She was happy, I think, for a while during this period—the society pleased her, Washington's Southern soul comfortingly familiar after her wanderings. She wasn't getting very far with the novel, and the interview must have seemed one way of thinking about writing and what she had written, of leaving a record, a literary testament, without having to write it down. She was happily social during this period, an ideal dinner guest: fresh to the city but already known for her stories, which were elegant, mannerly, and not terribly long. She was witty and charming, still beautiful and the kind of consummate flirt who could be trusted not to disrupt the established affections of the man seated next to her at dinner. (Two of my own beaux were permanently dazzled, given in her presence to an antique gallantry.) But all that charm and wit took a great deal of her energy, spiritual and physical. It did not leave much for piloting *Ship of Fools* toward its final harbor.

The interview was another kind of detour. We began on a late autumn afternoon in her dining room, the great black box of my rented reel-to-reel tape recorder settled on the round marble table. That day we drank iced tea with mint, but the next time she had made frozen margaritas in the Waring blender she'd bought that morning from the little kitchenware shop around the corner. We were both a little looser of tongue, but anxiety kept me tethered to the scripted questions, and nothing could disrupt her narrative flow, though she often veered off into tangential subplots and characters that for the moment were more interesting to her. Eventually I understood that the tequila had nothing to do with it, that the clarity of her language, which suggested a linear mind, was matched by a thought process that was more like a fast-moving spiral, collecting and discarding elements along its path.

Later I reflected that the workings of her storytelling mind suggested the source of two apparently incompatible facts about her work: that she wrote little, and that she always said she wrote the story "all in one breath," even though years later her papers proved that there were often many earlier fragmented discarded attempts. I think what she meant was that the story, with all its original false directions, took time to refine itself in her mind, both the conscious and the unconscious, before it could become a clear narrative with an ending that was inevitable. She once spoke of giving up an evening with friends because she knew the story was "ready." It reminded me then, and now, of the way housecats, even those awaiting a first litter, go into a fury of nest-making as they come close to giving birth: the instinctual knowing.

We became something like friends over the several months of the interview.[14] She was the wise and celebrated author, I was an acolyte of sorts, and most of all an uncritical admirer. She needed to be admired always, but surely never more than when that heavy book, so long promised, was still far from completion. My own view is that halfway through she didn't want to write it, wished profoundly that it hadn't been promised so publicly; that it could just go away like the biography of Cotton Mather, a hopeful beginning that was fundamentally incompatible with her gifts.

By the end of that year, my life was changing: I had decided to marry. Katherine Anne had become well enough acquainted with several of the men I knew ("dated" now has an implication that it didn't in 1959) to be included for cocktails or dinner parties they gave. Desmond Willson, the cultural attaché at the (very white) South African Embassy, was a favorite; another was a red-haired lawyer working on Capitol Hill whose intensity reminded her, she said, of a character in one of Julian Green's novels,[15] only handsome and well-mannered. She sat next to my future husband at a dinner party and found him "opaquely" charming and intelligent with his Oxford schooling and feudal past in Pakistan. She approved of gentleman admirers, even lovers, but was death on husbands. (I should have picked up on that earlier: her intense dislike of Leonard Woolf had come out in our interview, but I thought Virginia Woolf, who was not only a genius but a suicide, was a special case.)[16] Husbands, she clearly believed, were a liability to a writer, even an unproven one. She had liked Mueen until it came to our marrying.[17]

But I did marry, and we finished the taping that summer of 1960 and in the autumn I went off to Rawalpindi. Katherine Anne sent letters from the various places where she had sequestered herself to finish the novel. I missed the drama of its launching except for a terribly unhappy and angry letter about the "Little Brown men" who had turned the whole thing into a circus. Then there were the (few) negative reviews, by people who didn't like what they thought they knew about her politics (class, sexual or racial) or who just didn't think she rated a spot in the literary empyrean. She was unaccustomed to promiscuous fame. She had a best-seller and it brought her the first serious money she had ever had, but it cost her that formerly protected status as *rara avis*.

She did what I thought any woman in her shoes should do: she bought herself a substantial emerald ring and moved to Rome. I met her there in the late winter of

1963. I remember the time precisely because my second child was due in another month, and I had come armed with an introduction to a Roman obstetrician in case I didn't make it home. Katherine Anne was living at the Eden, a gracious old hotel that, predating air conditioning, offered large, high-ceilinged rooms and a tall French window opening out onto the trees of the Borghese gardens. It was a perfect choice for her, away from the noise of the Via Veneto but close enough to walk to Doney for an aperitif. Rome still showed some signs of the War, but the political left was strengthening, and the second wave, the "decadent soul of Europe" novels and movies, were being talked about, signs of the swinging city to come.

My older child, Tamur, was fifteen-months-old, firm on his own sturdy legs and with his Anglo-Pakistani nanny, Pamela, could play in the Borghese gardens while I visited Katherine Anne. We were each changed from the last meeting: she was a world-famous novelist whose book had been sold to the movies, and I, for all the years that divided us, was conferred at least a provisional adulthood by marriage and motherhood. Womanliness, at least.

We walked around the city, still easy, the fury of cars not yet dominating the streets. We took tea at Babbington's Tea Room beside the Spanish Steps and walked down to the Red Lion Bookstore to see what was new in English, then on to the antique shops near the Piazza del Popolo. Another day we took our morning coffee at Caffè Greco in that long narrow room of nineteenth-century furniture with walls dense with souvenirs of famous artists who had frequented it. And crossed the street to Gucci, and a shop that sold things by Balanciaga. She tried on a wonderful long hooded cape but didn't buy it—at least that day. I think she did buy a suit by Valentino. The Italian clothes of that moment suited her; they were refined but delectably feminine, closely fitted, with hand stitching and silk linings, made to be worn for a long time. And they were in wonderful colors, grass-green, sapphire, rose-red. Black was still associated with mourning, although that would soon pass. In a shop called Vanita she bought a white lawn peignoir with vast amounts of lace. We mused about whether the most beautiful lace was still being made by nuns.

She wasn't writing and as far as I could tell wasn't worrying about it. And I was in that dream state of late pregnancy in which you feel that everything you do is purposeful. Sometime during that week I asked her to be godmother to my child-to-be. I was sure this one would be a girl. Daniyal was born a month later, pretty, with long eyelashes and soft fair hair, but indisputably male. He was baptized Episcopalian (my nominally Muslim husband had observed at the time of our first son's birth that "it doesn't hurt the child and makes the grandparents happy") with Katherine Anne in absentia. She sent him a wonderful Roman silk blanket, pale pastels in pink and green, and later, what she called the official christening gift, a grand, ornate silver ewer, eighteenth-century Austrian. (It was stolen once years later from our farmhouse in Wisconsin. And when it was swiftly recovered from an apparently well-known local fence, he told the police he'd only given the thief $12 because it was too heavy to be real.)

We met most summers in the '60s. Once soon after she had taken a house in Spring Valley with several bedrooms, I was invited to come for the weekend with my own little Olivetti. We would work during the days and take our meals together, and spend the evenings talking and reading and listening to music. And so I arrived late Friday afternoon to a handsome, imposing house set high above the street. She must have been waiting for me because as I got out of the taxi she was standing in the open door, smaller than I remembered her, and more fragile. But she retained her beauty, barely webbed now in places with tiny lines, and her voice was the same, expressive and precise. She gave me a tour of the house, proclaiming the provenance of all the special pieces. There was the refectory table from a convent in Fiesole, the Victorian settee, the sixteenth-century cupboard from Avila. Some I remembered from the Q Street house, others had come from her recent European visit.

It was a beautiful twilight, and we took our mint tea out to her tiny garden with the green hill rising straight up behind it like a stage set. I suggested taking her picture before the light failed. She wanted to change "into something else" and returned in a diaphanous black negligee over a fitted long slip. I did not see it then, but when the pictures were developed, they were unexpectedly sad, even the set of her shoulders; in none is she smiling. Her posed pictures were often austere: she had been photographed often, particularly by her friend George Platt Lynes, and knew a trick or two about turning the face to offer the perfect line of her cheek-bones, but there was something in these pictures that I had never seen before. I wonder now if, having finally attained material security, she was set free to feel the older, deeper sorrows that practical troubles and fears had half-obscured.

When the light faded we went in to change for dinner, each of us in something pale, soft and loose, mine, and probably hers, from the Phoenix shop in Georgetown. Dinner was wonderful, I'm sure, but I can't remember what we ate. She was a great cook but a fussy one, who in spite of a taste for gadgets, cooked everything as she had learned to do it, from scratch. We talked till an early bedtime, each taking with us a couple of books to bed. But I woke to the clatter of someone in the kitchen a good hour before the agreed-upon time for breakfast. She was grinding coffee, had biscuits ready to go into the oven. There was a special sausage, and the makings of omelettes in tiny bowls set beside the stove. The coffee beans she had roasted the day before.

Lunch was quiche Lorraine, made properly, from scratch. And a perfect salad. In the afternoon we were to work, but I think, hope, that she slept. I already knew that I had to leave as soon as I could decently arrange it, that if I stayed she would very quickly dislike me. I finally called an old friend and asked her to send me a telegram requiring my immediate presence elsewhere. (I didn't know then that telegrams of that sort were to become Katherine Anne's own *modus operandi* for canceling dinners, appointments. Or that in extreme cases she would check herself into a hospital with likely real exhaustion.) The telegram came as we were sitting down to dinner, and in the morning I left.

She expressed regret and kissed me sweetly at the door, but I know she was grateful for the release. At first I wondered what I had done, later I thought that it was just that she couldn't bear to be less than a perfect hostess as she understood that role; anything else was a breach of long-ingrained hospitality. She was lonely and the house was huge, but she really didn't want to live with anything breathing that was larger than her beloved cats. (Years later I read a letter Caroline Gordon had written to Jean Stafford,[18] complaining of Katherine Anne that "you cannot depend on her for anything. The very thought of anyone depending on her makes her wild," adding at the end that it was probably necessary, "a protective bit of colouring that nature has given her. Without it I doubt if she could have done as much work as she has.")[19]

I should have been prepared for what happened a summer or so later when, on a hasty weekend visit to Washington with my boys, I called her just to see how she was. She sounded well, bright and happy, and urged me to bring "godson Daniyal" the next day for tea. Tea would be brief, I thought, and agreed. That night I spent an excess of energy impressing Danny with the honor he was about to be given and the elevated standard of deportment required. In the morning I confirmed that she felt up to it, and at four o'clock we climbed the steps to her front door and rang the bell. Nothing happened. I rang again—she could be in the basement, or the shower or on the phone. . . . . . And eventually crossed the street to telephone from a neighbor's house. No answer. We went back to our temporary digs, my mind rocketing through scenarios of her falling—she was given to falls, and if she had cats, doubly so. And no one would find her till, God knows when, the cleaning lady appeared. So I called again, letting the phone ring for an excruciating length of time. Finally someone picked up the receiver and silently put it down again. The next day in New York, I sent her a bland, cheery note saying I'd been sorry to miss her on this visit, and sent Daniyal a large stuffed animal from FAO Schwartz "from Godmother Katherine Anne."

There is a photograph of Daniyal and Katherine Anne taken as we are about to say goodbye to her at the Westchester Drive townhouse, so I know they actually met. He looks scrubbed to within an inch of his life, and has a rather glazed expression but is gamely attempting a smile. Katherine Anne is heavier both in body and spirit. For the first time she shows her seventy-nine years.

I did not see her again until the early '70s when I was on my way back to Pakistan. Bob Beach, the charming and capable assistant the University [of Maryland] had put at her disposal,[20] collected me from the Washington airport early one morning and drove me to her new home: a high-rise apartment with an elevator rather than the flights of stairs that had provided the occasion for so many falls. It was a Siamese-twin of a flat, two identical apartments joined, and she had made use of the rooms in ways which suited her own life and her rather eccentric collection of antique furniture.

That first morning we sat in a sunny former kitchen that she had made into a conservatory; with plants all along the wall of glass and an avocado tree that touched the ceiling. There was a tall bookcase of poetry—most of her other books had gone, with her papers, to the University of Maryland. I remember that there was a little kitchen nook, a table set in a booth. She insisted we celebrate our reunion with champagne, and wanted no help in providing it. So I was sitting in the nook when the phone rang on the wall behind me, and at a gesture from her, I answered it. "Darlin'" the voice said, a man's voice, southern-sugary, a lover's voice. "Oh wait, I'm not Katherine Anne." And set the receiver down. She was not a bit distressed, but poured the champagne into old etched glasses before explaining to the caller who I was and that we were celebrating my arrival with a mid-morning glass of champagne. I wandered around the room, and when the call dragged on, out into the apartment, where I could not hear her words. But I remember the tone and manner: confidently amorous. I was glad for her, and hopeful for myself when I became, unimaginably, eighty.

This was a happy visit. Her demons seemed at rest. She modeled for me the caftans I had designed for her in Pakistan—one midnight blue with an all-over appliqué of a wine-purple, a second of very delicate lawn, white on white that was perfect for her pink and white beauty. She was slim again and her new frailty made the white gown almost angelic. I took her picture in each, but not before she had done her make-up and arranged herself in proper poses. One that is before me now shows her resolute but tiring. She sits on her bed with the gilded floral headboard. An azure silk nightdress is crumpled under a smart black handbag that matches the wide black belt with which she had secured the blue-and-purple caftan. We were not going anywhere except to our separate naps, but the picture must be correct.

She must have been wearing, by then, the thick eyeglasses that were then necessary after cataract surgery, but I made no note of it, and she certainly did not

Katherine Anne Porter's godson, Daniyal Mueenuddin (*center*), with his godfather, David Martin, and his mother, Barbara Thompson Davis, October 1976. Courtesy Papers of Katherine Anne Porter, Special Collections, University of Maryland, College Park, Libraries.

wear them for the photographs. But they allowed her to live some facsimile of her old life—the apartment was filled with new books and her beloved spinet was there, with music on a shelf nearby.

I think we had a potpie of some sort that she said she had made in advance, the dough and the filling and the broth each separately and put in the freezer. It must have been chicken because I remember her instructions about thickening the broth with arrowroot, and flavoring it with three kinds of pepper (I had never heard of green peppercorns). The dishes were, I think, pink, and the flatware Tiffany gilt in a shell pattern. Roses in one form or another were everywhere: in the Redouté rose prints that she had always loved on the wall in the room where I slept, and in little sacks of pot-pourri hanging from doorknobs, dried remembrance of roses sent to her. I remember those two or three days as quiet and happy, my presence not a detectable burden but, I hope, some kind of blessing. We talked, but we also read in separate rooms and listened to Landowska on the record player.

Katherine Anne Porter in one of the glamour photographs by photographer George Platt Lynes, c. 1947. Courtesy George Platt Lynes II, trustee of the George Platt Lynes estate.

I am grateful for that memory, since the next time I saw her she was in a hospital bed, her face twisted by the stroke that deprived her forever of the use of her right hand, her writing hand. My sons were with me, but she wouldn't let them see her—they were almost men, after all, not made for the sorts of trouble and blight that women are born to—I think that was her unexamined conviction. Along with the certainty as deep that men must be pleased, shown the most perfect aspect of face and character; that something close to survival depended upon it. That surely must be the legacy of the handsome feckless father who did not provide even the minimum of security for his young children. All his life she had tried to win his approval, attention, love, and all his life it was withheld—most forcefully, I think, when he failed even to acknowledge the receipt of the copy of *Pale Horse, Pale Rider: Three Short Novels,* which she had dedicated to him.

I don't remember what we said to one another that day—it was not easy to understand her—but I know that her first words were to order me to her left side and that she cradled her useless arm against her body and I thought how like it was to a woman holding an infant at the breast. At her memorial service Sister Maura Eichner, who had been with her in those last years, read a poem drawn from that same image.

That spring afternoon was the last time I saw her, but on the program for the memorial mass a month after her death at the College of Notre Dame, I was pleased to see the photograph of her last birthday party. Not just that she was wearing the white-on-white caftan that I had given her but that she had a glass of what I'm sure was a fine red wine in front of her, and a cake with chocolate frosting that mysteriously had only 6 candles. In that picture she seemed in Yeats's lovely phrase, to have "wither[ed] into the truth."[21] She had lived longer than she wished, but she had endured, if not always with grace, always with courage, the terrible last years. Nothing was left to be spent.

35 / Rita Johns

Rita LeCoyer Johns (1916–2002), born in Baltimore, Maryland, was the second wife of Glover Steiner Johns Jr., the son of Porter's childhood friend Erna Schlemmer Johns. Glover Johns Jr. (1912–76), a 1931 graduate of the Virginia Military Institute and a highly decorated soldier in World War II, was the author of *The Clay Pigeons of St. Lô* (1958), an account of the arrival of the American unit he led into a French village that was almost totally destroyed during the Battle of Normandy. After Johns joined the faculty of the Virginia Military Institute, the gracious Rita was especially popular with the cadets, who paid tribute to her in an editorial in the cadet newspaper. Colonel Johns and his First Battle Group were selected by President John F. Kennedy in 1961 to lead the way through the Iron Curtain into West Berlin in the face of overwhelming Russian troop strength. In Berlin he was greeted by Vice President Lyndon Johnson and cheering German citizens. In Lexington, Porter was particularly charmed by the Johnses' young sons, Chip (1950–91) and Lee (1952–).

Source: Rita Johns, personal interview with Darlene Harbour Unrue, 29 October 1994, Austin, Texas.

My husband, Colonel Glover Johns Jr., called Katherine Anne "Miss Callie," and so I did, too. "Callie" was Katherine Anne's name in childhood, when she was a dear friend of my mother-in-law, Erna Victoria Schlemmer Johns, known as "Erna" in childhood but "Victoria" or "Vicky" in later life. Katherine Anne and Victoria always called each other "Callie" and "Erna." It's understandable that my husband would call Katherine Anne "Miss Callie." That's what he called her in 1913 and 1914, when he was a toddler and his parents lived in Corpus Christi, Texas, where Katherine Anne lived for a year or so with her first husband and babysat Glover when my mother-in-law had an appointment.

I hadn't met Katherine Anne until she came to teach for a semester at Washington and Lee University in Lexington, Virginia. Glover was Commandant of cadets at Virginia Military Institute, also in Lexington. Glover adored "Miss Callie," and she returned the affection. We often invited her to our house for din-

Katherine Anne Porter with Major Glover Johns Jr. and other military men at Virginia Military Institute, in Lexington, Virginia, who are lifting her onto a tank, 13 April 1958. Courtesy Papers of Katherine Anne Porter, Special Collections, University of Maryland, College Park, Libraries.

ner, and whenever I held a tea, I always included her, although I think she enjoyed the mixed-company dinner parties more than the all-ladies teas. She was a fascinating woman, very beautiful, and flamboyant. I thought of her as perpetual motion. She talked and talked, but when someone else spoke, she would stop and listen attentively. She often referred to the six books she had in her mind ready to be written down.

She was a great success at Washington and Lee. She was the first woman invited to teach there. In the several months of her term, she gave four or five lectures, and people came from miles around to see and hear her. I don't think she liked the town much, though. It probably was too parochial for her, and the temporary apartment she was given was not very attractive. She also was ill with pneumonia that winter and seemed debilitated much of the time.

While she was in Lexington, it was well known that she was involved in a May–December relationship with a young naval officer whom she frequently met in nearby towns for romantic rendezvous. She made no effort to be discreet about it and had no reluctance about bringing his name up in conversation.[22]

For all my mother-in-law's affection for Katherine Anne, I'm sure she didn't approve of her unconventional life and her several marriages. Victoria was strait-laced and perfectionist, although shy and kind-hearted at the same time. In some ways happy-go-lucky Katherine Anne seemed nearly her opposite. But Victoria would never have expressed disapproval of Katherine Anne, and there was no mistaking the bond between them. Victoria visited us in Lexington while Katherine Anne was there, and they had a lovely time reminiscing. One of them told a convoluted and funny story about a time when they were children and had climbed into the hayloft of the Schlemmers' barn. Katherine Anne had climbed down safely while Erna fell, unhurt but embarrassed.

Before Katherine Anne left Lexington, the chairman of the English Department had a dinner party for her, and Glover and I were among the guests. While a butler served coffee, Katherine Anne entertained everyone there with stories about her past life and humorous stories about persons she knew.

Several years after she left Lexington, I visited her in Georgetown, where she had a rented house on Q Street. I took my two young sons, Chip and Lee, with me because I wanted them to be exposed again to Katherine Anne. She was so vibrant and beautiful, even in her seventies, and she was good with children. She didn't even have to work at it. My boys were completely enchanted with her.

Mary Flannery O'Connor (1925–64) was born in Savannah, Georgia, the only child of Regina Cline O'Connor and Edward O'Connor, the latter of whom died when Flannery was fifteen years old. She attended the Peabody Laboratory School, Georgia State College for Women, and the Iowa Writers' Workshop. In 1951, having been diagnosed with the hereditary lupus from which her father had died, she returned to the ancestral farm in Milledgeville, where she lived out her remaining fifteen years by writing two novels, thirty-one short stories, many reviews and essays, and letters to numerous friends that included Betty Hester, Robert Lowell, Elizabeth Bishop, Porter, the mystery writer Cecil Dawkins, and the classics translator Robert Fitzgerald and his wife, Sally. She was a devout Catholic whose religious beliefs as well as the Southern Gothic tradition infused her fiction.

Source: *Letters of Flannery O'Connor: The Habit of Being,* ed. and intro. Sally Fitzgerald (New York: Farrar, Straus and Giroux, 1979), 260, 275, 276, 416.

To Cecil Dawkins, 22 December 1957
I have never met Miss K.A.P. All the men who know her seem to like her as I strongly gather she has a way with them, but I know a few women who seem to like her too. I have friends in Nashville who know her rather well and they say she's always pleasant. So many catty remarks circulate and people always suppose that there is rivalry between women writers. If so, I always figure they are not the best writers.

To "A" [Betty Hester], 4 April 1958
Katherine Anne Porter read in Macon on the 27th and the next day the Gossetts[23] brought her over to have lunch with us. She was very pleasant . . .[24] When she asked me where we were going in Europe and I said Lourdes, a very strange expression came over her face, just a slight shock as if some sensitive spot had been touched. She said that she had always wanted to go to Lourdes, perhaps she would get there some day and make a

Katherine Anne Porter, Flannery O'Connor, and one of O'Connor's "chickens" that Porter admired, at O'Connor's home in Milledgeville, Georgia, April 1958. Courtesy Papers of Katherine Anne Porter, Special Collections, University of Maryland, College Park, Libraries.

novena that she would finish her novel [*Ship of Fools*]—she's been on it 27 years. After that the conversation somehow got on the subject of death—there were two professors from North Carolina and the Gossetts and us and her—in the way that death is discussed at dinner tables, as if it were a funny subject. She said she thought it was very nice to believe that we would all meet in heaven and she rather hoped we would but she didn't really know. She wished she knew who exactly was in charge of this universe, and where she was going. She would be glad to go where she was expected if she knew. All this accompanied by much banter from the gentlemen. It was a little coy and a little wistful but there was a terrible need evident underneath it. . . .[25]

To Cecil Dawkins, 14 April 1958

Miss Katherine Anne was very nice indeed. Very pleasant and agreeable, crazy about my peacocks; plowed all over the yard behind me in her spike-heeled shoes to see my various kinds of chickens. I didn't hear her read but most of the people I talked to who did thought she read well. They say she had on a black halter type dress sans back & long black gloves which interfered with her turning the pages. After each story, she made a kind of curtsy, which someone described as "wobbly." She's about sixty-five. She's been on her novel 27 years and says all her friends call it "you-know-what." I hope I won't be on mine 27 years from now.[26]

To Cecil Dawkins, 8 November 1960

I have been recuperating from Minnesota,[27] and then an Arts Festival at Wesleyan attended also by Caroline [Gordon] and Miss K. A. Porter. Caroline spent the weekend here after it . . .[28] and one night of it, we had a lot of them to supper. Katherine Anne remembered to inquire about a chicken of mine that she had met here two years before. I call that really having a talent for winning friends and influencing people when you remember to inquire for a chicken that you met two years before. She was so sorry that it was night and she wouldn't get to see him again as she had particularly wanted to. I call that social grace.

37 / James Ruoff

James E. Ruoff (1925–86), born in Seattle, Washington, earned a B.A. from the University of Washington and an M.A. and Ph.D. from the University of Pennsylvania. He held faculty positions at Alfred University, Washington State University, Wichita State University, and City College of New York and was a Fulbright lecturer in Turkey in 1977 and 1978. In addition to *The Crowell Handbook of Elizabethan and Stuart Literature* (1973), he published numerous articles in scholarly journals.

Source: James Ruoff, "Katherine Anne Porter Comes to Kansas," *Midwest Quarterly* 4 (1963): 305–14.

Pale, thin, diminutive, archly erect and poised, her small freckled hands folded sedately in her lap, she seemed at first glance to resemble a chic version of Whistler's mother. But this initial impression of frailty and serenity was offset by the shock of wild gray hair, the alert blue eyes that flared like blown coals, and the firm eloquence of the voice that was falling on our ears like strange music. "As a little girl in Texas I was brought up a Catholic," she was saying. "But my father, Harrison Boone, now, he was a free-thinking man. One morning he stopped me as I was on my way to church to celebrate the Immaculate Conception. 'Immaculate Conception!' he said, 'Girl, d'you know what in thunder that means?' When I told him I did, he pointed to the *Complete Works of Voltaire* on the shelf. 'See those?' he said. 'Now you go ahead and read 'em so you and I will have something to talk about!'"

It was late afternoon, September 28, 1961. We were gathered in the Provincial Room of the Campus Activities Center at the University of Wichita. The speaker was Katherine Anne Porter, author of *Flowering Judas, Ship of Fools,* and a half dozen or so of the greatest short stories written by an American. Erect as a Buckingham guardsman, she sat in a straight-back chair and smiled calmly at the college students and faculty packed three-deep along the walls and jammed together at her feet. The small room was acrid with cigarette smoke and the odor of black coffee left unattended in a hundred cups. Somewhere in the room a student stirred to ask a question: "Miss Porter, where do you find your material?"

"It's wherever *I* am—in fact, dearie, I'm finding it right now," she responded quickly. And then, as if in pursuit of an elusive idea behind the laughing faces, her energetic eyes searched out the student who had asked the question, and she began to talk directly to him, as if they were completely alone. "You don't get material by peeping or prying or looking over transoms," she said quietly. "You live and it comes. Life's licking you in the britches all the time, if you only know it. If you go looking for your material you may put into your writing what really doesn't belong to *you*. I didn't look for Laura in 'Flowering Judas'—she was then and is now a very dear friend who never did anything in life—like the man in Henry James' story 'Beast in the Jungle.'"

She was a superb teacher. There was candid affection in her eyes and voice, and every word seemed to arrange itself behind the other with compelling force and accuracy. The subject turned to her contemporaries. Robert Penn Warren, she declared emphatically, was a great poet but not a true novelist. He was sacrificing poetic genius to satisfy his readers' demands for novels. "I've told Red a hundred times to leave fiction alone and go on with his poetry, but he won't listen to me." The real masters of fiction were Ernest Hemingway, Joseph Conrad, Eudora Welty, and James Joyce. She owed so much to Joyce, she said, that she could never be critical of him. "Like Eliot and Pound, Joyce was one of my important experiences. *Dubliners* was a revelation to me—it showed what could be done with the short story. To my generation, Joyce was a tremendous influence. He gave us courage and confidence. I can't tell you what a breath of fresh air he was. It was time for a break, and he made it. I don't know what we would have done without *Dubliners* and *Ulysses*."

She still read Hemingway, she said, for his short stories. "Go back to the 'Big Two-Hearted River.' All of his good things are right there!" As for Mary McCarthy,[29] her explorations into childhood were best, the rest of her work too caustic. "About her early times, as in *Memoirs of a Catholic Childhood,* she has a sense of wonder. But Eudora Welty is more sunny, more radiant." The University bell rang through the halls outside and she added wryly: "Ah, Mary's bell tolls for us!"

What about William Saroyan and F. Scott Fitzgerald?[30] She considered the question for a moment. "I don't care for Saroyan at all," she said at last. "He will not discipline himself. He runs off the edges, and he can't *think!* I know he's one of the sweetest, gentlest people, but he doesn't know how to stop to ask himself what he's doing. . . ."[31] As for Scott Fitzgerald, well, for a long time I couldn't read him because I knew the people he was writing about too well. In fact, I stayed in Mexico to avoid that crowd in New York. *Tender Is the Night* has some good passages, and so has *The Great Gatsby*. But poor Fitzgerald!" She bristled indignantly. "An artist has no *right* to have such feelings about those cheap, nasty, rich people he was so afraid of!"

What writers had influenced her most? "Laurence Sterne[32] was the first one who made me think I could write," she recalled affectionately. "That wonderful style with all the dashes! It looks easy, but it's terribly difficult. Through the years, though, I've had greater sympathy for Henry James than for almost any other writer. . . .[33] You know, I first started writing when I was five. I started a novel called 'The Hermit of Halifax Cave.' I had my hero going fishing and doing other such things until I couldn't think of anything more for him to do and had to quit the novel." As she talked about her own writing habits, her hands suddenly came to life and stroked the air as if they were molding clay. "For many years I had to work up a story slowly, and with many revisions—one story I revised seventeen times—but now I've learned to be a first-draft writer. I write at top speed and then go over the story again with a pen and there it is." She laughed with a kind of triumphant gaiety, then suddenly became serious. "The speed is not important, because I never intended to be a fifty-book writer—why should I print my studio litter? I haven't published a fraction of what I've written. I have four bushels of manuscripts I've never tried to publish—forty short stories, and five novels I started when I was young and didn't know I was a short story writer.[34] Once in a while a story can be brought out of storage and revived, though. Recently I printed one that had been lost for thirty-five years. It was based on something that happened to me when I was twenty, something that presented a powerful problem to me, something I couldn't avoid. A long time ago I made three revisions but somehow couldn't bring it off. Then, thirty-five years later, I rewrote it in twenty days from the first version, which, after all, was the right one. It was a long story called 'Holiday,' published in *The Atlantic Monthly*."

A student asked how she came to write the collection *Flowering Judas*. "I was so sure of the title story I wrote it in one day and part of a night," she said. "'María Concepción' took seventeen days. 'Flowering Judas' began one night in Mexico as I was walking down a street and passed a window where I saw a young girl I knew sitting in a chair, a book in her lap, and in another chair there was a great fat man plucking a guitar. I went inside and sat with the girl until the man left. I didn't write 'Flowering Judas' until ten years later, but the whole story began with that glimpse through the window. The publisher printed the manuscript just the way I wrote it, with all kinds of mistakes in punctuation and capitals."[35] She laughed. "I understand that edition is now quite a collector's item!"[36]

Of her story "Rope," she stated: "I'd heard lots of quarrels among couples I knew and found in them all the same pattern—a structure like a five-act drama. 'Rope' is the distilled essence of all those fights I'd heard." Of "Noon Wine" she

said it had taken but seven days to write, but "thirty-five years before that to prepare for it. And the genesis of that final version," she added, "took me one whole
summer." She referred to one of her most popular stories, "Theft." "It's about
a woman who leads a sacrificial life," she observed: "She had a strange sense of
alienation. No one could get near her. Someone gave her a purse with gold pieces
and it was lost. She accused the waitress.[37] The woman *really* wanted to commit suicide but didn't know it, so she killed herself bit by bit. But this isn't the
story," she concluded. "There's a transmutation, a chemical change that makes it
fiction."

A student posed the question every English instructor hears in his sophomore
literature courses: do authors employ symbols consciously? "Well, you don't *put
in* the symbols," she replied kindly. "You see, symbols take care of themselves.
Anything can be a symbol, but it must never be forced. I'm often asked about the
symbolism of the silver dove and the engraved ring in 'The Grave.' I used these
symbols only because they were really there in the experience on which the story
was based. My brother and I found those objects in my grandfather's grave. Of
course the dove is a symbol. It's symbolic of peace, security, love, and lechery. But
it's also the Holy Ghost and the innocent love of children. The ring is the serpent
biting its tail, a symbol of immortality." She paused, adding reflectively: "At the
time I wrote 'The Grave' I didn't know the ring was also symbolic of exploring
the past...."[38]

But what about obscurity? "Well, you don't have to know everything about a
work the first time you read it," she countered easily. "I wonder now what there
could have been about T. S. Eliot that *ever* puzzled me! As for my own stories, I
wrote strange and rather weird things, so that at first they wouldn't even publish
me because I was such a recondite writer." She laughed. "Recondite! Look at me
now—I'm no more mysterious than a goldfish floating in a bowl!"

Obscurity was one thing, isolation from society quite another. A writer, she
insisted vehemently, must never be alienated from the community, and the de-
liberate isolation of writers like J. D. Salinger she considered as enervating as alcohol or drugs.[39] "Any such alienation from society is death," she asserted. "You
may live in an attic, and you'll probably have fine company if you do, but first
you have to become a human being...."[40] It was equally dangerous for a writer
to become so involved in one corner of society as to lose his perspective. As examples she cited Richard Wright, Ralph Ellison, and James Baldwin.[41] "I can't
read them," she declared. "I'm so tired of all that hatred and poison that I think
I'll just sit this one out, if you don't mind. They've all had such horrible lives—
such horrible experiences—that it's left them with dreadful minds. Baldwin, I
think, is nearly crazed—not at all sane." She suddenly grinned, and one could tell

from the expression in her eyes that she was laughing at herself. "You see? I just won't talk about them at all!"

Everyone was curious about her new novel, *Ship of Fools*, which was to be released by the publisher later that month.[42] Now that the long work was finished, she could talk about it, and she approached the subject with all the enthusiasm of a fisherman describing the big catch that did *not* get away. "Nobody ever fought a novel as I did that one. It took me twenty-one years to get that novel written, and I quit every chance I found. But it won," she said and then, wonderingly: "460,000 words! Is it possible? The title *Ship of Fools* I borrowed from Sebastian Brant's *Narrenshiff*, published in Basel in 1494. I found the title when I was in Basel reading about Erasmus of Rotterdam, and I thought 'That's *my* title—I'll just borrow it. Brant doesn't need it anymore.'"

A question from an English instructor: "Did *Ship of Fools* end the way you had originally planned it?"

"It's exactly the same," she replied. "In fact, I wrote the last three pages first and kept working toward that conclusion. The idea of the novel is basic and simple—the ship of this world on its voyage to eternity. But this was a real ship that started from Vera Cruz and went to Bremerhaven. It was my first voyage to Europe, just after *Flowering Judas* came out and I'd received a Guggenheim. . . .[43] I'd been on voyages before, but there was something about this one that was totally different. For one thing, 1931 was a crucial year, with revolutions in Mexico and South America, and Mussolini in power in Italy. In Cuba the bottom had fallen out of the sugar market and there were shipping strikes. Sugar fields were burning, idle ships choked the harbors, and all the workers brought to Cuba from Spain and the Canary Islands were being deported by the government. In Havana we saw them driven aboard ship like cattle. . . .[44] We had a twenty-eight day voyage. Aboard ship were a half dozen nationalities and as many religions and castes. That ship was like a basket of snakes on a hot stove. People were drawn together by religion, separated by language or nationality; drawn together by nationality, separated by caste or politics. You see, all my life I'd been a completely free agent experiencing one thing and then moving on to experience something else, but aboard that ship I was stuck—stuck with people I never dreamed existed—and I started keeping a diary of everything I saw and heard. Strangely enough, I don't think I spoke a half dozen words to as many passengers, yet I couldn't take my eyes and ears off them. . . .[45]

"When we arrived at Bremerhaven I sent my ship's log to Caroline Gordon—Allen Tate's wife—in the form of a long letter,[46] and afterwards, in Berlin, I wrote a poem about the voyage,[47] but it was interrupted after forty-two lines. Three or four years ago I added some lines to the first version and published it as 'After a

Long Journey.' A few years after I left Germany, Caroline Gordon returned my letter because she thought I might find use for it in my writing. Although the voyage was still working in my mind, I put the letter away and never looked at it again except to get the time right, the phases of the moon, the tides, and so forth. All the rest was novel. At first, though, I tried to make it a short story. With 'Pale Horse, Pale Rider,' 'Noon Wine,' and 'Old Mortality,' *Ship of Fools* was to be the fourth in a group, but it simply ran away from me. . . ."[48]

"Why did you experience such difficulty with it?" someone asked. "Were there too many characters in it to fit the short story form?"

"No, I just didn't *want* to write a novel," she said emphatically. "I was baffled and frustrated because I wasn't able to work my material into the shape it wanted to become. And *I* was wrong, of course. It grew and developed, and with its growth my own view of the world changed. I came to see that something had happened aboard that ship which was quite stupid—that it wouldn't have happened if the people opposed to it had taken hold and not let it happen. The point is, I had seen these criminals—these *clowns*—like Hitler, and was stricken by an idea: if people like this could take over the world! Of course there were all the good people who didn't believe in the clowns, but they still let the clowns commit the crimes good worthy people would commit if only they had the nerve. How else to account for the collusion in evil that enables a creature like Mussolini, or Hitler, or Huey Long,[49] or McCarthy (make your own list, petty or great) to get hold of things? Who permits it? We *know* we're not criminals—we're not evil. We don't *believe* in that sort of thing, do we?" Her penetrating eyes made a swift arc among the young faces gathered on the floor around her. For a brief moment the room was so quiet the clock on the wall could be heard throbbing like a drum.

A student cleared his throat to phrase a mindless but heart-felt question: "Miss Porter, what can we do about the world situation today? What do you think we ought to be doing to avert disaster?"

"Oh, dearie, it's too late now. It's too late!" She smiled grimly. "The tragedy of our times is not an accident but a total consent. Anyway, my novel is a tiny drop of water to illustrate this vast ocean of accord. For me as a writer, being on that ship was a godsent experience, although I wouldn't have been able to see any of these things if I hadn't seen them first in Mexico. Still, in Mexico there was always something good about it—in Mexico there was always a chance of salvation. As for all the evil that threatens us here and now, I must say we haven't an alibi in the world. We let all the evil come upon us." She paused for a moment, then added: "Well, that's the theme of my novel. And it's not mentioned once in the story. Find it for yourself."

Having almost reached her four score and ten years, she would never, in all probability, witness the ultimate consequences of our human folly on this planet.

We who would live after her were already eager to begin picking her frail bones. "What about all those manuscripts you mentioned?" someone asked.

"I'm leaving my papers to the University of Texas," she replied. "They seem to think I'm the only writer Texas has produced. Actually, there are plenty of young ones coming up—George Garrett, Walter Clemons,[50] William Goyen—who have perfectly wonderful talents. The University of Texas is naming a big new library center after me, with a special room for my papers—and, well, I have to do something in return, don't I?"[51] She sighed and folded her gnarled but delicate hands in her lap. She seemed then to become as tiny, shy, and incredibly fragile as the little girl who had stood before her towering father and tried to explain to him the meaning of the Immaculate Conception. "So I guess I'll wind up in a dark, tight place after all," she said. "Too bad—I have a terrible case of claustrophobia!"

But it was impossible to sustain even for a moment the incongruous idea of her death. Through her well-wrought works of art the firm voice would go on forever reassuring us that "Beauty is truth, truth beauty." And to the many Kansans who listened to her on that September day, she will be remembered not as an aged woman but as a youthful artist still head over heels in love with living.

6
New York, Washington, DC, and Maryland, 1962–1973

Ship of Fools was published on 1 April 1962, and Katherine Anne Porter became a wealthy and yet more celebrated writer. She discovered, however, that commercial success sometimes has an artistic price. Exhausted after what she called the "hullaballoo" surrounding the publication, she spent a month in Europe. When a few unfriendly reviews appeared in the summer and fall, she escaped to Europe for a year. She might have suspected, but did not articulate the thought, that her creative energies were spent, for after 1963 she wrote no new fiction. Instead, she began to settle her affairs, spiritual and financial. She thought she wanted to own another house, but ownership proved beyond her. She selected her attorney, made a will, tapped a biographer, placed her papers in the University of Maryland, College Park, and assigned literary executors and trustees. She returned to the Roman Catholic Church. She sat back to enjoy the company of friends, old and new.

38 / Frederic Prokosch

Frederic Prokosch (1908–89), American novelist, poet, critic, and translator, was born in Madison, Wisconsin, and educated at Haverford College, Yale University, and King's College, Cambridge. He was cultural attaché of the American legations in Portugal and Sweden. He moved around in the United States and especially in Europe, becoming acquainted with a large number of literary persons. His works include the poetry collections *The Somnambulists* (1933), *Death at Sea* (1940), and *Chosen Poems* (1945); and the novels *The Seven Who Fled* (1937), *The Skies of Europe* (1941), *Nine Days to Mukalla* (1953), and *The Missolonghi Manuscript* (1968).

Source: Frederic Prokosch, *Voices* (New York: Farrar, Straus & Giroux, 1983); this excerpt was published as "The Nightmare of Literary Life," *Harper's* March 1983: 58–59.

Monroe Wheeler, who was head of the Museum of Modern Art, gave a party one evening in honor of the Sitwells.[1] Edith and Osbert had arrived in New York for a farewell visit.[2] Poor Osbert was very ill, suffering from Parkinson's disease, and poor Edith was very bitter, nursing her persecution mania. [. . .]

The guests had assembled and there was an air of cynical expectancy. The Sitwells were a legend, but a moth-eaten legend. There had been some rather thinly veiled attacks on the Sitwells recently. But all were eager to see the Sitwells and even to rise to their defense, provided that the Sitwells were appropriately ingratiating.

Marianne Moore sat in a corner, looking pallid and timorous. Edmund Wilson sat on a couch, leafing through *The Unquiet Grave*.[3] Three young painters stood in a corner, discussing the music of Paul Hindemith.[4] A young composer stood by the bookcase and stared at the first editions. Near the table, next to a rubber plant, sat Katherine Anne Porter.

She looked so sad and lonely that I wanted to comfort her. She was a beautiful woman with stupendous eyes and foam-white hair. I was puzzled by the martyr-like intensity in her eyes. I sat down close beside her, eager to console her in her anguish.

She lifted her glass and stared at me accusingly. "A horrible thing they've done!"

"Who? The Sitwells?"

"No! The Swedes!"

"What have they done?"

"Giving that prize to a mediocre hack like Steinbeck!" Her voice shook with rage. She gripped her glass feverishly. "It was all very well to give the prize to William Faulkner. There is an integrity in Faulkner which I thoroughly respect. I objected not in the least when they gave the prize to Hemingway. There is a flavor in Hemingway which deserves to be recognized. But the Swedes must be mad. Pearl Buck was bad enough. But to give that silly prize to a sentimental hack like Steinbeck!"[5]

Edmund Wilson came up and stood by the table impenetrably. He had a petulant fat face with a high, looming forehead and a babylike expression of benevolent implacability.

"I've been leafing through this strange little volume of Connolly's. Palinurus, he calls himself. But it's obviously Cyril Connolly. He guides us in his boat through the swirlings of the Styx. Very clever, that conception, and he attacks it with dexterity. Cyril Connolly has a certain way with words that is felicitous. As a rule I distrust all this verbal virtuosity, but in the case of Cyril Connolly it is more than virtuosity. It is clear that he has suffered. He has been tortured by acedia."

"Are they coming or not?" said Miss Porter rather crossly.

"Who?" said Wilson.

"The Sitwells!"

Wilson looked puzzled. "Are we waiting for the Sitwells?"

"So it seems. Look around. They are positively twitching with excitement. They look like at bunch of flies waiting to pounce on a Camembert."

Edmund Wilson cocked his head. "A most intriguing notion. I have never thought of the Sitwells as resembling a Camembert, but now that you mention it I see what you mean. I do not pose as an authority on matters Sitwellian. I liked *Before the Bombardment* and I was amused by *Rustic Elegies*. I browsed through *The Gothick North* and found it only mildly stimulating."

There was a hush of suspense. All the faces turned simultaneously. There was a rustling in the vestibule and the curtains stirred expectantly.

It was Edith who entered first. She was less angular than I expected, and more massive and myopic. [. . .]

She was followed by Osbert, who looked rather startled. He moved in sudden jerks, as though groping his way through a thicket. He started toward the window, then abruptly recovered himself. He headed for the bookcase and stared at it in bewilderment. Monroe Wheeler took him gently and tactfully by the elbow, and Osbert started to glide across the room as though on casters.

"I would like you to meet Miss Moore," said Monroe Wheeler coaxingly.

Osbert lurched uncontrollably in the direction of Miss Porter.

"Ah, Miss Moore! Delighted to meet you. I find your poems irresistible. They remind me of seashells. Or birds' nests. Or paperweights. You know the kind I mean, full of swirlings and squigglings. . . ."

"This is Miss Porter, not Miss Moore," said Monroe Wheeler nervously. "Miss Moore is a poetess but Miss Porter is a raconteuse. I am sure that you've read *Flowering Judas,* haven't you, Osbert?"

I crept furtively toward the sofa and sat down by Edith Sitwell.

39 / E. Barrett Prettyman Jr.

E. Barrett Prettyman Jr. (1925–) is the son of Lucy Courtney Hill Prettyman and Elijah Barrett Prettyman, the latter a prominent U.S. Court of Appeals judge. He earned a B.A. from Yale University in 1949 and an LL.B. from the University of Virginia in 1953. From 1953 to 1955, Prettyman served as a law clerk to U.S. Supreme Court justices Robert H. Jackson, Felix Frankfurter, and John M. Harlan. He became an associate with the law firm of Hogan and Hartson in 1955 and was named a partner in 1964. In 1963, Prettyman served as special assistant to U.S. attorney general Robert F. Kennedy and was an aide to Presidents John F. Kennedy and Lyndon B. Johnson from 1963 to 1964. He was also the first president of the District of Columbia Bar Association. In 2007 he was named "Lawyer of the Year" by the *American Lawyer* magazine.

Source: E. Barrett Prettyman Jr., "My Years with Katherine Anne—as Friend and Lawyer." This essay, written specifically for this volume, is published here for the first time.

In 1962, the year after my own book, *Death and the Supreme Court,* had come out and won the Mystery Writers of America and Scribes Awards, I began and finished reading *Ship of Fools.* Katherine Anne's novel had sold well but had also received a number of unflattering reviews. I liked the book enormously, including some sections that had been panned, and as I finished it late one evening, I felt the urge to tell her so.

I had heard that she lived in an apartment in Georgetown and so, without expecting anything helpful, I looked in the Washington, DC, telephone directory. There I found a "K. A. Porter," and even though it was almost 10 o'clock, I called the number.

She answered the phone herself, and I was immediately full of apologies. I told her that I had just finished *Ship of Fools,* that I had loved the book, and despite the late hour, had just felt the need to convey my admiration. Rather than being upset, she sounded both flattered and grateful. We began talking about various chapters, scenes, and characters.

As the conversation wore on, however, it became apparent to me that Katherine Anne was quite despondent. In fact, she appeared to be in almost a self-destructive mood. I suddenly asked, "Miss Porter, don't you think I should come see you?" She immediately grasped my concern over her mood and said, "Yes, come tomorrow morning."

And so it was that I went to see her the next day. At the time, she was seventy-two and I was thirty-seven, almost half her age. I liked her immediately. She was full of vigor and rapid-fire conversation despite the despondence that I knew was there. As in the conversation the night before, she soon lapsed into tales of loss and fatigue. I did the best I could to make her feel alive, successful, and productive. After almost two hours, I left her but promised to meet again.

The following year I sent her my book. She wrote back, "Your explanation of the workings of the Supreme Court is the first satisfactory one I have ever read." This was typical, I was to learn, of her kindness, her desire to please, and her tinkering with the truth.

As Justice John Harlan explained to me later, he was sitting next to Katherine Anne at a dinner in 1966, four years after I met her. She was complaining about her need for a good lawyer to handle her numerous problems and particularly to write her will. He said, "Well I thought you knew Barrett Prettyman." She replied, "Of course I do." And he said, "Didn't you know he is a lawyer—and a good one?" (I had clerked for the Justice on the Supreme Court.) And Katherine Anne, looking somewhat sheepish, said, "I did know that, but I just never thought of him that way."

The upshot of that conversation was that Katherine Anne wrote me in May of 1966 asking me to write her will.

In a book about Katherine Anne, the author implies that I had little contact with her during the years between our first meeting in 1962 and the signing of her will in 1966.[6] However, I did see her episodically, and frequently exchanged calls with her during this period. It is true, however, that our relationship professionally intensified after I worked extensively on her will with others in my firm. The will was signed on 3 December 1966.

The following year I legally established a Board of Trustees of the Katherine Anne Porter Foundation, with the goal of distributing funds to potentially worthy writers and performing other good deeds. At a meeting of the Board in 1967, attendees included, among others, Eudora Welty, William Humphrey, Glenway Wescott, Katherine Anne, and myself. The Foundation was later dissolved when members found they could not regularly attend its meetings.

Perhaps a brief outline of the time I spent dealing with Katherine Anne over the two years following her will signing will give some idea of my heavy concentration on her trials and tribulations as well as the fun times we shared.

Thus, in 1967, despite my absence on a railroad merger case in Chicago and many weeks spent in wartime Vietnam for a Congressional committee, I visited Katherine Anne on at least fourteen occasions and at the same time we exchanged calls at least twenty-nine times during the same year. A number of those visits and calls occurred when she was in the hospital.

The subject matter of our discussions included taxes, her contracts with Delacorte, a book being written about her, the Foundation formed under her will, her obligations to Little, Brown, lost notes, and a codicil to her will. All of this was in addition to the many calls and visits with others on her behalf and research relating to her many problems.

My Vietnam trip continued into 1968. I also traveled extensively that year on behalf of Robert Kennedy's campaign for the presidency, and engaged in funeral arrangements after he was assassinated. In addition, I had many clients, conferences, court appearances, and speeches. Yet my diary shows that during 1968 I visited Katherine Anne—at her home, on the way to an airport, and in Annapolis—twenty times, and we called each other forty-one times. The subjects we discussed included a projected book of her essays, a threatening letter, a second codicil to her will (which was signed 1 May), finances, insurance, the *Ship of Fools* film, negotiations with Dell, a house she wanted to buy in Annapolis, and much more.

So it went. My relationship continued on a personal basis—we remained great friends until almost the end—but that relationship was interspersed with hard work on her behalf.

In those next years I dealt with disputes over what she owed her maid, bank loans, a contract with the actor Keir Dullea,[7] taxes, carpeting, royalties, a lease on a new apartment, a threatened suit by a storage company, Medicare, the disposition of her papers, and her frustration over attempts to write a book about Cotton Mather.

One biography of Katherine Anne accounted for all this work and my dealings with other authors by stating that I craved to be out of the legal profession.[8] Nothing can be further from the truth. As the son of a judge, I was imbued with legalese from childhood. I became totally enthralled as soon as I took my first law classes, and my excitement mounted when I clerked for three successive Justices on the Supreme Court. In practice, I loved my cases, including argument in the high court, and I never once thought of changing professions.

My fascination with the literary world, which led me to the Presidency of the PEN/Faulkner Foundation, came about purely because of my love of books and my admiration for many who wrote them. It was not an attempt to escape the law, but an extracurricular activity the way some people play golf or watch football.

The matters I worked on for Katherine Anne were all discussed, at one time or another, at breakfasts, lunches, and dinners she and I would enjoy at her homes and apartments. She was a marvelous, imaginative cook, and I always looked forward to those meals that were part work and part gourmet.

At some of these meals the occasion was enlivened by guests—usually writers such as Robert Penn Warren, his wife Eleanor Clark, Glenway Wescott, and Monroe Wheeler. At one dinner in New York City in November 1970, the attendees with Katherine Anne and myself included William Saroyan, John Cheever, Tillie Olsen, Kay Boyle,[9] Jean Stafford, Peter Taylor, and John Barth.[10] Another event in New York that we attended together resulted in Truman Capote hiring me to act as his attorney in putting together a television documentary on the death penalty.[11]

Also in 1970, my then-wife and I held a party at the 1925 F Street Club to celebrate the publication of Katherine Anne's *Collected Essays and Occasional Writings* (which she very kindly dedicated to me). The assembled group gave her a book, *Adam Bede,* inscribed by Henry James to the English novelist Rhoda Broughton. Katherine Anne later re-inscribed it to me, and I bought it from her estate after she passed away.

Among my disparate duties during this period (one which I failed to carry out) was to find all the facts supporting the premise that Dylan Thomas "attacked" her during a party (pushed her down some steps) to rebut the then current play *Dylan.* Another, more successful, duty was to prepare her for her disposition in a case (subsequently settled) involving her jewelry. And I spent most of one morning with the police breaking into Katherine Anne's house to determine, after many attempts to contact her, whether she was all right. (She was.) At other times, however, she had less luck and landed in the hospital from falls, broken bones, and various illnesses. We had many hospital visits.

Despite those down periods, she enjoyed many up periods too. Her birthday parties at the University of Maryland were always a joy, and she described her adventure to me enthusiastically when she returned from a trip on the *Playboy* Yacht to view a shuttle takeoff.[12] I also took her to a small college, where I was struck by her extraordinary ability to speak—fluently, intelligently, persuasively, and without notes. The young audience was enthralled. Katherine Anne's enthusiasm for her subject—writing and writers—showed through in every line she spoke, and at the end, the students gave her a long standing ovation. Sometimes I thought she would have benefited from a dual career, as writer and speaker.

Beginning in 1973, she began discussing the importance of choosing an Executor in her will who could select successive literary trustees. These trustees would care for her papers and whatever money was left to give to promising authors. She offered the job to several people, but because each in turn could not serve, she finally chose me. Despite the fact that she knew well how to change her will with codicils, I remained her Executor even through the very difficult times to come and after her death.

During almost all my friendship with Katherine Anne, we included expressions of love in our correspondence and conversation. This has confused many people who did not know us well. The explanation is simpler than they suspected.

My impression of Katherine Anne, formed early on, was that she was never terribly happy with real life, despite the confidence she had in her own writing. But she was totally taken with, immersed in, and pleased over her imaginary life.

In this latter life she could profess love with utter devotion. The various people she chose in her imagination to love her back were flawless, they saw no defects in her, and they never stopped loving her until she stopped being interested in them. That was the life she attempted to live, and when it worked, it gave her comfort and relief.

I detected early on that I had become one of her chosen ones, and since I knew for a fact that she never aspired to another level of love above a simple declaration, I was perfectly content to play my role with conviction, for it made our relationship acceptable on both sides.

But make no mistake. I knew that we were never in love, and so did she. What we had was in a way more solid and grounded than that. We truly cared for each other, respected each other, and liked each other. We delighted in each other's company, we were never bored, and we could speak freely and without boundaries. That kind of relationship is very rare.

I left in January 1977 for a six-month sabbatical granted by my law firm, and body-surfed my way around the world, starting in Peru and thereafter following the sun. Two days after my return I called on Katherine Anne and found her in terrible physical and mental condition. She had suffered a series of severe strokes, resulting in partial paralysis and sporadic paranoia. Some people who came to see her after my return thought she "looked fine" or was "in good spirits," but those of us who were close to her and met with her often knew that she was lacking the capacity to control her assets and to make wise decisions. Her loyal nephew, Paul Porter, joined me in petitioning a Circuit Court to name Paul as her legal guardian. The court appointed two psychiatrists to examine her, and they reported back that she was, indeed, unable to care for herself. And so Paul became her guardian.

This convinced Katherine Anne that everyone close to her was in a cabal to steal her money and property. She "fired" me; excoriated Paul; turned against her publisher, Seymour Lawrence, and her long-standing friend Glenway Wescott;

Katherine Anne Porter and attorney E. Barrett Prettyman Jr., 19 January 1974. Courtesy Papers of Katherine Anne Porter, Special Collections, University of Maryland, College Park, Libraries.

sought the return of her portrait from the University of Maryland; and drew more and more people into her web of deceit.

Since Paul was now in charge of her affairs, and I had been "fired," I saw virtually nothing of Katherine Anne over the next several years until her death on 18 September 1980.

In looking back, I find an utterly fascinating woman in Katherine Anne. The fluency I described at the small college never left her, so that even at teatime or over the phone, her conversation sparkled and lit up like that of no other. She was accident prone, giving her something to talk about when all else failed, which it seldom did. She spoke in grammatical sentences, and paused to make paragraphs at just the right points. There was often a sadness in her, which was endearing, and one never knew whether she was living primarily in the real world or in that wonderful world of her imagination.

She had a lovely face. It is fascinating in reviewing pictures of her over the years to see that face develop, as if she was allowing only so much advanced age to intrude. Her smile was real. Sometimes when she was writing, you wanted to crawl inside her head to see just how the wheels meshed and the genius took over and the right words tumbled out in the right order to make a story no one else could make.

She was a woman of conscience, as when she returned her medal to the American Academy of Arts and Sciences because the Academy refused to award its medal to Ezra Pound. But she could also be up to tricks, and one had to be watchful not to accept at face value everything she told you.

Altogether, a grande dame, a lady to care for and about. I know I did.

John Prince (1922–), a Virginian and a graduate of the University of North Carolina and the University of Missouri, was a friend of Marcella Winslow, through whom he met Katherine Anne Porter in the early 1950s. Prince, who had studied at the Cordon Bleu in Paris and worked in a catering business in Washington, DC, shared an interest in cooking with Porter, who had taken a few classes at the Cordon Bleu herself. He often praised Porter's cooking talents, and Prince and his wife, Catherine, frequently shared dinners and parties with Porter after she rented a house in Georgetown on Q Street, not far from the Princes' house on Twenty-ninth Street. Between 1959 and 1964 Porter and the Princes were good friends, and the Princes helped her in a number of practical ways that included finding an accountant for her (Harry Perry) and escorting her to social events such as the surrey races at Foxhall to celebrate her seventieth birthday (1960) and the party Atlantic–Little, Brown threw in 1962 to celebrate the publication of *Ship of Fools*. They also became well acquainted with her friends Glenway Wescott, Monroe Wheeler, and Eudora Welty. The friendship between Porter and the Princes unraveled in 1964, after she reneged on the purchase of a Georgetown house that John Prince, who was working for a real estate firm at the time, had brokered with difficulty. When he heard that Porter had blamed him for the financial and legal mess she created, he wrote up an account of the sequence of events that led to the end of the friendship and placed it with his and his wife's papers at the University of Maryland, College Park.

Source: John Prince, untitled and unpublished reminiscence, Papers of John and Catherine Prince, Special Collections, University of Maryland, College Park.

In the fall of 1963, Mina Curtiss put her Georgetown house up for sale.[13] It was a handsome, restored brick house, and she had spent a great deal of money on it—including the putting-up of eighteenth century English paneling in the drawing room. I was given an exclusive listing until February 1, 1964, for the sale of the house. Mrs. Curtiss placed an asking price of $114,000 on her house, and because of this high price, it didn't sell.

Katherine Anne returned to Washington from her second European trip [1962–63] and settled down at the Hotel Jefferson in a tiny apartment. She came to dinner with Catherine and me and told us that she was going to buy a house in New Jersey near Glenway Wescott. We told her that we thought it was a fine idea. However, a few days later she said that she had given up the idea because "too many people had gotten into the act."

I had thought for some time that the Curtiss house would be perfect for KAP. She had been buying crystal chandeliers and large pieces of elaborate furniture that would require large, ornate rooms. This house had these rooms, a delightful private garden, and a fine pink bedroom with a small kitchen unit outside. (Katherine Anne had fallen twice down the steps of her house on Q Street when she got up in the night to go down and get something to eat. I thought having a kitchen outside her bedroom would stop this. Also, there was room for an elevator to be installed when she could no longer make the stairs.)

I discussed this with Catherine. I didn't really want to get into any business arrangement with her, and we didn't know if we really wanted her across the street. We had been called many times when she was sick on Q Street. I had done most of her banking for her, and we used to take her food and cook for her when she wasn't well. I knew that there would be many such occasions again, but I felt that she needed to get into a house of her own, with her own things around her, if she was ever going to write again. Catherine and I agreed that I should show her the house—only if she asked me to find her a house.

In December she did ask me. She wanted me to look into a house she had passed in Georgetown for rent. The rental was $650 a month. I told her I thought that such a large rental was foolish, and that while I had hesitations I was going to show her one house for sale. I explained that the price was far too high; that I knew she could not afford $114,000; but I thought she could get it for possibly $90,000.

I took her in the house (there was an H. A. Gill sign outside the door), and she fell in love with it. She said, "Honey, you know my weakness," and later she said, "Don't try to save me from myself."

I explained that I had an exclusive listing until February 1, and that I would know if there were any offers on it. I also explained that I thought $20,000 in cash would buy the house, and that monthly payments including principal, interest, and taxes would be under $500 a month. Also, I told her that the interest and taxes would be tax deductible, which would help her $3000 a month income.[14] She had said that she could easily pay $500 a month. (She was paying $583 a month for rent at the time.) Katherine Anne said that she could get the $20,000 from Little, Brown by threatening to go to Hollywood as a consultant for *Ship of Fools*.[15]

After this talk on the sidewalk in front of the house, I never initiated another discussion about the house. She called Catherine several times and talked about it. On the day before New Year's Eve she called Catherine again, and she said, "Honey, I think I want that little old house." She said that Little, Brown would give her the down payment if she could get the house for $90,000.

We picked her up on New Year's Eve and took her to the Biddles' for a party.[16] All during the party she kept after me about the house. She wanted me to call Mina Curtiss and see if she could have the house for $90,000. I told her that the best way was to sign a contract offering that amount and then see if it would be accepted. She didn't want to do this. She called again on New Year's Day, and I reluctantly agreed to call Mrs. Curtiss on January 2.

I called the next morning and talked to Mrs. Curtiss in New York. I told her that I had a verbal offer for her house from Katherine Anne Porter for $90,000. She said at once, "She can't afford my house." I told her that Katherine Anne had made approximately one million dollars from her book and that she said that her publisher would give her the down payment. Mina Curtiss said that she would consider it. She called back in a half hour to say that she would accept if she got the money at once. She was buying an apartment in New York, and she didn't want to sell securities. I told her that we would make it a thirty-day settlement, and she agreed.

I called Katherine Anne and told her that she could have the house if she settled in thirty days, and she said, "Then I can't have it. I can't get the money that soon." She started to go to pieces over the phone, and I told her to calm down and that I would come over at three o'clock and we would talk about it. She agreed.

Mr. Gill, my broker, offered to hold her down payment check for twenty days if she had money surely coming in. However, I went over to see Katherine Anne at the Jefferson that afternoon with the idea of calling the whole thing off.

She was waiting for me, and I was amazed to find her calm and collected. As I came in, I said, "Katherine Anne, nobody is trying to force you to do anything you don't want to do." She then said that she had made up her mind that she wanted the house, and the only problem was money. She said, "Honey, I haven't been telling you the truth. Little, Brown has said that they will advance the money on a preface I am writing for an anthology, but it isn't $20,000; it's $15,000." She said that she had wanted it to be $20,000 and then imagined it was. She showed me a letter from Little, Brown stating that they would send her $15,000 as soon as they received the preface.[17]

We had a long talk to try to work out some way for her to get the house. I told her that Mr. Gill would hold the deposit check for twenty days. She asked who he was, and I explained that he was my broker. She said, "I thought you were on your own," and I said no; I was a salesman for the firm of H. A. Gill and Son.

She said that the preface was almost done and that it was only a preface, not a story, and she could easily finish it in two weeks—if only people would let her alone. She also said that she would be getting money in and she could make up the other $5,000. But she said that she couldn't go over $90,000. Also, she was paying $500 a month at the Jefferson; so she could make the payments easily.

I told her that we could draw up a contract contingent upon either a $70,000 loan (twenty years) or a $65,000 loan from the bank and a $5,000 second mortgage taken back by Mrs. Curtiss.

She said that she would give me a $15,000 check for down payment then. I told her she didn't have to make it that large. She said, "No, I know I am getting this much." She wrote a check payable to H. A. Gill and Son for $15,000 and handed it to me. I promised again that I would hold the check for twenty days. I then said that I would go back to the office and write up a contract and bring it back for her to sign that afternoon.

I drove back to the office and handed the check to Mrs. Nancy Volckmann, our sales manager. I remember saying, "I'll regret this 1000 times before I'm through."

Mrs. Volckmann wrote up an H. A. Gill contract for the sale of the house. She made the contract contingent upon a loan, and I drove back to the Jefferson with it. KAP was expecting me. She was in high spirits and said she had just called Seymour Lawrence in Boston and that he was delighted that she was buying the house. She wanted to sign the contracts at once.

There was a desk in her room, jutting out from the wall, and I made her sit down across from me. I then went carefully through the contract and explained it fully to her. She appeared to understand it all, and so I had her sign four copies. I then signed them and put them in my pocket.

Next, I gave her a lecture on extravagance. (She was having her emerald ring reset with diamonds, and she had just bought a large emerald pin for several thousand dollars. Also in one morning in Venice she spent $2,000 on glass—including a glass block with colored glass fish in it.) She said, "I know. I'll be good. I'll send these back," and she went to her dresser and took out two long strands of pearls she'd just gotten for $800.

I told her that I really thought that the house was the best thing for her and I left. I sent the contracts off to Mrs. Curtiss that night, and I felt that everything was settled. Mrs. Curtiss signed the contracts and returned three copies.

I talked to Katherine Anne several times that week, and she seemed bright and cheerful. The following Monday was Twelfth Night, and we had invited her for a roast goose. We had asked three other people, and Katherine Anne called and asked if we could include Rhea Johnson, the man who lived in her basement apartment on Q Street, and we did.

When she arrived on Monday, I gave her a copy of the contract. We had a gay evening, and after dinner, we all went across the street to see that house Katherine Anne had bought. She seemed delighted with it and kept asking people if they didn't think it was pretty.

I didn't talk to her again after that. I was busy with another house, and we had requested an appraiser for Riggs National Bank to inspect her house to see about the loan.

On Friday night, while we had dinner guests, the door bell rang, and I was handed a Special Delivery letter. It was from KAP, announcing that she was giving up the house. Saturday morning I called John Gill and Mrs. Volckmann, and we met at the office. I gave them the letter and asked if they thought there was any way to cancel the contract. John Gill said, "No."

I said that I knew what had happened: the pressure of a deadline had come up, so she was running away. Once when Seymour Lawrence came down from Boston with orders not to return without some promised pages of *Ship of Fools,* KAP locked herself in her room and refused to see him. She claimed that she was being persecuted. She could finish if "they would only leave me alone." Catherine and I took her to the airport the next morning to fly to California, and once she left the house, she was gay and relaxed.

John Gill decided that the thing to do was to tell her that we could get an extension of time. He called the Jefferson, and her room didn't answer. I called Seymour Lawrence in Boston and told him what had happened. He said that the preface was almost finished and that arrangements had been made for the money as soon as it was received. He agreed that she probably had panicked because of the deadline and felt that an extension would help. He also said that he was going to see her in New York the next week at the opening of the play *Dylan* with Alec Guinness. [. . .]

I decided to call Glenway Wescott to see if she was at his brother's estate in New Jersey. Glenway said that she wasn't due there until the next week. She was at the Jefferson accepting only long distance calls. He said that he would be talking to her again, and I told him I had been trying to reach her, and that I would leave a letter at the desk for her. John Gill, meanwhile, had tried to reach her lawyer at Little, Brown in Boston.

The next day was Sunday, and it was snowing. I wrote a letter to Katherine Anne, telling her that I had tried, but was unable to cancel her contract. I said that it was out of my hands. However, I said, Mr. Gill thought he would be able to get her an extension and that I would do anything I could to help. I left this at the desk of the Jefferson Hotel for her. I never had a reply, and I never wrote her or tried to call her again.

On Monday, Mr. Gill talked to Mr. Thornhill in Boston and told him the situation. Since no one could reach Katherine Anne, Mr. Gill called Mina Curtiss and read her the letter. She was not surprised. She said that Katherine Anne had gone through life breaking contracts, and she was going to teach her a lesson. She wanted money from her. Mrs. Curtiss referred John Gill to her Boston lawyer. The next day, Mrs. Curtiss called to say that a friend had gone to the opening of *Dylan* and sat just behind Katherine Anne. She heard KAP tell someone, "Oh, I've given up the Georgetown house."

Mrs. Curtiss' Boston lawyer referred the case to the Washington firm of Covington and Burling. From this point on, the case was handled by lawyers. These lawyers insisted that the check be cashed. I objected because I had given my word that it would be held for twenty days. I was overruled. The lawyers for Mrs. Curtiss said that she had lost that consideration when she cancelled everything and refused to communicate with us. Mr. Gill took the check down to the bank and put it through. It bounced and was sent back marked "Exceeds drawer's available balance in checking account." In the meantime, the house was appraised for the full price.

We didn't hear anything from Katherine Anne until the day that had been set for settlement. I was sent down to the title company to be on hand. When I got there, I was told that Miss Porter's lawyer had asked for an extension.

Mr. Thomas Wadden of Edward Bennett Williams' office called the Gill office that afternoon and said that Katherine Anne had retained them. I told him the entire story, and later I told the same office's Peter Taft the story. Mr. Taft said that Katherine Anne was scared. I told him that I was sorry. We had tried to help her, but now it was completely out of our hands.

Several weeks later, John Gill was called by Covington and Burling and asked if we would give up all claim to commission. He said that if we did this, Katherine Anne and Mina Curtiss would come to a mutual settlement. I agreed at once, and John Gill agreed.

When the release came, some weeks later, I signed it to end the whole situation. However, had I known what Katherine Anne's claims against me were, I should have refused and let the whole story be brought out in court.

41 / Michael Scott

Michael Scott, a former student at Loras College, in Dubuque, Iowa, was working in Washington, DC, in the summer of 1964 when he met Katherine Anne Porter through his former professor Raymond Roseliep (1917–83), with whom Porter had been corresponding since 1960. A diocesan priest and poet, Roseliep seemed to have an amatory interest in Porter that she did not return.[18]

Source: Michael Scott, "A Classic Manner," *The Spokesman* 63 (Spring 1965–66): 19–22.

An evening with Katherine Anne Porter is something like a moveable feast: you not only remember it, but the experience grows and becomes an image of reality which is both true and beautiful.

Father Roseliep, my English professor at Loras College in Dubuque, was spending his summer as Georgetown University's poet-in-residence, and I was working for the U.S. Department of Agriculture. We were enjoying lunch at the 1789, the campus restaurant and pub, and were having a grand time deciding upon the week's activities when he posed the question: would I be able to escort Katherine Anne Porter to his poetry reading the coming Friday evening? I was taken back a bit, but there wasn't much I could say, except yes.

The humid Friday in Washington's impossible summer arrived. As I left for Katherine Anne Porter's house, I tried to imagine what she would be like. I entertained myself with various visions, oblivious to the fact that the car needed gas. I drove along the tree-lined streets of Washington, a city in which getting lost seems to be a habit with me. As I turned a corner, the car sputtered, choked, and coasted down an incline and stopped against the curb. As it happened, Katherine Anne Porter's house was only a few blocks from where the car had quit, but this wasn't going to help me get her to the poetry reading.

The house nestled on a corner lot. It was large and impressive, in the Elizabethan style, with a sharply gabled roof and panelled sides. The entryway was hidden, like a heavy monastic door, beyond the wide stone steps. I walked up the steps, lifted the brass door handle, let it fall, and waited. It wasn't very long before the door opened, and there stood my hostess in a dazzling white evening gown. Her smile was gracious and her voice had a particular friendliness which set me at ease. She invited me in, and as we began a tour of her house, we got acquainted.

She didn't hesitate to tell me about her paintings, imports, keepsakes, and antiques. When we went into her library, she pointed out the fifteenth-century walnut table which was centered in the room. There was a fireplace green with age on one wall, and her shelves of books scaled the walls around the rest of the room. As we walked into the dining room and living area, she switched on the gold and silver chandelier, which flooded the walls with light. The room seemed very dignified. I remember now that she had bought quite a few things in Venice, and the chandelier was one of her prized imports. There were many little wall lamps located around the room, and Katherine Anne went about turning them on, assuring me that she enjoyed the effort.

As we walked into the entryway, she ruffled the copper tuft of hair on her statue of Eros, the god of love. She took her wrap from the chair, and I suddenly realized that I had forgotten about the car. Abruptly, I blurted out the difficulty with more than a little embarrassment. I expected the bit of sympathy which I got. Katherine Anne made light of it and called a service station. I left to get the car and arrived back at the house within a few minutes, and we were on our way with only ten minutes to spare.

We arrived at the Georgetown University Union at precisely five minutes to eight. I parked, opened the door of the car and helped Katherine Anne onto the sidewalk. All the while she chatted merrily about diplomacy and the punctuality required for social affairs in Europe. As we entered the large double doors of the union, all eyes focused on Katherine Anne. Her white hair was lustrous in the light. She smiled and moved gracefully, stopping for slight moments only to gather her thoughts. Katherine Anne seemed to accept everything within her sight, and she reminded me of a wind that swiftly takes up paper scraps into the sky. She talked of the small child sleeping in the foyer, the woman resting in a chair, the blooms lining the globe in the center of the lobby. And as she spoke, she revealed the sensitive, detailed workings of her mind. Katherine Anne radiated a genuine love for all that she saw and knew. She was the flower who had drawn the sun and was now glowing and could not help being seen. She smiled and chatted simply.

Once in the Hall of Nations lecture-room, we sat toward the front with the others who had gathered for the reading. The highlight that evening was a sixty-one line poem Father Roseliep had just written for Katherine Anne. He approached the title with hesitancy. All was silent as he read. I felt as a child next to this lady who had "mingled on deck with lovers and fools." While he read, she responded as a lady, with tears. She sat delicately on her chair and watched, almost in a trance. "That was lovely," she said to me, and as he began to answer from the lectern, she interrupted, "Father, that makes me so very happy, thank you."

When the reading was over and the listeners had gone, we slipped over to the 1789 for lobster and wine.

The host led us to a table in the middle of the dim, colonial room. The atmosphere was old and inviting, with a cold fireplace and a small statue of a young slave offering a tray. The parchment menus crackled as we talked over them.

It would be trite to say that she is charming—many people seem to be just that but are usually bored and boring. Katherine Anne betrays a sincerity which lets her rise above the stereotyped image of a literary personality. She gives the first impression of being vain, but this soon disappears, and you know it is really a genuine brand of humility. She is approachable and, in a way, untouchable in her simple but classic manner.

Katherine Anne's frail fingers lowered the coffee cup from her lips. She laughed at our jokes and told a few of her own, always making sure that everyone enjoyed them. The conversation was spontaneous. Plumbers, paperboys, gardeners, Napoleon and his Courvoisier moved into the talk and somehow moved out as quickly as they appeared. She spoke of the history behind her gabled house in Washington, her family, and her fabulous emeralds which glimmered softly in the midnight light of 1789.

It was Friday and we all settled for lobster in one form or another. Katherine Anne said she liked anything from the sea and Father Roseliep pretended he did, having always claimed a Protestant stomach.

We walked to the car and then drove home. As Father and I escorted her to the door, she insisted that we come in and have "one for the road." We sat at the walnut table in the library, sipping wine, and chatting about war, college, jewels, books, love, and just people. Delicate yellow light streamed down the shelves of books and onto the table where Katherine Anne presided. She spoke quietly and continuously, almost statically. Leaning on our palms, Father and I listened intently to this woman who had certainly concerned herself with all of man's suffering, foolishness, love, and hate.

Before we left, Katherine Anne autographed my copy of *The Leaning Tower*. I remembered how she had graciously signed a menu for our waiter as we left the 1789.

She wrote in the book a favorite passage from Pindar which at the time she didn't quite remember correctly. But a few days later, I received in the mail a correction of the passage.

Dear Michael:

I didn't quite remember Bowra's translation from Pindar after all—I'll type it for you—

Beauty which creates
All sweet delights for men
Brings honour at will,
And makes the false seem true
Time and again.

42 / Enrique Hank Lopez

Enrique Hank Lopez (1920–85), editor, lawyer, and writer, is believed to be the first Hispanic American to graduate from Harvard Law School. He edited the Hispanic literary journal *Diálogos,* served as a consultant to the Ford Foundation, and promoted bilingual education for children. His books include *Afro-6* (1969) and *The Harvard Mystique* (1979) as well as *Conversations with Katherine Anne Porter.*

Source: Enrique Hank Lopez, *Conversations with Katherine Anne Porter: Refugee from Indian Creek* (Boston: Little, Brown, 1981), xiii–xviii.

In January of 1974, just a few months before her eighty-fourth birthday, Katherine Anne Porter bought her own coffin from a mail-order cabinet shop in Arizona.[19]

She had once asked me to buy her a plain simple Mexican coffin with rope handles, the kind she had often seen at peasant funerals in rural Mexico. "I'm bound to die fairly soon," she told me. "And I don't want to be buried in one of those garish overpriced caskets that funeral directors get rich on. So I'd be much obliged if you'd get me a plain wooden box with some good strong rope for handles."

When I resisted her suggestion, she smilingly accused me of being excessively squeamish and later asked her nephew to buy the coffin. When he also declined, she somehow located an advertisement in a mail-order catalogue and forthwith ordered a fairly satisfactory coffin.[20] Although it wasn't as plain and simple as she hoped it would be—the joints were too smoothly sanded and the long brass hinges were a bit too ornate—the six-foot pine box was ready to be painted Mexican style.[21] Having provided the coffin with a winding sheet of fine Belgian linen, which she had bought while teaching in Liège, she propped it against the rear wall of her closet and calmly turned her attention to more immediate concerns.

Most people would say this was a ghoulish thing to do, but it was actually quite logical and uniquely sane. Her entire life was unique to the rarest degree, unique and suspenseful. Indeed, as one follows the often incredible twists and turns of a long career filled with heartbreak and triumph, high drama and low comedy, one is inevitably reminded of Mme. Du Barry's final words as she was led to the guillotine: "My life is incredible. I don't believe a word of it!"[22]

During our first conversation in the lobby of a Mexico City hotel, Katherine Anne Porter told me about a Nicaraguan poet she had met in the early twenties. "He was one of the most evil men I've ever known," she said. "An absolute scoundrel, who thought nothing of seducing the teenage daughter of his best friend and then bragging about it. Yet there was something strangely compelling about Salomón de la Selva,[23] a certain sinister magnetism that made him hard to resist. He was one of three such men that I've known in my life. . . ."

But just as I was about to ask her the names of the other two scoundrels, someone interrupted our conversation, and she didn't tell me about them until nine months later.

Miss Porter made several such elliptical remarks that first afternoon—tantalizing half-finished references to marijuana, revolution, sex, literary vendettas in New York, the trials of Ezra Pound, political intrigues in Mexico, and the horrible nightmare tragedy of Hart Crane—touching upon each subject with just enough personal involvement to pique the interest of even the most detached listener. Consequently, since I had instantly become a very "attached" listener, I came away from the initial interview feeling intensely frustrated, each of my carefully prepared questions having provoked a chain reaction of numerous other questions that (most probably) would never be answered. She herself, in a disturbingly speculative and self-mocking manner, had posed most of the queries, as if she regarded her own life as a perpetual enigma.

"There are no limits to this woman," I told one of my colleagues. "She's known everyone from Diego Rivera to Ernest Hemingway,[24] and there's very little she has not experienced."

But there was something strangely sad and lonely in the way she lived. She had been so restless and so chronically dissatisfied. She had lived in at least fifty different places—in barren rented rooms, half-furnished apartments, a rented house now and then—moving at least once a year, sometimes two or three times in a single year, always in wistful pursuit of something permanent and stable. And in her restless wandering, she had been married three times and lived with four or five lovers,[25] perhaps unable or at least unwilling to form any permanent attachments. Yet she had a profound and deeply personal commitment to her career as an artist, a commitment that was never abandoned.

I first met Miss Porter at a coffee-and-rum reception following her lecture at the Instituto Cultural Norteamericano in the winter of 1964. In fact, the rum-and-Coke was the first thing we talked about.

Holding a rum-and-Coke someone had given her, she took one sip and said,

"This is much too sweet. Don't they have any bourbon and plain branch water around here?"

"Whiskey is too expensive in Mexico," I said. "This *instituto* is sponsored by the U.S. Embassy, and they always economize at these cultural functions."

"Now, isn't that typical of our State Department," she said with a wry smile. "They'll spend millions to back some stupid dictator, but when it comes to something like this, they give you cheap rum instead of good bourbon."

Setting aside her highball, she took coffee instead. It was then that I introduced myself as co-editor of *Diálogos,* a Mexican literary magazine, and promptly asked if I might interview her for our special issue on American writers.

"I'll do anything for Mexico," she said. "I've always considered it my second home."

The following afternoon we met in a remote corner of the mausoleumlike lobby of the Hotel del Prado, my bulky tape recorder snuggled under a long narrow coffee table in front of a leather couch, where we sat almost shoulder to shoulder. I had partially concealed the microphone behind a bulbous red vase filled with colorful paper flowers.

"I'm glad you've got all that machinery out of sight," she said. "I always get a bit self-conscious when I see a tape spinning round and round."

"I feel the same way," I said, reaching down to adjust the volume so as to catch the full resonance of her soft, mellow, slightly accented voice.

She was wearing a stylish pale green dress and a single strand of pearls, and although her hair was chalk-white and wispy as gossamer, she looked more like sixty than seventy-four. Her clear blue eyes were especially youthful, now gently amused by some human foible, then coolly analytical a few moments later.

"Where shall we start?" I asked.

"Why not start at the middle—and go backwards and forwards," she said. "I guess the middle happened right here in Mexico."

So we talked for nearly four hours, my questions ranging from her adventures in revolutionary Mexico to her early childhood in Texas, to Germany as the Nazis were coming to power, to Paris, "where Gertrude Stein was throwing her weight around," to the Greenwich Village of the frail Edna St. Vincent Millay, and "grumpy" Edmund Wilson, to the many other places where she lived during what she later called "the restless pilgrimage of my soul." But every morsel of remembrance was but a mere hint of her come-what-may life-style, her perpetual face-to-face exposure to all kinds of direct experience. That was her phrase: direct experience. "I didn't want my life filtered through other people. I had to see and feel for myself."

About nine months later a small portion of that interview—written by me and cross-checked by her—was published simultaneously in two magazines, the

English version in *Harper's* and the Spanish version in *Diálogos*.[26] Subsequently, while in New York negotiating certain matters for my Mexican law firm, I phoned her home in Washington, and she immediately invited me to dinner. "I'll fix you the best Mexican meal you've ever had." Then an hour later she called me back and said, "It's silly for you to fly down just for dinner. Why don't you come before noon, so that I can serve you a perfectly mediocre lunch. Then you'll be sure to appreciate the *chiles rellenos* and *mole poblano* that I'm planning for dinner."

Needless to say, I accepted without a moment's hesitation, and we had a marvelous twelve-hour conversation interspersed with excellent food (it was clam chowder for lunch) and a fine sourmash bourbon "with just a smidgen of branch water." She was one of the most engaging raconteurs I'd ever known, wickedly humorous at times and then profoundly philosophical. She seemed so alive and expressive, it was difficult to believe she was fast approaching eighty.

But I also learned that she was no longer writing, that she had not published any fiction since *Ship of Fools,* not even a brief short story. Keenly aware of the writer's block which had always plagued her, I was soon convinced she would never write an autobiography, that no one would ever read of the incredible people and events she had been telling me about in such vivid detail. Several later visits, all of them replete with often-hilarious personal anecdotes and remarkably candid self-analysis, further confirmed my impression that she was "talking" her autobiography rather than writing it. To say the least, that was a disheartening thought.

Then one evening, as we were having an after-dinner brandy with Barbara and Norbert Schlei[27] at the Rive Gauche restaurant, she turned to Norbert and said, "I want you to know that Hank is relieving me of the responsibility of ever having to write again."

Flattered but also puzzled by her remark, I later asked her, "What exactly did you mean, Katherine Anne?"

"Well," she said, pursing her lips and frowning slightly, "I've hesitated to ask you, Hank, because I know how busy you've been with your international law practice—but I'm going to be selfish anyway. As you no doubt realize, I won't be able to write my autobiography. I'm too old and too tired. But I'd like you to write a biography about me."

"Of course," I said without a moment's hesitation. "But I'll have to tape record some additional interviews."

"We can talk as much as you want," she said. "But let's keep the recording machine out of sight."

Happily accepting that condition, I then somewhat hesitantly said that I preferred not to write an "approved" or "official" biography. "From what you've already told me, you've been involved in considerable controversy," I said. "So I'd like to explore—as freely as possible—what others have said about you and your involvement in those controversies."

"Fair enough," she said, an amused glint in her eyes. "I wouldn't want you to write one of those mushy worshipful biographies, which no one would believe anyway—certainly no one who's really known me. But there is one favor I'd like to ask. . . . I'd prefer that you not publish your book 'til after my death. It's bound to be controversial, and I'm just too old and weary to deal with any more conflicts."

Quite obviously, I readily agreed. And within six weeks I abandoned my office in Mexico City and temporarily moved to Washington, DC, to undertake a series of daily interviews that lasted more than a month, later supplementing them with additional weekend sessions after I had permanently established a new home in New York City.[28] Most of our talks took place in the comfortable tastefully furnished living room of her two-story brick house in one of the more fashionable areas of the capital. But for reasons I could never fathom, she seemed to save some of her choicest stories for the dinner hour, which naturally enhanced the flavor of the superb dinners she had prepared. I've never eaten better food, nor enjoyed more fascinating conversation.

"I'm telling you things I've never told anyone—not even to myself," she said one afternoon. "But I guess there's no point in holding back at this late stage."[29]

William Raymond Wilkins (1928–) grew up in the redwood country of northern California. After receiving a B.A. from Humboldt State College in 1951, he joined the U.S. Navy, where he eventually rose to the rank of lieutenant commander. In 1952 he married Fern Stahl, and during his navy career the couple and their two children, David, born in 1954, and Robin, born in 1957, traveled widely. He served twice at National Security Headquarters in Maryland before retiring in 1974. After he left Porter's employment in 1977, he worked for the assistant superintendent of the Maryland School for the Blind and then as a volunteer for the University of Maryland Libraries.

Source: William R. Wilkins, personal interviews with Darlene Harbour Unrue, 27 May 1995, Baltimore, and 13 August 1997, College Park, Maryland.

The day in early November 1968 when my wife, Fern, and I met Katherine Anne Porter was the saddest day of our lives. Our fourteen-year-old son, David, had been killed by a drunk driver several days earlier, and Bob Beach, Fern's cousin, was driving us home from David's burial at the Arlington National Cemetery. Our daughter, Robin, and my sister Eleanor, who had come from California, were with us.

At the time, Bob was employed by the University of Maryland as presidential assistant for university relations, and among his duties was that of liaison between Katherine Anne Porter and the university, which had given her an honorary doctorate in 1966 and to which she had donated many of her manuscripts, letters, and personal belongings. He asked whether we minded if he stopped by her apartment to drop off some papers. Of course we didn't mind. He went in and came back out quickly to tell us that nothing would do Miss Porter but that we come in and have lunch with her and her other guest, who happened that day to be Glenway Wescott. It was an especially thoughtful and gracious gesture. Her sympathy and kindness touched us deeply.

After that day we saw Katherine Anne occasionally either with Bob or by ourselves when Bob asked us to stop by her apartment to pick up or drop off something. In 1976, a year or so after I retired from the navy and was looking around for something interesting to occupy my time, Bob called to say that Katherine Anne needed an assistant who could help her with a variety of tasks. He thought it would be the perfect job for me. "Would you be willing to undertake it?" he asked.

I called Katherine Anne and said, "Are you looking for help?"

She said cheerfully, "Yes, I need all kinds of help. Can you start Monday?"

I said yes and never regretted it.

I stayed on with her for a little over a year, and I was with her most days from nine in the morning until four or five in the afternoon and sometimes beyond. She dictated letters that I typed up and mailed, I answered the phone and took messages, and I tried to help her sort through her boxes and baskets of papers and photographs that were stacked all over the apartment. I helped her put together her memoir of her participation in the Sacco and Vanzetti affair.[30] During the fourteen months I spent with her, I also worked on a cookbook with her (we got as far as corn pone and mint juleps) and her biography of Cotton Mather, trying to combine her notes and previously published pieces into a coherent whole.[31] It is one of my regrets that this was never completed.

When I let myself into her apartment in the mornings, or when Fern went with me to help with the shopping, Katherine Anne would sing out, "Coffee's on the stove." And then, "Come on in here, Baby" (or "Babies," as the case might be), "there's kissin' goin' on."

Fern, Robin, and I became Katherine Anne's friends. We took her to movies (*Snow White* was one of her favorites), introduced her to a nearby farmers' market, and escorted her to gala functions such as a memorable one at the Jewish Center that should have been a delightful occasion for her—but wasn't, because the crowd was large and she felt penned in. I also suspected that she was frustrated because she wasn't so much the center of attention as usual, despite the fact that her friends Robert Penn Warren, Eleanor Clark, and Monroe Wheeler were there and greeted her affectionately.

Although we weren't present at her eighty-second birthday party hosted by the University of Maryland, we heard about the event from Bob Beach. In the middle of the party, which Katherine Anne was enjoying immensely, loud and persistent sirens interrupted the festivities. After someone went to get a radio, Katherine Anne and the celebrants learned that George Wallace,[32] who was running for president, had been shot during a campaign rally at a nearby shopping mall. With all her guests hovered around the radio listening to the coverage of the assassination attempt, Katherine Anne's birthday party was ruined. "I never did like Wallace," she announced.

Katherine Anne was outspoken about other persons she liked and disliked, whether politicians or other writers. She adored Eudora Welty. "She is one of the saintliest persons I know," she told me. But of Norman Mailer[33] and others who wrote what she considered gratuitous filth, she said, "Honey, everybody has a bathroom, and everybody has a bedroom in his house, but I haven't the slightest interest in what they do there."

Katherine Anne loved to have people around her and to entertain them. She often insisted that we have dinner with her. Sometimes Bob, or another friend, was included. These dinners almost always took place in one of the two kitchens in her double apartment, the one with a bar that functioned as an informal dining room. "We got an eatin' kitchen and a drinkin' kitchen," she would say, "and we're havin' dinner in the drinkin' one." When she entertained more formally in the dining room, it was always elegant. Her dinners were superb, for she was a wonderful cook and proud of it. She referred to herself as a "Cordon Bleu dropout" since she had taken a course at the school in Paris but earned no certificate. She said she learned to cook a boar there.

She had her own ideas and techniques when it came to preparing food. "You'll have to explain hamburger to me," she said. "I haven't the faintest notion what hamburger is." She boiled down broth, especially chicken and lamb, and then strained it through four layers of cheesecloth. She called it "sop" and froze small portions of it for soup stock and other uses.

It was apparent that she loved to cook. Almost every single day I was there she would go to the kitchen at eleven o'clock, no matter how bad she felt or how depressed she was. Cooking seemed to cheer her up, and if there were guests for lunch, all the better.

She always poured good wine at her dinners, whether formal or informal, and she loved to take an afternoon break and serve champagne to me and anyone else who had dropped in. If someone demurred, she would say, "You can't NOT take it, my dear." And she would talk and talk, telling one story after the other. I remember one she told about an event at the Museum of Modern Art attended by Mrs. Rockefeller, among other members of affluent high society. Mrs. Rockefeller, who was standing by Katherine Anne, said to one of the hostesses, "How lovely. Did you plan it?" "No, it just happened," said the woman sarcastically. "Oh, I know," said Mrs. Rockefeller, "like a dividend."[34]

Katherine Anne was as proud of the furnishings and art pieces in her big apartment as she was of her cooking. She had a big chandelier that she didn't think sparkled enough. I took it to a specialist in Georgetown, who took it apart and cleaned it. She was delighted and enhanced it further by hanging on it a Christmas ornament Fern had made, probably a thank-you to me for restoring the sparkle. Her guest rooms were gorgeous, as was her own bedroom. Right across from her bed was a dresser with a mirror and a picture of two little cherubs with plump bottoms. "I've had that since 1919," she told me. "In the hospital during the influenza epidemic I thought I was dying of thirst. And then I saw that picture and thought it a good omen. I asked for it, and I've kept it ever since."

Until her first major stroke early in 1977 I found Katherine Anne merry, funloving, and witty. She had a great sense of humor, although sometimes barbed and aimed at one of her acquaintances or a former friend. At one of the events in her honor at the University of Maryland, her then current physician showed up in a tuxedo with a bright yellow cummerbund and bowtie. "He looks like a five-hundred-pound canary," Katherine Anne whispered to me. After one of her dinner parties, Fern asked whether she could help Katherine Anne clear the table. "No," Katherine Anne replied, "that's what that wretch does in the mornings," referring to a maid who found it impossible to please her.

Her standards might have been difficult for household help to satisfy, but she generally wanted to please others, even those who tried to take advantage of her. One man in a small town in Mississippi sent her a copy of *Ship of Fools* and asked her to sign it and return it to him. She did that, and soon two more copies arrived with the same request. She complied again, but when three copies arrived with the same appeal, it was clear that the man, who owned a bookstore, was selling the autographed books. When I took the letter to her, I jokingly said, "You do whatever you like, ma'am, as long as you say no." Immediately came "Awww, Honey, shouldn't we make the gent'man happy?" When I suggested that he was up to no good, she said devilishly, "Oh well, in that case, Honey, write him a polite little note and tell him to wash his hands and face, comb his hair, and go to hell."

She was generous with almost everyone, including me and my family. Right before Robin was married, Katherine Anne took out a big rope of pearls and gave them to her. Fern said, "Oh, Katherine Anne, we can't accept that," but Katherine Anne dismissed the protest. "Honey, every little girl has to have a strand of pearls." We had to stop expressing admiration for things in her apartment because she would say, "Honey, you just take that." We did accept, however, on her insistence, the peacock feathers Flannery O'Connor had given her. (We later donated them to the University of Maryland.)

When the first major stroke occurred in February of 1977, Fern and I visited the hospital as much as we were allowed, and I did what I could to keep her apartment orderly and her correspondence current so she could make the transition home as smoothly as possible. I wrote to her friends to tell them that although she was seriously ill I could see that she was fighting. Outwardly I was guardedly optimistic, but for the next several weeks I privately wondered whether she was trying to survive or to die. When the doctors finally agreed that she could return home, it was clear she would need around-the-clock nursing care. She was partially paralyzed, and she fluctuated between cheerfulness and paranoia. Sometimes she blamed me (along with her nephew Paul Porter and her lawyer, Barrett Prettyman) for her condition. Other times she told me how grateful she was for my help. With the second major stroke in April, the part of her brain that controlled speech was severely affected. Her distrust of many of us who were most concerned about her intensified. After she had a seizure near the end of April, I felt as though I was inexplicably and permanently on her bad side, despite the fact that her rages and firings were interspersed with apologies and pleas to return. Then in May there seemed to be a miraculous remission. It was if some crisis had passed and Katherine Anne was her old self. She began to dictate notes again and was interested in her business affairs. While I had no doubt that there would again be periods of distrust, I felt that if there were happy spaces, too, I would hang on and do all that I could to alleviate her suffering. I wanted to see her through this heartbreaking time in her life. Barely a week later, however, she turned on me with such a vengeance that nothing I could say in protest penetrated her distrust. Although I knew it was the illness, I also knew that nothing was to be gained by trying to reason with her. Regretfully, I bowed to the circumstances and left her employment. I wrote to Toni Willison, her friend for many years and one of those whom I had kept abreast of Katherine Anne's progress and setbacks, "It is *not* our Katherine Anne at all, but a frightened, frustrated little lady who just cannot command death to come soon enough."

I wasn't bitter. As I said to Toni, "How could I be? While her mind was her own, we shared respect for one another and a pleasant affection and I know in my heart that she did not dismiss me from her mind. So, actually it is less hurt than just regret not to be allowed to help as long as I could, to provide the affection and kindness which are so therapeutic. But, I also firmly believe that we interact in one another's lives for purposes we may not know about."

44 / Kathleen Feeley

Kathleen Feeley, School Sisters of Notre Dame (1929–), author of *Flannery O'Connor: Voice of the Peacock* and numerous articles and book reviews, received her Ph.D. in English from Rutgers University. She was president of the College of Notre Dame of Maryland for twenty-one years. Subsequently, she received two Fulbright teaching awards, one in India for six months, and one in China for a year. She was visiting professor at the Catholic University of Australia for a year, teaching in Brisbane, Canberra, and Melbourne. Presently she is professor of English at Catholic University College of Ghana, West Africa.

Source: Kathleen Feeley, "In My End Is My Beginning."[35] This essay, written specifically for this volume, is published here for the first time.

Following hunches (a.k.a. responding to inspiration) has led me to meet persons and visit places that would be outside my usual experiences. Such a hunch led me to call Katherine Anne Porter on the phone in late November 1970. I had learned that she lived in College Park, not far from Baltimore and the College of Notre Dame of Maryland, where I was President-elect. I told her that I deeply admired her stories and used them for my literature classes, and that I would very much like to meet her. She responded graciously, and we arranged a date.

Sister Maura Eichner, poet and chair of the English Department at CND, went with me. Katherine Anne welcomed us in her beautiful apartment (actually, two apartments converted into one), and we talked. Or, to be honest, she talked and we listened. In the corner of the living room, we saw her hand-carved coffin. The apartment was filled with beauty: fine crystal, sparkling chandelier, fresh flowers. Before we left, we invited her to the College of Notre Dame for Mass on 8 December. Actually, I wanted to invite her to be the opening speaker for a series of lectures by prominent women that I was planning, but I thought that rekindling her Catholic sensibilities would be a good beginning of a relationship.

A college car picked her up and brought her to Baltimore. The special liturgy for the Feast of the Immaculate Conception was filled with beautiful singing; the chapel was aglow with candles.[36] She walked up to receive Holy Communion, holding my arm. (She was still recovering from hip surgery.) As we returned, Sister Maura noticed tears silently coursing down her cheeks.

A small dinner party followed the service. Katherine Anne sat at the head of the table taking stock of the six School Sisters of Notre Dame who were dining with her. Later, Sister Maura wrote of this dinner in an article published in the *Baltimore Sun*: "[Katherine Anne] had such tender, funny recollections of her early school life in a convent boarding school in the South that she quickly warmed to the sisters, especially the older ones who still retained their long black dresses and veils.

"She was dressed for dinner that night in an off-white brocaded shift; there was a touch of the oriental in the delicate embroidery at the neckline. [She] sat at the head with the same abbatial charm that had been Edith Sitwell's. She ate little. She was a marvelous raconteur, and we listened to stories about her friends: her admiration for Robert Penn Warren, her early recognition of the talent of J. F. Powers,[37] her appreciation of Peter Taylor and his wife,[38] her dislike of Steinbeck. She recalled friends of Greenwich Village days: Dorothy Day, Caroline Gordon, Allen Tate.[39]

"She was poor then, but she dreamed of having, sometime in her life, her birthstone, an emerald. She touched the emerald in the brooch on her breast, glanced down at the stone blazing from her ring. 'So,' she went on, 'when *Ship of Fools* became a film, and for the first time in my life I had some money, I bought an emerald.'

"She smiled at us, turned to the sister on her right and asked, 'Would you like to try it on?' Of course we would. Each of us did. It had been a long time since any of us had worn a ring, much less a radiant emerald."[40]

I went with her on the drive back to College Park. She was exhausted. I waited while she prepared for bed, and tucked her in.

Sister Maura and I visited her again on Shrove Tuesday, 1971. She made French crepes for us, and served them with honey; we drank champagne in tall, crystal flutes. She was celebrating her own Mardi Gras on the day before Lent began. On this visit, I asked her to be the lead speaker for Notre Dame's Year of the Woman, a year-long series of lectures by distinguished women. She accepted.

For the opening lecture, the auditorium was crowded. Katherine Anne walked onto the stage dressed in a white pants suit, splendid with sparking sequins. I introduced her, and put a microphone on her lapel. She walked up and down the stage, charming her audience with her stories about her life. Each story seemed to point to the same conclusion: dare to do what you want to do with your life, no matter the cost. She was an ideal role model for the women in the audience who were contemplating a return to formal education.

For the next four years, Sister Maura and I took the senior English majors to visit KAP as part of the senior seminar. The students were charmed by her lively wit and poignant reminiscences. She was charmed by their insightful questions. On one occasion, one of them asked—thinking of "Pale Horse, Pale Rider": "Was Adam real?" She sat up very straight, pointed behind her shoulder, and said, "He's so real; he's right here."[41] This Porter session was always the highlight of the seminar.

One year we visited her on 15 May, bringing a beautifully decorated birthday cake. She loved celebrating her birthday with our students. She blew out her birthday candles while we sang birthday blessings to her.

Our Board of Trustees offered Porter a Doctor of Humane Letters degree, *honoris causa* at our 1973 commencement, and she was very pleased. However, she had been at Governor Lehman's College in New York that spring, and had over-exerted herself. She could not attend. We waited until the next spring, when she was strong again, and took the ceremony to her apartment. We brought a small audience, dressed her in cap and gown, and presented her with Notre Dame's hood. Sister Maura read the citation, while KAP stood in regal splendor. Refreshment for all finished the ceremony.[42]

As she declined in health, our visits became fewer. In July 1977, Paul Porter, her nephew, called to ask if I could come to see her. He thought she would be comforted by the presence of Catholic sisters. I was away at the time, but Sister Maura went. She recorded the visit. "I visited her alone, and found her in bed with her right hand under her blue blanket. But her left hand, which held mine firmly, pulled me down to her and held me fast, was intensely strong. Toward the end of that visit, when I said I did not want to tire her, she released my hand and carefully put back the blanket to cradle her helpless right hand in her left. She spoke of and to her right hand, tenderly. She reminded it of all the writing it had done; she reminded it of what good cooking and baking it had done. She felt that she wanted to praise it now, not to disown it when it was helpless."

When I returned to Baltimore, I went for a visit. Lying in her lovely bed, she talked, but with difficulty. I was sitting quietly in her bedroom, stroking her hand, when her nurse came in to attend her. I left the room, walked into her study in the next room, and studied the books in her bookcases. On a hunch, I took *The Confessions of St. Augustine* from the shelf. Her name was on the flyleaf, and under it, she had written this quotation from *The Confessions:* "It doth make a difference whence cometh a man's joy." In my several readings of *The Confessions* I had never noticed that sentence. It came to me in a flash that these words characterized her life, including her declining years. She knew the source of her joy—her own indomitable spirit. Her joy resided in herself, her writing, her accomplishments. Even though she was suffering what Teilhard de Chardin called "passive diminishment" at the close of her life,[43] her sense of joy was abiding. When I re-

Sister Kathleen Feeley, Katherine Anne Porter, and Sister Maura Eichner at Porter's apartment in Westchester Park Towers, College Park, Maryland. The two nuns from Notre Dame College in Baltimore guided Porter to a reconciliation with the Roman Catholic Church in 1970. Courtesy Papers of Katherine Anne Porter, Special Collections, University of Maryland, College Park, Libraries.

turned to the room and mentioned that epigraph she had chosen to inscribe in her copy of *The Confessions,* she stroked her right hand and said, "My writing hand. It served me well. I still love it."

On another visit, she asked me to bring a priest to see her. I invited a priest friend of mine who was a literary man; I knew he would connect with her.[44] He went back several times to see her. In her last year, she reverted to her early childhood. She liked to keep her rosary in her hand. We talked about spiritual things; we talked about death. She was ready for such conversations. Deep down, she was a very spiritual person. I don't think one could write the way she did without depth of spirit. She was deeply spiritual, but not overtly religious. Every time I went to see her near the end, I always prayed with her—prayers that she knew, the Our Father, Hail Mary, and also spontaneous prayers of blessing.

When I was informed about her death on 18 September 1980, I arranged for a Requiem Mass to be held in Notre Dame's chapel the next day. A few weeks later we had a Memorial Mass for her family and friends. I was deeply touched to see Eudora Welty, tall and slightly bent, enter the chapel and make her way slowly to one of the pews. Then I recalled that Katherine Anne had written a splendid introduction for Welty's first book of stories. Heart speaks to heart. Eudora Welty remembered.

As I reflect now on the relationship that began with that first phone call, I realize how blessed I was to have a deep relationship with a woman of her artistic and spiritual caliber. I will always remember that "it doth make a difference whence cometh a [wo]man's joy,"[45] and how Katherine Anne Porter lived out that epigraph to the end of her life.

45 / Maura Eichner

Maura Eichner, School Sisters of Notre Dame (1915–2009), is the author of several books of poetry, including *Bell Sound and Vintage* (1966), *What We Women Know* (1980), and *Hope Is a Blind Bard* (1989). Her poetry has been published in many journals, including the *Yale Review* and the *Hopkins Review*. She was chair of the English Department at the College of Notre Dame of Maryland for many years and won the Theodore Hesburgh Award for her Outstanding Contribution to Catholic Higher Education. A native of Brooklyn, New York, she received an M.A. from Catholic University of America. She met Porter in 1970 and with Sister Kathleen Feeley and Father Joseph Gallagher remained Porter's dependable spiritual adviser until Porter's death.

Source: Sister Maura Eichner, S.S.N.D., "Try It On," *Four Quarters* 21.1 (1971): 39.

Try it on

you said. And so I did.
Cleopatra's moss green
emerald with its beaten
silver galleries hid

the third of my finger bone.
I remember spaces of time:
Pliny's gold lion with an eye
of emerald; the talisman stone

of Charlemagne and the rose
of carven beryl that some say
Cortez brought back; how a
woman in childbirth knows

its poignant healing
yet the virgin wears it for

her purity. O I give it
back. Let it beget

upon your hand a mystic tree
of blessing on whose green
veined boughs birds sing
eternally.

Source: Maura Eichner, S.S.N.D., "Visit to Katherine Anne Porter: after the stroke," *America* 15 November 1980: 302.

Visit to Katherine Anne Porter
   after the stroke

When I came into your room, Beloved,
(pale horse, pale rider
tethered to the espaliered geraniums)
your left hand pulled me
down past the paraphernalia
of oxygen tent and mask.

You talked of intensities
of living, telling me
that dying will be part
of your answer to the call
that life has been. I crouched
at the delta of a river

I, too, travel though hardly
understand. But when you released
my hand, to draw from under
a blue blanket, your bloated
useless writing hand, cradling it
as though it were an idiot child,

you said—*a good creature,*
and not to be disowned now.
I trembled for both of us.
Of many gifts I have received,
it is that hand, beloved,
I hold in the reliquary
of a doubter's heart.

46 / Clark Dobson

Clark Dobson (1939–), who began his career as a high school music teacher, holds M.B.E., M.S., and Ph.D. degrees from Florida State University. He was an associate director of the Association for Supervision and Curriculum Instruction and served as a professor and administrator at George Mason University and the University of South Carolina.

Source: Clark Dobson, "An Unforgettable Decade." This essay, written specifically for this volume, is published here for the first time.

I met Katherine Anne Porter in 1970. At the time, I was a young academic, with a passion for books and writing. I loved Katherine Anne's work, and the very idea of meeting her was beyond belief.

The occasion was lunch at the Army-Navy Club in Washington, DC. It had been arranged by my friend Jack Horner,[46] who had been introduced to Katherine Anne by the University of Maryland's Bob Beach. Bob served as an informal liaison between the University President's office and its newly minted Doctor of Humane Letters.

There were four of us sitting around a small square table, with Katherine Anne just to my right. I really can't remember many details of the conversation. I was probably so awed and overwhelmed that much of it went right over my head. My memory is that she was charming, witty, fun, and very petite. She was small in stature, but large in presence. At one point, when the conversation had turned to sex, she leaned toward me and said in a low voice, "I was married and divorced three times, and I never cared that much about it." That one line has remained with me for a long time. After this meeting, we became friends and saw quite a lot of each other until her death in September 1980.

Katherine Anne and I shared a love of music, especially opera. Among her favorite singers were Maggie Teyte, Jennie Tourel, and Denise Duval.[47] One year, she decided that she would prefer celebrating her birthday at the opera, rather than at the impressive annual celebration arranged by the university. Jack Horner and I managed to get last minute, peanut gallery tickets to *Die Fledermaus*[48] at the Kennedy Center. She sang and conducted through most of the performance, to the amusement and enthusiasm of the audience seated around us.

An even more memorable operatic occasion was a later trip to Wolf Trap Farm Park for a performance of Prokofiev's opera *War and Peace*. This was a performance Katherine Anne was very enthusiastic about attending; so we arranged for four tickets (two down front for Katherine Anne and me, and two in the rear for Jack and Addie Hubbard). Jack and Addie were not opera lovers and probably dozed during the less dramatic and loud parts of the performance.

Addie is an important person in Katherine Anne's later life, but not often mentioned. She served for a while in an odd and complex role of companion, nurse, housekeeper, and chauffeur. They argued constantly, but were actually very close and affectionate. Katherine Anne seemed to appreciate Addie's innocence, genuineness, and lack of sophistication. At one point, I can remember her referring to Addie as a bird among the vipers. One unforgettable story about Katherine Anne and Addie had to do with their attendance at a notable funeral. After the service, Addie was driving their car in the funeral procession. They suddenly ran out of gas, but were able to coast to a nearby service station. Katherine Anne never forgot the incident, and never ceased to remind Addie of it.

While Katherine Anne and I waited for *War and Peace* to begin, she told me the story of the baroque pearls she was wearing that evening (along with her bird's-egg-sized emerald ring). It seems that after *Ship of Fools* was published, and she finally had a bit of surplus money, she went to a New York City jeweler to buy some long-desired pearls. When she had selected the pearls, the jeweler asked "how many?" Katherine Anne replied "I'll take three yards!" When she told this story, which was often, she always used a measuring motion with her hands to emphasize the point.

I also learned a great lesson about Katherine Anne that night, and perhaps about great artists in general. I can remember her touching my arm and pointing upwards. In the rafters of the Wolf Trap auditorium were a large number of technicians I had never realized were there. They were all silhouetted against a blue sky that reminded me of a bottle of "Evening in Paris" perfume, a rich dark cobalt blue. In an interesting and perceptive way, she had captured the uniqueness and beauty of the moment. I realized that, even in her eighties, she missed very little in the world around her. I think that storing up impressions like this one was an important habit for her. She simply saw everything, and she saw it differently than I did.

Another example of this gift of perception and memory occurred in a much earlier telephone conversation. She shared the memory of a childhood experience, when she had seen a group of mourners carrying a coffin across a railroad trestle. The cemetery was on the opposite side of the river from the village and its church. Her description of the procession, the coffin held aloft, the early morning light, and the mist rising from the river below seemed very real, as if she had just experienced them. She had stored the memory away for a long time, perhaps in anticipation of an inspiration to use it.

Katherine Anne also had a long memory for real or imagined slights or disagreements. Sometimes they popped to the surface in surprising ways. In one of Truman Capote's last publications, he described her as one of the two most beautiful women he had ever known. I couldn't wait to telephone her with the news. I was taken aback when her response to the quote was ". . . that aborted fetus!"[49]

Another long held memory was about Glenway Wescott. She and Glenway had disagreed over some issue at the National Institute of Arts and Letters many years before. She had never forgotten it, and seemed never to have forgiven him for it. She always spoke of him as if he had long been dead (even though I knew he was alive and well). When Glenway decided to come down to College Park for one of Katherine Anne's last birthday celebrations, I was curious to see how she would react to his physical presence. Even in the same room she never seemed to acknowledge his reality. It was as if a wraith or spirit was there. Even after this visit, she continued to refuse to consider him among the living; at one point, even saying to me, "You know that Glenway is dead."

My most enduring memory, though, is of Katherine Anne's generous and loving spirit. You only had to mention the names of past and present friends (many of long standing) to get a burst of warm and enthusiastic recollection. Among these were Cyrilly Abels, Cleanth Brooks, Allen Tate, Robert Penn Warren, Monroe Wheeler, Barbara Harrison Wescott,[50] Eudora Welty, and Isabel Bayley. For those she saw as faithful and loyal friends, she remained the same lifelong.

She seemed to think of me sometimes as an aspiring writer, and at times our relationship seemed to be that of mentor and student. One of the most dramatic examples of her generous spirit in my case was a telephone call I received one weekend (during the final years when she was generally bedridden), asking me to come at once to College Park to see her. Because she was so insistent about it, I was concerned and made a quick trip to her apartment. When a nurse took me into her bedroom, I was stunned to find Robert Penn Warren, Eleanor Clark Warren, and their daughter. Katherine Anne had asked me to come simply because she thought I would enjoy (and probably gain something from) having the opportunity to meet him.

In Joseph Blotner's biography of Warren, this visit to Katherine Anne is mentioned, and how dreadful he felt about it.[51] This bothered me when I read it because my recollection was so completely different, especially of her obvious pleasure at having them there. After thinking about it, I realized that his very negative memory was based on his shock at seeing Katherine Anne's physical deterioration and difficulty in speaking. His memory was of the sprightly and dynamic friend she had been just several years earlier. For me, who saw her more regularly, the decline was much more gradual and less shocking.

The final several years, though, were difficult ones. She could no longer write, except for signing a shaky K.A.P. Her speech was sometimes halting, and it was sometimes impossible to remember a particular word or memory. It was helpful if the person with her was familiar with her life and the many stories she loved to tell. Then, a missing word, place, or incident could be supplied and her frustration considerably reduced. During these last years, there were regular visitors (a kind of on-going support group) that included me, Jack Horner, Kevin Foley,[52] Monroe Wheeler, Jane DeMouy, and Sister Kathleen Feeley. Sister Kathleen also brought other nuns, and an occasional priest, who provided a spiritual support that meant a great deal to Katherine Anne. This relationship was so important to her that she arranged that these same nuns would conduct her memorial service on the first anniversary of her death.

For many friends of Katherine Anne, the famous Mexican pine box coffin was a symbol of her sense of fun and delight in entertaining (if not shocking) people. For some time, it was kept in a hall closet where she could show it off to departing guests by opening the coffin, stepping inside, and commenting on the "fit." Later, it was placed on two sawhorses in an unused guest bedroom. When Hank Lopez wrote in 1981 that she had been buried in the coffin, it was actually sitting on the rafters of our garage. Later, I moved it into my library where it rested more appropriately against shelves of books. This is where the coffin inspired a beautiful poem, "Katherine Anne Porter's Secret," by Carolyn Kreiter-Foronda, the current poet-laureate of Virginia.[53]

How did I acquire the coffin? It was surely serendipitous that Jack Horner and I were helping Katherine Anne's nephew, Paul Porter, clear her apartment after she had moved to the Carriage Hill Nursing Home. Paul had planned to destroy it, but we persuaded him to let us keep it. This is how it made its way, finally, to its appropriate home in the Katherine Anne Porter Room at the University of Maryland.

The coffin is just one of the symbols that represent, for me, Katherine Anne's character and personality. Like most great artists, I suppose, she was an uncommonly complicated person. In addition to being one of our greatest writers, she was also an actress. She loved an audience and had a multitude of stories to entertain them, always using her expressive hands to emphasize the drama. She loved and hated deeply, and never seemed to hesitate to express either feeling in her life

Addie Hubbard, Clark Dobson, and Katherine Anne Porter, 13 August 1971, McLean, Virginia, where they dined before attending a performance of Prokofiev's *War and Peace* at Wolf Trap. Courtesy Papers of Katherine Anne Porter, Special Collections, University of Maryland, College Park, Libraries.

or writing. She was a survivor and was far stronger than her frail and frequently ill body would indicate.

During the decade that I knew Katherine Anne Porter, she was a very kind and supportive friend. I began as an admirer of her writing, but soon loved, as well, her wit, sense of fun, theatricality, and wisdom. What a remarkable ten years it was.

47 / M. M. Liberman

Myron Mandell Liberman (1921–95) earned a B.A. from Lafayette College in 1943 and an M.A. from New York University in 1946. Both a fiction writer and a critic, he was an instructor at the State University of New York at Buffalo when he began studying Katherine Anne Porter's fiction. His book *Katherine Anne Porter's Fiction* (1971) followed his *A Preface to Literary Analysis* (1964, with James Kisane and S. P. Zitner), *The Practice of Criticism* (1966), and *Maggot and Worm and Eight Other Stories* (1969). His article on Porter's *Ship of Fools* ("*Ship of Fools* and the Responsibility of the Novelist") brought him to the attention of Porter, who was grateful for his defense of her novel and turned to him when she needed a trustee for her literary estate after several others had declined.[54] For many years he was a professor in the English Department at Grinnell College, in Grinnell, Iowa.

Source: M. M. Liberman, "Meeting Miss Porter," *Georgia Review* 41 (1987): 299–303.

On my office wall is a picture of Katherine Anne Porter looking, because of her garb, strikingly nun-like, and bringing to mind the disloyal young woman in "Flowering Judas." It is identified in Miss Porter's hand as *Photograph by Manuel Bravo, Mexico 1931*. The inscription reads: *For Mike Liberman in College Park, October 1973—memento of a happy meeting and many hopes and plans—Katherine Anne.*

The "meeting" to which Miss Porter refers is the weekend I spent with her at her urgent invitation following a phone call from her young Washington attorney, who asked me to become her literary executor.

To write of this experience is no labor of love and I would as soon forego it, but one day someone will write a decent biography of Miss Porter. That scholar will have scoured Miss Porter's personal library and taken note of her marginalia in my 1971 book, *Katherine Anne Porter's Fiction*.[55] He or she may well wonder about these comments and, in this connection, her motives for inviting and dismissing a rather long string of literary, as she smilingly put it to me, "executioners." What follows here is my explanatory footnote to that as-yet-unwritten biography.

In 1969, early in the course of my research on Miss Porter's fiction, I got into some unsettling business. I had written to the McKeldin Library at the University of Maryland, where I understood that the bulk of Miss Porter's papers were housed, asking for a general description of these holdings. In response I received word from some librarian that my request was out of order since no one was to look at this material. Some days later I received a call from a Mr. E. Barrett Prettyman, who identified himself as Katherine Anne Porter's lawyer, telling me that Miss Porter was extremely upset because she had heard that I was poking around in her letters and was going to publish them. He demanded to know the truth. I assured him that I had not seen nor had I any interest in her letters, that I was not writing a biography, and that Miss Porter was getting some very suspect misinformation. This seemed to satisfy Mr. Prettyman, who sometime later agreed to meet me in Washington, where I told him of my difficulties with the Maryland people. He found this difficult to believe, for after all Miss Porter had stipulated quite clearly that "reputable scholars" would have access to her papers. He finally agreed to speak to Miss Porter about this, which he evidently did, for I was later to hear from him that she had set the Maryland librarians straight.

To hear from Mr. Prettyman again in 1973, after years without contact, was unexpected enough, but his invitation to be Miss Porter's literary executor took me very much by surprise.[56] I had been years before encouraged to write my book on Miss Porter's work for several reasons, not the least of which was a letter I had once received from her addressed to "Dear Miss [sic] Liberman," telling me that a piece I had published on *Ship of Fools* was the best she had seen and much appreciated by her since the novel had been so unfairly maligned and grossly misunderstood. But, as I told Mr. Prettyman, she had never acknowledged my book, a copy of which I had sent her on publication two years earlier, and I supposed she didn't like it. No, she "loved" my book, Mr. Prettyman assured me. Peter Taylor, her present trustee, wanted out; Miss Porter was getting quite old, had been unwell, and was very anxious to have her affairs in order without delay. I agreed to visit her as soon as I conveniently could.

I took a plane to Baltimore a few weeks later after receiving three telegrams from Miss Porter. One of them contained the contention that she "wished they would just let me die," but another assured me that I would be quite comfortable if I visited her, since she had a "housekeeper" who would meet me at the airport and attend to the amenities. Yet I had to wait in the Baltimore airport for what seemed a very long time before I was paged. I was beginning to think I had dreamt all this Porter matter and hoped I would soon wake up. Then a plump, breathless, middle-aged lady asked me if I were Mr. Liberman and introduced herself as Miss Porter's "housekeeper." She was Mrs. Hubbard. "Call me Mother Hubbard," she said with a big grin. I felt a little better for this gracious note of humor, the very first, I realized, since I had taken a professional interest in the nation's most accomplished writer of short fiction.

As we drove through heavy freeway traffic, Mrs. Hubbard apologized. Miss Porter had mislaid my letter and could not remember what day I was to arrive, and she, Mrs. Hubbard, had been summoned at the last moment from her home to find the letter and pick me up.

The Miss Porter who greeted me was indeed old, bent, and wrinkled; her hand was hard as a claw, and she had a beakish face to match. Still, I could see the very pretty young woman in her, the girlish self-styled fluttery debutante, ageless in her graceful belle-of-the-cotillion gestures and bodily postures, whom I had met and admired years ago at a writer's conference in Connecticut. I reminded her of that occasion, but she could not recall it.

How I appeared to *her*, of course, I cannot certainly say. But later in the weekend—it was when we were drinking a lot of bourbon on empty stomachs—she allowed that I did not seem to her to be "very Jewish." I was struck dumb by this flaming impertinence for which, of course, there is no appropriate response. To have replied, "Is that good or bad?" could only have generated God knows what further discomfiture on my part (with embarrassment, perhaps, on hers) and in all likelihood my early departure for home without a plane reservation. I chose to pass her remark off as ingenuous tongue-rattle.

Dinner on the Friday evening of my arrival was pleasant enough. Miss Porter had invited Mr. Prettyman (who could not recall our earlier phone discussions or meeting) and his wife to join us; the conversation was polite and unforced, with a little badinage tossed now and then in my direction. They were interested in knowing if I were a Democrat or Republican. Miss Porter asserted that it would be a good thing if Richard Nixon were assassinated. (The force of her statement made it memorable enough, but it received ironic emphasis the next evening when her phone rang. Miss Porter wondered aloud who might be calling, since her number was unlisted. It was a friend in the State Department who informed her that "We have no government," and reported to her the events subsequently known as the "Saturday night massacre.")[57] When we finally decided it was time to sleep, she said, "See you in the morning." I said, "O.K." She said, "O.K. yourself."

Saturday morning I showed up for breakfast uncomfortably shaved, bathed, and dressed. Miss Porter was in her perpetual dressing gown. She told me straight out that on the next day I was to show up similarly attired. There were several robes in my closet I could wear, she told me. (I breakfasted Sunday morning disguised as Glenway Wescott, clothed indeed in his very robe. "Poor Glenway was a trial.")

The apartment Miss Porter occupied I never expect to see again in kind. It was in fact two semicircular apartments made into one, so that there were two of everything—including bars. Walking from one bar to the bathroom I had the disconcerted sense of arriving where I had been. Fortunately, my room was equipped with a massive radio, and I would, over the long Saturday, once in a while plead fatigue and sneak back there to listen longingly to an inning of the World Series.

As for Mrs. Hubbard's housekeeping, it consisted of some desultory dusting and shopping, while Miss Porter did the cooking (which was good enough, what there was of it). Who, after all, needed lunch after an ample breakfast of two fried eggs, bacon, toast, and coffee—especially when we could sit around all day and talk, talk, talk and drink?

All weekend I heard that Allen Tate was the "wickedest" man she ever met. Malcolm Cowley was "that lug." "Red" Warren had shown up once with his "awful Italian wife,"[58] and refused to eat her kidneys which she had spent a whole day cooking. Faulkner sentimentalized his Negroes. John O'Hara at least knew what he was talking about. The only man she really ever loved was John Peale Bishop, who once met her at the Museum of Modern Art and rushed over to where she sat and kissed her foot.

In my inexcusable innocence I had supposed that I had been summoned to Miss Porter's side to go over the necessary details of my future trusteeship and to look over what papers she still retained. Nothing of the sort. Lawyer Prettyman, though amiable enough, was elsewhere in thought and spent little time with us. Miss Porter, herself—though making the gesture of showing me her study, scattered with piles of letters, manuscripts, and works-in-progress—persisted in hovering over me all weekend, making it impossible to read one full paragraph of anything.

She left me alone for fifteen minutes once. I found my *Katherine Anne Porter's Fiction* on her shelf and opened it with curiosity. I cannot recall the precise wording of the marginalia in Miss Porter's hand, but the sense stays with me clearly enough. There were a great many notes in the spirit of "No, no, no" and "Never, never, never" and "Wrong, wrong, wrong" and "Stupid stupid stupid"—as well as a number of locutions ordinarily deemed improper for the eyes of young children. Where I had quoted from published interviews it was, "I never said that."

When Miss Porter came back to the study I didn't hear what she said. I was tired and depressed and wanted nothing so much as a walk around the block. Unfortunately, the apartment building was surrounded by bridges and freeways.

Miss Porter hoped that she wasn't boring me. No, of course she wasn't.

Mrs. Hubbard drove me to the airport on Sunday. She said a great deal I intend to keep to myself, along with some specific advice: "If you have anything to write to her about, send it to me and I'll see that she reads it. Otherwise it'll just set there."

At Christmastime I received perfunctory greetings from Miss Porter, but a few months later a letter came from Mr. Prettyman informing me that I was no longer Miss Porter's trustee. She had decided that because of the very personal nature of some of her papers she wanted a certain lady, an old friend of hers, to take over.[59]

I wrote to Mr. Prettyman to say that I didn't appreciate being picked up and put down in such a manner. Mr. Prettyman replied at some length that he was sorry I felt that way and was turning my letter over to Miss Porter. Miss Porter then wrote to me to say that she thought, after all, she was doing me a favor.

7
Texas and Maryland, 1974–1981

Katherine Anne Porter's 1976 birthday party in her homeland, described by Charlotte Laughlin, was the highlight of her last years. Although Porter talked about writing more books, she knew at some level that none was going to be written. Only *The Never-Ending Wrong,* an account of the Sacco-Vanzetti affair and her participation in protests surrounding it, was to be published in 1977, and then only with the help of her assistant, Bill Wilkins, who was able to piece together drafts she had begun in 1927. It was also in 1977 that the debilitation that had been building for years accelerated with the onset of severe strokes. Most of her longtime, dear friends lived too far away—or were themselves too frail—to visit often. Although Rebert Penn Warren, Eleanor Clark, Monroe Wheeler, and Isabel Bayley came when they could, she depended for the most part on nuns, a priest, and a group of young people, including Jane DeMouy, Jack Horner, Clark Dobson, Rhea Johnson, and Ted Wojtasik, to brighten her days. Lynn Darling covered the birthday party held a year after her death that brought together Porter's nephew Paul Porter and many friends to celebrate her long life.

48 / Charlotte Laughlin

Charlotte Laughlin (1951–) was born in Brownwood, Texas, and received her Ph.D. in English literature from the University of Texas, Austin, in 1975. From 1975 to 1983 she taught English at Howard Payne University in Brownwood, Texas, leaving as an associate professor in 1983 in order to be a full-time mother, including home-schooling both her children from kindergarten through high school. She returned to adjunct teaching at Howard Payne from 1999 to 2002 before assuming a teaching position at McLennan Community College in Waco, Texas. In 1990 she spoke at the dedication of the Texas State Historical marker erected in Brown County in Porter's honor.

Roger Brooks, president of Howard Payne University from 1973 to 1979, corresponded with Katherine Anne Porter several years before he broached to her the idea of bringing her to Howard Payne to receive an honorary degree at the commencement that coincided with the week of her eighty-sixth birthday. When she accepted, he also planned a birthday party and an excursion with a faculty entourage to the Indian Creek Cemetery, where Porter's mother, Mary Alice Jones Porter, is buried. Brooks sent Charlotte Laughlin and Alta Ada Schoner, two young English professors, to the Dallas–Fort Worth airport to pick up Porter and deliver her to his office on the Howard Payne campus.[1]

Source: Charlotte Laughlin, "How I Accompanied Katherine Anne Porter on the Last Great Pilgrimage of Her Life." This essay, written specifically for this volume, is published here for the first time.

In May 1976 airline security allowed those greeting travelers to wait on the concourse directly in front of the door to the plane. Accompanied by another Howard Payne University English professor, Dr. Alta Ada Schoner, I stood holding a bouquet of roses as we anxiously awaited the arrival of eighty-six-year-old Katherine Anne Porter. We were nervous because we'd been told that she was temperamental, even self-centered and demanding. We knew a bit about her changeability. In the preceding weeks, she had promised to attend a seminar dedicated to her works, only to back out, and then, once again, promise to attend.

Her earlier decision not to attend had sent the seminar planners into a state of near panic, and I had jokingly volunteered to have my grandmother masquerade in her place. As we waited, I wondered whether our trip to Dallas would prove futile, whether Miss Porter would not be on board the plane after all.

At that moment the doors opened. A stewardess emerged and saw us waiting with roses in hand. She said, "You must be here to greet Miss Porter. You are certainly in for a treat!" And we were. Miss Porter emerged with a smile meant for the runway and the pop of flashbulbs. "For me!" she exclaimed, dipping her face into the roses and proclaiming them "heavenly." We needn't have worried about making conversation because she carried on with non-stop expressions of gratitude and delight, regaling us with the story of her flight. The stewardess whispered, "See what I mean?" We did, indeed. Miss Porter was in her element: a gracious lady, a *grande dame,* an actress, a creator, a storyteller. Twenty-four, a first-year assistant professor with newly minted Ph.D. in hand but very little life experience, I was in awe.

We used a wheelchair to take Miss Porter to baggage claims and then to Alta Ada's car, which awaited for our nearly three-hour journey from the Dallas–Fort Worth airport to Brownwood. All the while, Miss Porter laughed merrily about the advantages of age and how nice it was to ride in her chariot attended by two such lovely ladies in waiting, who had come all this way and gone to all this trouble for her, sounding as surprised and in awe as I felt. If she momentarily faltered for something else to praise, she again inhaled her roses and proclaimed them "divine, heavenly, so wonderful, and all this for me!"

On the drive to Brownwood, she talked about many subjects, the landscape, the expanse of blue sky, how it had looked just that way when she was a child. A little over halfway into our journey, she began to tire, and we stopped in Stephenville at a restaurant where we were the only mid-afternoon patrons. After being seated at a table, sipping some water, and perusing the menu, Miss Porter was again bubbling over with delight: "Pecan pie! And black coffee! Oh, I haven't had a true pecan pie and black coffee in so long. It's so good to be back in Texas—to think, pecan pie!"

She ate with gusto, with a sensual delight I imagine must have characterized the way she had gone at everything in her long life. She told us she wanted to treat us, that she wanted to give us a champagne dinner, then added quickly as if she feared she might have offended, "But I do understand that Baptists have a different attitude toward champagne than do Catholics. My mother was a Methodist, my grandmother a Presbyterian. I understand. But I do love champagne!" We assured her she was a guest whose wishes would be respected, that while we abided by university rules when on university time, as we were then, our personal beliefs did not equate tee-totaling with morality. That was all she needed to launch into

a story of her nephews' learning to drink like little gentlemen and how modera-
tion, a bit of wine or good drink with meals, was so much preferable to prohibition, that it had a better chance of leading to a moral life than did extremism.

During the second half of our car trip, Miss Porter was a bit more subdued,
as if the pecan pie had left her feeling mellow and drowsy, and she herself feeling
more at ease with her two young hostesses. I didn't realize how truly keyed up she
was until we crossed a bridge over a little creek identified by a Texas Highway Department sign as "Indian Creek."

There are a lot of creeks in Texas and at one time there were a lot of Indians
in Texas, so we have more than one Indian Creek. But when Miss Porter saw the
sign, she started. "Indian Creek?" she cried. "Oh, go back, go back! That's where
my mother's buried, you know. That's why I've come! Please go back!" Even after
we explained that this wasn't *her* Indian Creek, Miss Porter remained restless and
nervous and once said, "If I'd known how long the drive would be, I wouldn't
have come. This is too much, too much."

By the time we arrived at the Holiday Inn in Brownwood, Alta Ada and I were
about as nervous as Miss Porter. We worked quickly to register her and get her
settled into her bed to rest. She was tired, for after all, she had been traveling for
more than seven hours that day, and her physical exhaustion added to the nervous
apprehension about visiting her mother's grave, and the place she, too, planned to
be buried, an apprehension she had so valiantly attempted to hide with her afternoon's patter of small talk and praise for everything we did for her.

That night, or perhaps the next day, we had dinner with Miss Porter and Alta
Ada's parents, Dr. and Mrs. Paul Cates. When I hesitated to ask that my steak be
well-done and cause the others to wait, Miss Porter burst into laughter. "Don't
you ever apologize for wanting your steak well-done. You've ordered like a true
Texan, and there's nothing better to be in the whole world! My father wanted his
meat burned on the outside and brown in the middle. Oh, Charlotte, dear, you're
the salt of the earth." She spread her arms wide to include everyone at the table
and proclaimed, "It's wonderful to be among Texans again!"

It was at this dinner that Alta Ada mentioned the New Testament epigraph
to the third section of *Ship of Fools,* titled "The Harbors": "For here we have no
continuing city" (Hebrews 13:14a). Although everyone at the table knew that the
verse continued, "but we seek one to come," we also knew that Miss Porter had
chosen to end her epigraph without that hopeful conclusion, prophetic of what
St. Augustine later called the "City of God."[2] We asked Miss Porter to explain
why she had stopped where she did, and the conversation waxed theological.
Everyone talked about the chapter as a whole, that the "here" was the world in-
habited by all human beings, not just the world of the Hebrews shortly before the
destruction of Jerusalem or that of St. Augustine and his contemporaries before

the fall of Rome.[3] As we discussed issues related to Hebrews 13 and to the great "faith chapter" of the Bible, Hebrews 11, which precedes it, Miss Porter listened and nodded, and made appropriately appreciative noises. But it became clear that she did not share the bright vision of the city to come for her ship of fools; their harbors, like the city that doesn't continue, were to be chaotic, spiraling downward into the destruction soon to engulf the literal Germany where they disembarked. Miss Porter's vision of humanity seemed to be a vision of original sin, of human evil in all its destructive power, without any clear hope of redemption, without any abiding faith in something better, in something more. But I believed I detected a tiny lifeline of possibility for hope and faith in the way she emphasized "here" when she repeated, "For *here* we have no continuing city . . . ," implying that elsewhere we might.

I left the dinner pensive, wondering whether Miss Porter herself felt content in the promise of grace or if she was approaching the end of life without it. I thought that if she had her grandmother's clear Calvinist sense of original sin without the concomitant hope of grace, Miss Porter's flamboyance and determined merriness had a darker underside.

I did not accompany Miss Porter to the Indian Creek Cemetery to visit her mother's grave because I was working at the HPU seminar where scholars and critics gathered at the first symposium dedicated to her works. But I had been present when she said that she wanted to have a picnic in the cemetery and to make a day of it. Mrs. Elva Dobson and Mrs. Almola James accompanied her and saw to it that everything was done just as Miss Porter wanted. Mrs. Dobson told me that as she stood before her mother's tombstone, Miss Porter quoted bits of the poem "Anniversary in a Country Cemetery,"[4] which she had written to memorialize the only other visit she had made to her mother's grave,[5] and that she talked to her mother as if long-dead Mary Alice Porter could hear her.

HPU personnel had set up lawn chairs beneath the spotty shade of mesquite trees and provided the picnic Miss Porter wanted. Pictures taken by HPU photographer Joe Underwood show Miss Porter, dressed in a lovely white pantsuit with flowing sleeves, gesturing with arms wide as I had seen her do from the time we met her at the airport. Clearly, she was again the actress and creator, the storyteller of her own life.

By the time I next saw her, the afternoon's emotional toll on her was obvious. She was agitated and overwrought, terrified she was dying of a heart attack. Dr. Roger Brooks, then president of HPU and the originator of the idea of a seminar devoted to her works, assured her by phone that he was sending her his personal physician, Dr. Seal Cutbirth. But before he arrived, several English professors from HPU, unaware of Miss Porter's nervous exhaustion, had arrived from the seminar at her hotel room. Someone politely introduced English teacher Bill Crider with the courtesy title associated with his Ph.D.—"Dr. Bill Crider."[6]

"Oh, doctor! Doctor!" Miss Porter cried grabbing his hand. "My heart is racing, and I'm having difficulty breathing. . . ."

It was Bill who nearly had a heart attack as he attempted to disentangle himself from her misapprehension, quickly explaining that he wasn't "that kind of doctor!" The real Dr. Cutbirth arrived shortly, listened to her heart, and used his best bedside manner to calm her and assure her that she was just overtired, perhaps overheated, and over excited from her happy afternoon.

At some point that afternoon, I asked her to sign my copy of her little book *In Defense of Circe*. "I love this book!" she said. "The marbled paper is so lovely! And Circe deserves a defense. No one can turn men into pigs unless they already have a pig nature. She only showed them as they were. That's what writers do, you know, and often we get blamed for it just as Circe was blamed. Showing the people's piggish nature doesn't make you very popular, so I wanted to defend her."

HPU had planned a lovely banquet in Miss Porter's honor one evening of the seminar, complete with a birthday cake to celebrate her birthday later that month. She dressed with care in a white Mexican wedding dress she had bought in Mexico many years before and had me carefully mark a copy of the book containing her poem "Anniversary in a Country Cemetery" so that she could read it as part of her banquet speech. But before we were to leave for the banquet, someone brought a copy of the local newspaper, *The Brownwood Bulletin,* into her room. Earlier in her visit, she had spent some time in Dr. Brooks's office happily autographing multiple copies of her books. The *Bulletin* had printed a picture of that activity in the story about the upcoming banquet and birthday party. Unfortunately, the photographer had taken a side view, which showed the sagging neckline normal for someone in her eighties.

If we thought Miss Porter had been overwrought after her visit to her mother's grave, it was nothing compared to her rage over that picture. "It's cruel! Wanton cruelty! Why would anyone print such a picture!" were just a few of her outcries as she flew into a full tantrum. "I won't speak at the banquet tonight. I can't speak. How could I speak after that horror!"

We finally convinced her to at least attend the banquet. Alta Ada's husband, George Schoner, had arrived to drive us, and as we helped her out of the room, I still had the book in my hand; but with a flamboyant wave of hers, she ordered me to leave it in the room as she wouldn't be speaking. I placed it on the bedside table, and we all drove off to Sid Richardson Hall, once a grand old hotel but by then converted into a boy's dormitory for HPU. We would be late, but at least we had succeeded in getting the guest of honor to the banquet.

The entrance of the old hotel was still beautiful with marble floors and an elegant chandelier. A lovely dining hall called the Gold Room was reserved for special occasions such as the banquet. Miss Porter looked admiringly at the pink marble and sparkling chandelier, but we were still nervous about having to tell everyone gathered to hear her speech that she wouldn't be speaking after all. As Miss Porter made her late entrance, everyone seated in the elegant Gold Room stood and applauded; and that turned the night around. Miss Porter once more spread her arms wide as if embracing the whole roomful of people.

"For me!" she exclaimed as she had done over the bouquet of roses we gave her at DFW airport. "These people are here for me! I must speak for them. Go and get my book!"

Alta Ada, George, and I looked at each other, pleased but surprised. "I'll go get it," whispered George, as he took the key and slipped away, returning with the book less than a half hour later.

The standing ovation she received on entering the Gold Room had revived the veteran artist within Miss Porter. In her speech, during which she stood and held the microphone unaided for forty-five minutes, she distanced herself from the emotional experience of the afternoon, combined it with an emotional experience of fifty years before, and formed them into a verbal creation expressing her theory of art.

Sensing that the speech might seem rambling, Miss Porter provided an explanation: "I don't write my speeches, and don't even think them. I just get up and talk, and I never know what I'm going to say till I hear it. But I do somehow get a shape in it, and we'll get back and touch base before this ends."

She did, indeed, get back and touch base. She wove together her homecoming and the story of a Mexican art show she assembled and thought lost, only to discover it many years later in another city, to form her thesis that "everything cannot be lost . . . you cannot really lose everything, no matter what!" Her Texas origins had not been lost because she had synthesized them to produce her literary art.

Miss Porter's speech that night was itself an artistic creation, one, which despite her exhaustion and heightened emotions, she offered in defense of her faith that life has meaning and that while much can be lost, and will be lost in the vicissitudes of life, "you cannot really lose everything, no matter what!"

At the conclusion of her speech, a giant white birthday cake with candles blazing was wheeled out, and the audience sang "Happy Birthday." Her arms flew out in that gesture now familiar to me. But this time I saw it not only as her wanting to embrace the whole scene—the cake, the audience, the whole event offered her by her HPU hosts—but also as her opening herself up to everyone there, to the whole experience, to all of life, that everything would not be lost, that despite the inevitable losses of life, she would fight for it all, that anything lost would literally have to be wrenched from her embracing arms.

A night later Miss Porter wanted to have a champagne and escargot dinner for all the planners of the seminar, and once again George Schoner was our chauffeur. As usual, Miss Porter's hands gestured dramatically as she spoke, emphasizing her insistence that Dr. Cutbirth's name originally must have been "Cuthbert" and mine must have been pronounced "Lachlan" and other such small talk. Later as she happily drank champagne and told stories, her fingers fluttering as always, she suddenly missed her emerald and diamond ring, the one she had bought with proceeds from *Ship of Fools*. Her emotions ever volatile, she looked frantically about. Everyone looked for the ring. I even crawled on the floor around her chair and beneath the table, patting the multi-patterned carpet as I searched for the ring. George Schoner again saved the day by going to search the car, where he found her ring resting on the carpet. It must have landed there unnoticed as she had expressively swished her hands while telling one of her many stories.

At Sunday afternoon's HPU graduation ceremony, Miss Porter was to receive an honorary doctorate. Certainly, she had received many more prestigious honors, but she seemed as delighted as a small child playing dress up as we helped her into graduation robes and mortarboard complete with golden tassel. "At last, my dears," she said to me and Alta Ada, "I shall be doctored as you are. We will all be doctors together!"[7]

Everyone expected her to receive her honorary degree and be seated, but she was energized by the pageantry and theater of the graduation ceremony and by the audience. And she truly seemed to love the thought of passing something on to young people. I think that was part of the reason she was always so kind to me and Alta Ada; she seemed to enjoy the company of women fifty or even sixty years her junior, almost as protégées.

I did not drive Miss Porter back to Dallas at the end of her four-day visit to Brown County. When she and I had said goodbye, she had called me "baby" and urged me to be true to myself, to live my life and no one else's. Later that month, she invited me and Alta Ada Schoner to visit her in Maryland, ostensibly to plan for a Katherine Anne Porter room at HPU, which she would furnish with some of her own furniture and copies of her books in their editions. But I think she also invited us because she had truly enjoyed being "one of the girls" again, of being in the company of the young.

When we arrived, we were greeted by Miss Porter and her assistant, Bill Wilkins, who was as gracious as she was. When he left about 5:00 p.m., she announced that she would now put us to work cooking. "I have white wine and fresh fish, if you'll only uncork the one and cook the other! I'll tell you how." She led us to the kitchen, telling us where to find utensils and ingredients, all the time telling us about the marvelous "feesh deesh" a Mexican woman had taught her to cook many years before in Mexico. So following Miss Porter's instructions, we cooked the "feesh deesh."

After dinner, conversation turned to family. Miss Porter told us that "The Jilting of Granny Weatherall" had grown from a late-night conversation with friends over wine, just like the one we were having that evening, that she and friends in Greenwich Village had been drinking wine late into the night when they began talking about their grandmothers. She said the characteristics of Granny Weatherall were a compilation of the memories shared that night and that her own grandmother had been the one who dug postholes in the hard-packed, sun-dried earth of Texas. Thinking of our conversation the month before about "no continuing city," I commented that despite all Granny Weatherall's good work, the priest had been in the house the second time and the "bridegroom" had not come. "Was it because she had never forgiven the man who jilted her?" I asked. "Is that why she couldn't go to heaven?"

"Oh, I don't know. Maybe she did, maybe she didn't." Miss Porter brushed the question away with her fine fingers. "We all have too much to forgive." She paused; then her voice became nearly mischievous. "But the first bridegroom had given her plenty."

I'm sure I looked genuinely puzzled because I was. "The baby," Miss Porter said. "She fainted you know." She laughed merrily at the dawning recognition on my face.

The second night I spent in her apartment, after Bill left, Miss Porter again drank wine and talked of Mexico, of drinking tequila while licking salt and lime and of smoking marijuana, "Only once. I didn't like it a bit. Wine and tequila are both much better!" She talked of the flowers in Mexico and in San Antonio and how she maybe should have bought some land instead of an emerald ring, but concluded that she had enough land in the flowerpots on her balcony. As she talked some more of flowers in Mexico, her face lit up. "You know, I saw the most extraordinary thing in Mexico. Plain wooden coffins painted all over in gay-colored flowers. When it came time for me to think of my coffin, I wanted one of those and tried to get my nephew Paul to order me one, but he didn't want to, didn't want me to think about my death, I suppose, or thought I was being morbid. But I got one without him. I found a wooden coffin in a mail-order catalogue and ordered one, but I had to pay someone else to paint it. It didn't come painted. Do you want to see it?"

I'm sure we looked puzzled because she laughed merrily and said, "It's here! I'm comfortable with the reminder of death; I don't mind the coffin being here; come and take a look."

She led the way to a hall closet, opened the door, and pointed to the coffin, cov-

Charlotte Laughlin (*left*), Katherine Anne Porter, and Alta Ada Schoner at the Howard Payne University graduation, 8 May 1976. The faculty, staff, and townspeople celebrated Porter's approaching eighty-sixth birthday and awarded her an honorary degree. Courtesy Papers of Katherine Anne Porter, Special Collections, University of Maryland, College Park, Libraries.

ered with what looked like a white linen sheet. "My shroud," she said as she swept it away revealing the pine box painted with red and yellow flowers and twining green leaves. She was showing off the coffin as proudly as another woman might have whipped out baby pictures of grandchildren.

"Would you like to take a picture?" she asked. And so we did. I'm looking at the picture now as I write this and remember that long ago happy day in which she stood beaming by her own flower-bedecked coffin. She had quoted "For now we have no continuing city" and left out "but we seek the one to come." She had written of the death of Granny Weatherall when the "bridegroom" didn't come. But as she stood smiling by her own coffin, I felt that Miss Porter faced her own death with some measure of hope. Or was it to be found in Yeats's phrase in "Lapis Lazuli"—"Gaiety transfiguring all that dread"?

The next morning we said goodbye, Miss Porter waving and gaily making plans for our next meeting. But I never saw her again. We exchanged a few letters. In one, she sent me a signed photo of herself, the one her nephew Paul had taken of her sitting in a white sunhat among the potted plants on her balcony, the plants that contained "all the land I need" according to her. She had personalized her photo, "For sweet merry Charlotte" and signed it. I smiled when I read the inscription because I thought of her, not me, as the merry one.

The papers read at the seminar and Miss Porter's banquet speech I so painstakingly transcribed from a scratchy audiocassette were never published. No Katherine Anne Porter Room came to fruition at HPU. Her first biographer, Joan Givner, despite a glowing article she had written for *The Dallas Morning News* ("A Fine Day of Homage to Porter"), pilloried all of us at HPU in her *Katherine Anne Porter: A Life* as small-minded, grasping, controlling, and bigoted.

Despite these disappointments, however, I believe Miss Porter was right in her banquet speech when she asserted that the worthwhile, the beautiful, can never be completely lost. You can't lose everything. Her fiction and her life were contradictions of dark visions, fierce hope, merriment, and a courageous love of life. I remain honored to have witnessed some part of that and to have participated in honoring her and making her happy in those days we were together.

In a personal letter to me after she returned to Maryland in May 1976, Miss Porter wrote: "I have been a little exhausted since our grand festival in my homeland, but the happiness of those wonderful days will be mine for life—it is a marvel to remember."

It is, indeed.

49 / Joseph Gallagher

Joseph Gallagher, a retired priest of the Baltimore diocese, is also a former editor of the *Catholic Review* and a frequent contributor of articles to the *Baltimore Sun*. He is the author of *To Hell and Back with Dante: A Modern Reader's Guide to* The Divine Comedy (1996). Katherine Anne Porter greatly admired Dante, one of many literary and spiritual subjects she found to discuss with Father Gallagher.

Source: Joseph Gallagher, "Katherine Anne Porter: The Last Candle Is Out," *Baltimore Evening Sun* 30 September 1980: A11.

When I first visited the sickbed of Katherine Anne Porter, we both thought it would be her deathbed. Like Old Nannie in her story "The Last Leaf," the 87--year-old writer was "expecting her own death momentarily."

In person and over the phone she was to speak to me constantly about dying. "I'm going to die, and I'm going to do it as soon as I can." "I need to die." "I'm busy dying; it's the hardest job I ever had."

In 1977 she had suffered a stroke which left her writing hand useless. I met her in January 1978 when she lived on the 15th floor of the Westchester Apartments near College Park. She had nurses around the clock, and during my thirty subsequent visits over the next twenty-eight months, she was always in bed, except for the two or three times I found her in a wheelchair.

Last April she was transferred to a new and final bed at a nursing home in Silver Spring. I paid her a last visit a few days after her ninetieth birthday in mid-May. A woman friend who had written a dissertation on the role of women in Miss Porter's fiction was her sole companion at the end,[8] which occurred at 4 p.m. on Sept. 18.

At last she had the peace she had earned. A handwritten note on the door of her Westchester suite had requested that in view of her need for rest and quiet, uninvited callers should consider themselves disinvited. Some autograph hunter had clipped away her signature.

Inside that suite I was allowed to see the simple but gaily colored coffin that she kept in a closet. I also saw on her walls several pictures she had taken of the poet

Hart Crane when she befriended him in Mexico in the early 1930s. It was on his way back from Mexico to the U.S. that he leaped or fell to his death from a ship.

In a lighter vein she confirmed for me a legendary story: Late one night, at a writers' colony, an overwrought poet banged on Miss Porter's door. "Katherine Anne," she said, "I'm going to commit suicide, and you're the only one I care to tell about it." "Well, thank you dearie," replied Miss Porter escorting the lady to the door; "be sure to let me know how it turns out." (There was no suicide.)[9]

Propped up in bed beneath a gilt-edged painting of the Madonna and Child, she seemed a tiny woman indeed. But hers was a face still marvelously alive, and crowned with elegant silver-white hair. You were struck at once by her engulfing smile, her ingratiating Southern voice, her wit and her feistiness. When she couldn't find some word she was looking for, she might grow mightily vexed, or she might mock herself playfully with a string of nonsense syllables.

She was a softie, this Texas-born relative of Daniel Boone (and also of William Sydney Porter alias O. Henry, and of Cole Porter.)[10] During a violent summer storm she recalled how as a child she loved to lie on the ground during such storms. "Don't you know that's dangerous?" her wifeless father asked. "Sure I do," replied the youngster. "And that was that."

On another occasion she spoke about the consolation of having done your best—"Angels can do no more." Then after a slight pause, she added: "Or maybe they can. I'll see them soon and ask them."

I mentioned W. H. Auden's remark that life is a blessing even when we cannot bless it.[11] "Darn him," she joked; "he would say that. That's what I've always tried to say in my stories."

She gave me a copy of her *Collected Stories,* which won for her the Pulitzer Prize and the National Book Award [in 1966]. Of these 26 stories, "Pale Horse, Pale Rider" is the favorite of many, with its theme of war, sickness and self-sacrificing love. "It really happened to me," she said; "it was my first experience of death, and it changed my whole life. But I don't regret it." Her eyes brimmed with tears as she recalled the Adam of the story (actually Alexander) who died after nursing her more than sixty years earlier.[12]

Those tears belied somewhat a comment she made after listening to the Prayers for the Dying contained in the Roman Ritual. "This message we have of tenderness and love—it's the only thing that breaks me up [. . .]."[13]

Katherine Anne also gifted me with a copy of her *Collected Essays* [1970]. In it she had written: ". . . only the work of saints and artists gives us any reason to believe that the human race is worth belonging to." Educated for a while in a convent school, she told me she had once thought of becoming a nun, but the sisters said that her call was to the world. Nevertheless she pursued her writing career as a genuine vocation and endured a built-in asceticism by refusing to sacrifice her integrity to popularity.

This copy of her essays is enriched with her own handwritten comments and footnotes. For example, in the text she lists some of her favorite playwrights, but leaves out George Bernard Shaw.

"And Shaw," she scrawled at the bottom of the page, "what about Shaw? I knew and adored his plays before I knew any of these others, and yet to leave him out. Shame on me."

After working on it for 20 years, she published *Ship of Fools* in her 72nd year. With it she finally achieved popularity and affluence. The latter allowed her at long last to buy some jewelry containing her birthstone, emerald. Sad to say, she was not permitted to wear any of these hard-won and dearly-prized trophies in her final years. Her court-appointed guardian felt legally responsible for them and put them under lock and key.[14]

A third book she gave me was the text of a symposium on her writings.[15] In this volume too she added choice comments. One critic speaks of her story in which a wife "dispassionately" murders her rival.[16] Miss Porter had underlined the adverb and jotted in the margin: "Better take another look at this story."

The same critic asserted that the most noble of her characters are confronted with the obliteration of hope. "The tiny particle of light must always be snuffed out," he wrote. In reaction to which she wrote: "Why, no! The particle of light still lives."

This gallant woman has at last achieved her death, but her artistic vision of the roots of human tragedy lives on in many particles of light embedded in her writings. For myself, a high point of that vision glows in the only passage in *Ship of Fools* which is emphasized by italics:

"What they were saying to each other was only, Love me, love me in spite of all! whether or not I love you, whether I am fit to love, whether you are able to love, even if there is no such thing as love, love me."

Love was italicized in her own long life. Someone once remarked to her: "Katherine Anne, wherever you have lived, there have always been people who loved you." She had a memorable explanation: "Well, I always loved them first, and that sort of helped them get used to the idea."

50 / Ted Wojtasik

Ted Wojtasik, born and reared in Connecticut, is a visiting faculty member in Creative Writing at St. Andrews Presbyterian College in Laurinburg, North Carolina. He holds an M.F.A. in fiction writing from Columbia University and a Ph.D. in twentieth-century American literature from the University of South Carolina. He is the author of three novels, *No Strange Fire* (1996), *Collage* (2004), and *Wild Animal Nation* (2006), in addition to numerous short stories. During the fourteen months of his friendship with Porter he kept a journal, which along with notes he made and letters he wrote during that period provided the starting point for this memoir.

Source: Ted Wojtasik, "The Final Year of Katherine Anne Porter." This essay, written specifically for this volume, is published here for the first time.

My life has always been a series of serendipitous moments—moments that have changed my life, in good ways and bad. As a young man, in mid-May of 1979, just out of college, with a degree in philosophy from George Washington University, I met Rhea Johnson (pronounced just like Ray)[17]—that was one serendipitous moment. When I discovered that he was a long-standing friend of Katherine Anne Porter, I started to read my way through her work, and he eventually made arrangements for me to meet her—that was another serendipitous moment that altogether altered the entire course of my life in the best way possible.

Tuesday, 10 July 1979, Rhea Johnson and I went to Katherine Anne Porter's apartment in College Park, Maryland, so he could visit her and I could meet her. He had been friends with KAP for more than twenty years, since the time he was a boarder in the basement apartment of a house she rented in Georgetown. It was a clear, warm day when Rhea and I drove out in a friend's car. I was nervous and excited, and Rhea said to bring along my Porter books because if she were up to it, she would autograph them. Of course, I did, although it seemed somewhat silly—the meeting alone would have been enough. That first meeting was blissful because it was the first time I had met anyone of literary stature under friendly terms (visiting terms). Just to talk and to laugh. She did autograph my books in a shaky right hand, merely marking down her inimitable initials K.A.P. with a blue felt-tip pen.

She lived in a huge apartment at the end of a long corridor on the fifteenth floor of a tall apartment complex. On the door to one apartment entrance there was a note that said she was ill, needed quiet, not to knock at either of these two doors unless you had an appointment, and not to call unless she had asked you to. There were two doors because there were two separate apartments, opposite each other, at the literal end of the building with an inside wall knocked down between two back bedrooms to make one large apartment, odd in that each one was an exact replica of the other, as though you were stepping into a mirror: identical kitchens, dining rooms, living rooms, balconies, bedrooms, and bathrooms.

Her caregiver answered the door and led us to her room. There she lay, upright in bed, white-haired, frail, wrinkled, and lovely. Robert Penn Warren described her eyes as "brilliant dark-violet eyes"—that's close to the mark. You could see how beautiful she must have been in youth. Of course, there were photographs to prove that. She had suffered a series of strokes a few years before that made her bedridden with her right arm and leg paralyzed. Rhea sat down on the foot of the bed, and I sat down in a chair. She was bright and bubbly and talked, talked, talked. Her voice was soft (somewhat hushed), inflectional, and slightly impaired by the strokes. The window was open, and if a plane flew overhead or some noise outside was too loud, I would lose her voice.

She had nurses around the clock. They were not, or at least not all were, registered nurses but women acting as caregivers or practical nurses to bring her food, to give her medication, to bathe her, to change her bedclothes. Rhea said to me that he wished I had come onto the scene three years earlier when she was still in her "prime," as it were. She was "quite a gal" up to the moment before the flesh began to fail.

Letitia, the caregiver, soon brought tea and Oreo cookies, which Katherine called "those black cookies." It was simply delightful. Tea, sunshine, and listening to Katherine Anne Porter: *Ship of Fools* Porter, *Noon Wine* Porter, Pulitzer Prize–winner Porter. I asked questions about Virginia Woolf and Aldous Huxley. I asked her if she had ever met them, and she quipped, "Honey, there are very few people I *haven't* met."

Tuesday, 6 November, I met with KAP in the afternoon all by myself. Prior to this, I had discussed with Rhea the possibility of compiling, editing, and publishing her letters. He asked her about it, and she thought it was a wonderful idea. She said for me to "come right over." I was ecstatic. The opportunity was vast, incredible. Together, Rhea and I spoke to her Monday night on the telephone, and we set up the next day as the time to visit. And so I went. She was ebullient and friendly and said that she would have to tell me all about her life and her work. She held my hand almost the entire three hours I was there.

That day she told me about Hart Crane, that "sad story." In her bedroom, at the literal end of her life, she had several framed black-and-white photographs of him. Despite all the difficulties of dealing with him in Mixcoac, I suppose that over time she must have reconciled herself to the fact that his abusive and self-destructive behavior that eventually ended in suicide was a result of his alcoholism and his own conflicted views on his homosexuality.

Shortly before this visit I had gone home to Connecticut to see my family, and while I was there I had read *Of Human Bondage.* I asked Katherine Anne whether she had ever met Somerset Maugham. "That sorry old man," she said. She related a story when both he and she were at a party in New York and he beckoned her to come over to him, which she steadfastly refused to do, so he came over to her and told her she had an attitude. "You don't like me very much, do you?" he asked. "Well, I wouldn't exactly call it *love,*" she replied. Then they changed subjects and got along well for the rest of the evening.

Around Thanksgiving I made a trip to New York to see Paul Porter, Katherine Anne's nephew who had power of attorney and oversaw all her business affairs. He wished to meet the young man who had suddenly initiated this literary project to collect KAP's letters for publication. The meeting was pleasant enough, and Paul eventually did grant me permission to do research in the McKeldin Library at the University of Maryland where her papers were archived.[18]

The Monday after Thanksgiving I brought Katherine Anne a bottle of Chateau Fourcas Hosten-Listra Haut Médoc (1975) and *The Habit of Being,* a recently published collection of Flannery O'Connor's letters. We drank some wine and talked, but she wasn't feeling well, and it was not one of our better visits. Rhea had warned me before my first visit alone with her that she was a difficult person to deal with. He told me how once she didn't speak to him for three months.

Thursday, 29 November, I spent two hours with Katherine Anne in the afternoon. I brought what I had done by way of organizing the letters and materials I had looked at while at the McKeldin Library the day before. We talked about her childhood, how her mother died and how her father was "terrified" by the loss of his wife. He wanted to enlist in the army, but her sister Gay told him there were other things he could do. He was never quite the same.

She noticed I was growing a mustache, and she related a story about how she and Gay had always told their father, who had a big, curled, waxed mustache, that he would look better without it. One day, while he slept, she and Gay snipped it off with scissors. He awoke, and he did look better and never grew another one until he was much older and then, too, a goatee. She said she liked to see a man's face, but "it's up to you" (I soon shaved my mustache off).

On the way to Katherine Anne's apartment I had read some short stories by Flannery O'Connor (laughing out loud, chuckling), and we talked about O'Connor, who, Katherine Anne said, "could give a blow and take one. She's a Catholic, you know." KAP liked the way she died: "pure innocence." I read to her one of O'Connor's letters in *The Habit of Being* when she recalled KAP's asking about one of O'Connor's chickens she had seen two years before. KAP said that the reason she liked that chicken was that it ran in the opposite direction from all the other chickens.

Monday, 8 December, when I went to see her, the day was cold and clear with white billowy clouds that dappled the blue. When I entered her bedroom, she lay there against the white pillows in a pretty pink nightgown with green and pink stitching. Her hair was puffy and nicely combed, her good knee was up, the lamp to her right was on, and she was gazing out the window: serene, calm, beautiful. She held a rosary in her good hand.

She turned to me. The light in the room, a mixture of cloud-filtered sunlight and a tincture of lamplight, cast a soft golden hue, accentuating her features and lines and curves of not only her face and hands but also the pillow and sheets and books scattered on her blanket. All objects seemed sharp (as hair is sharp after a haircut). And the room smelled clean with a hint of some kind of perfume, and I exclaimed, "You look wonderful today!"

She turned to me and said, "I'm dead."

"Oh, you're far from dead," I protested.

And she said that no, she wasn't dead, not yet anyway. And she was very articulate and bright as she began to question me about my progress on her letters.

She clutched a rosary while she talked. She told me to give Rhea "a sock in the eye" for not having visited her recently. She talked about how they met and how much she loved his cat, Bela Bartók. Then, because she thought I must have questions or things to say, she put her hand up to her mouth and said, "I'm not going to talk," and I laughed and said, "We'll see how long that lasts," and immediately she was off and running on another topic.

Saturday, 15 December, I visited with KAP for three hours, an hour longer than usual. She was spry and chipper: wonderful. She was dressed in a white nightgown with intricate lace about the neck and wrists and held her customary rosary beads. But this time she had a tube strapped around her face with a transparent green section against her nostrils to help her breathing. "Well," I said, referring to the oxygen mask, "I see we have on our jewelry today." She laughed and put on her glasses (the left lens was covered with adhesive tape because it was her left eye that was damaged by the strokes). She started reading what I had typed up. Every sentence or word would cause a flood of comment so that after twenty minutes we had gone through only one paragraph.

She laughed loudly at parts of the letters, and when we read over passages about little Mary Alice Holloway, her niece who died at the age of six, her voice grew soft and slow, and her words filled with emotion. She said at one point, "I don't cry easily now," but after the third reference to her "ineffable Mary Alice," she turned to me and said, "If I'm not careful, I may be crying on your shoulder." I said, "Fine, please do so if need be."

What lovely little phrases spilled out of her mouth. And how she loved going through the letters. At the end of my last visit she had told me that she believed in me. At the end of this visit she told me she liked me. I liked her; in fact, in a way, for an artist and a human being, I loved her. She was like some type of lost grandmother to me.

Friday, 21 December, I visited Katherine Anne before I went to Connecticut for Christmas. I brought some things of mine to give her: a funnily shaped rock I had scooped up off the ocean floor snorkeling in Nassau (she took it and kissed it and pressed it against her cheek) plus a single red rose. She gave me three very pretty ascots. On Christmas Day I called her from Connecticut to wish her a Merry Christmas.

Monday, 7 January 1980, I went to see Katherine Anne and discovered I had to defend myself. Apparently her suspicion was aroused after I had given her a paperback copy of her own *Collected Essays and Occasional Writings* and she saw again its dedication to Barrett Prettyman, her attorney. In the paranoia left by the strokes she ranted against her nephew Paul, her former editor Seymour Lawrence, and Prettyman, men she claimed had "stolen" her works and were responsible for her "situation." She wanted to know whether I was "in cahoots" with them. I defended myself strenuously and told her I had nothing to do with *The Collected Essays* and it had nothing to do with her letters.

She calmed down and talked of many things. She told me she had died three times: once when she was three, once in Denver during the flu epidemic, and once in Mexico, several years ago, when she went there on "some presidential thing."[19] She wanted to give me a book by Maurice Chevalier. She knew about him since she was in her twenties. She said that it was important "just to see how people are great in different ways." I told her I was reading Faulkner's *Absalom, Absalom!* She smiled, said she thought it wonderful, and mentioned how someone had compared her work to his.

Wednesday, 16 January, I met Ed Horner,[20] a friend of Katherine Anne's, and Monroe Wheeler at the National Gallery of Art in Washington, DC, in order to go with them to visit Katherine Anne. I had not met Mr. Wheeler before, and I considered the meeting, indirectly made possible by KAP, to be another serendipitous moment because he later became my mentor. She once mentioned to me how Monroe Wheeler and Glenway Wescott were lovers for forty years. "And I loved them both," she said. Which one did she love more? Monroe. And she said he told her, "I think you made the right choice."

On this day, although she was happy to see Ed and me, when Monroe entered the room she became so excited that she began talking too fast and became angry for not being able to speak more clearly. Ed Horner had to leave, and Monroe, KAP, and I settled down to talk, although I listened more than I talked.

On the drive out, Monroe said to me that if words could kill, then KAP's battlefield would have many corpses. He said she was at her best when she was criticizing someone: "poisonous darts in all directions."

Monday, 21 January, I dropped off a great multi-colored bouquet of balloons for KAP. The summer before, I had started to work in Washington for the then unique business started by Joe Delvecchio called Balloon Bouquets. Rather than delivering a bouquet of flowers, his business delivered bouquets of helium-filled colorful balloons. At the time I had no earthly idea what I was going to do with my life, and I was working for him just to pay my bills.

I hadn't planned to visit KAP that day, but she was so delighted with the balloons, which I tied to the bedpost at the end of her bed, that she insisted I stay. She started to rant against the three men she called the "curse," but I diverted her to literary topics. I told her I planned to finish reading Dostoevsky's *The Idiot* that night and that I thought I could see Dostoevsky's influence in Carson McCullers's work. I told her that, on the other hand, her own work seemed to exist in a vacuum. No influence. She liked that and went off on how "you hear your own music and it's up to you to put it down in your own way." She said she had never let anyone influence her writing. "What became art, I wanted it to be me," and she pointed to herself, to her head, to her ear. I said I was "trying to be a writer," and she said, "No, you *are* a writer. I can tell—you have it." I didn't know what "it" was, but I was pleased to hear her words.

Saturday, 9 February, when I visited KAP I saw that her mind was in the past more than usual. She talked a little about Gertrude Stein, saying that Alice B. Toklas was "lovely" and had told her she was "just a cook" at their house. KAP said that she herself was quite a cook in her day. She recalled some of her marriages. She said that her husbands would come home and there she would be at her typewriter. She recalled the sad death from cancer of her friend Cyrilly Abels. She mentioned that she herself would be dying soon. "It's about time," she said. She told me that she would be moving into a nursing home before long. She also told me I had very nice hands.

Tuesday, 4 March, when I went to visit KAP I took her *The Life of Katherine Mansfield,* by Anthony Alpers. KAP liked Mansfield but detested John Middleton Murry.[21] I remembered that in her Virginia Woolf biography by Quentin Bell beside the name Murry KAP had written in the margin "a hyena."[22] She also detested "that whole crowd"—the Bloomsbury and Garrington ones. She "hated" D. H. Lawrence and considered Frieda Lawrence "a fool." Katherine Anne had met Bertrand Russell in New York City when they were guests on CBS's *Invitation to Learning* discussing *Alice in Wonderland*. "He looked like a little boy," but she liked him. "I like his work." She said that Truman Capote once came for breakfast at her house and then wanted her to go out with him so he'd be "seen" with her. She wouldn't—she said she did not do those kinds of things.

Thursday, 13 March, KAP was in a grand mood when I visited. She spoke clearly and eloquently, and while I read from her letters she listened for an hour and a half, interrupting with laughter or "It's true, you know." Afterward we talked about religion and God and death. She had spoken to Monroe Wheeler that day, and they had talked about an after-life. He said, "You don't believe that, do you?" She leaned toward me and said she had replied, "I'm afraid I do."

Thursday, 27 March, KAP and I had a very pleasant visit. I brought her a Calla lily, which she liked, and I put it in a green vase on her dresser. Letitia brought in good black coffee, and Katherine Anne and I started talking. She was reading a book of selected poetry by John Malcolm Brinnin, whom she liked very much.

We went through more letters, and in one letter there was mention of a dream. She told me she rarely dreamed (only five or six times a year) but that she had had a dream about three or four weeks earlier: there was some human shape, she couldn't say whether it was male or female, and it was standing in front of her and said something like this: "Why haven't you become what you should have become?" And she asked, "What do you mean?" But it went away. She used a hand gesture to indicate how it disappeared.

Wednesday, 28 May, I visited KAP at the Carriage Hill Nursing Home in Silver Spring, Maryland, my third visit since her move there 28 March. I had visited her the day she moved in and was appalled then that she looked so unhappy and frightened. She had whispered to me, "I can't stay here." I had given her a long-stemmed, bloodred rose and tried to comfort her as much as I could.

On her birthday, 15 May, she had looked bad, and two weeks later she looked worse. I remembered that Rhea had said he thought a move to a nursing home would kill her. Her eyes were closed, her skin was dark, her fingers and everything about her looked bony. She didn't respond to the nurse who came in and left or to me: only groaned. I stood by her side looking at her noble head thrown back against the pillow and almost cried. A cleaning lady interrupted me. I told her to come back. I stroked KAP's hair and told her that I didn't know if she could hear me but to know that "I love you, very much." I stroked her hair, touched her face, and kissed her forehead. My dear, beautiful KAP. I thought that she would die soon.

Sunday, 1 June, I visited KAP and was surprised that she seemed much better than the last time. Jane DeMouy and Sister Kathleen Feeley were there but left shortly afterward. There was color in KAP's face, her eyes were open, and she was talking again. She drank some water and milk for me. When she spit up a little of the milk, I cleaned it up and told her, "Oh, don't worry, don't worry, it shows you're getting some spunk again." I told her she had to get up some strength and eat so we could talk and laugh again.

Wednesday, 30 July, I visited KAP and found her sitting up in her wheelchair, talking with her daytime nurse, Debby. After she was put back into bed, she held her rosary beads up and kept kissing them. She wanted me to hold her useless right hand, the hand that signed and wrote and typed, and hoped by some mysterious osmosis her drive and determination and genius would flow into me. But I felt sad. I read her a postcard that Isabel Bayley sent in an envelope that was unopened. I didn't think she read much at all. As I left, she said, "God bless you. I love you." I kissed her hand.

Monday, 8 September, I was nervous when I went to see Katherine Anne to tell her I was moving up to Rhode Island to open a Balloon Bouquets franchise. She was upright in bed, and the light from the window lit up her profile magnificently. She smiled and said she was happy for me. I told her I was picking up one of her habits—always moving about—and she smiled again at that.

When I was ready to leave, she looked at me wide-eyed and squeezed my hand tightly. "I love you—so much," she said. And I said, "Oh, Katherine Anne, and I love you, too." I kissed her forehead and cheeks and lips and hair and hugged her good-bye. I cried as I drove home that afternoon.

I wrote her every day after I left, and I already had dropped a letter to her in the mailbox 19 September when Rhea Johnson called to tell me she had died.

I traveled down by Amtrak to attend the Memorial Mass for Katherine Anne on Saturday, 18 October, which was held in the Gibbons Chapel of the College of Notre Dame of Maryland. Monroe Wheeler and Glenway Wescott were there, and afterward, on the walk over to the reception in Doyle Hall Lounge, Glenway made a curious remark: "You were her last lover or her last beloved."

As I write this memoir in 2007, it has been twenty-six years since her death. I'm now middle-aged. I mused over Glenway's remark for weeks after I found it in my notes. What little I know about love, in all its varieties and forms, I did come to love KAP as I spent more time with her. However, knowing KAP's proclivity

Ted Wojtasik, who became Katherine Anne Porter's friend the year after he graduated from college. Glenway Wescott described Wojtasik as Porter's "last beloved." Courtesy Ted Wojtasik.

for falling in love with younger men as she aged, I don't think she ever thought of me in terms of a "lover," as Glenway suggested, but certainly, perhaps, as a "beloved": a young man working with her on her letters, sharing stories, laughing, reading out loud to each other, discussing literature and writers, exchanging books, helping her, and just *being* there with her.

One of the most serendipitous moments of my life was the moment I stepped into KAP's bedroom on Tuesday, 10 July 1979. Unlike other writers (even KAP herself) who claimed to have started writing as a child or teenager or adolescent, I had never entertained the idea of becoming a writer—until I met Miss Katherine Anne Porter, my literary godmother.

51 / Jane DeMouy

Jane Krause DeMouy (1942–) is a Katherine Anne Porter scholar who retired from teaching in 1984. Since then she has worked as a journalist for National Public Radio, a feature writer for newspapers and magazines, and a science writer/editor at the National Institutes of Health. She is the author of *Katherine Anne Porter's Women: The Eye of Her Fiction* (1983). She received her B.A. from the College of Notre Dame of Maryland and her M.A. and Ph.D. from the University of Maryland, College Park.

Source: Jane DeMouy, "Elegy for Katherine Anne," *Virginia Quarterly Review* 75 (1999): 504–10.

September 18, 1980—It is not quite 5 p.m., and Katherine Anne Porter is dead. She has expired in the true sense of the word, breathing out the last of her life imperceptibly. I am standing at her side holding her hand, looking at the notches on the ticking clock, the time moving on, even as Katherine Anne has moved beyond it. This visit has become the last of the many I have made to be with her during the last two years of her life. There have been no profound—or even simple—last words, no enigmatic questions posed nor secrets betrayed, just a quiet bowing out—a step, step, slide behind the final curtain and out the stage door.

Her last breath came and went quietly, but her death had not. It is no mistake to say Death was her familiar, as it must have been for most people born when dying typically occurred, not in the sterilized and remote world of a hospital, but in the next room. Her mother's death in childbirth when Porter was barely a toddler may have been one of her first memories, and her own life was threatened by tuberculosis and the influenza epidemic of 1918 when she was still a young woman. Not surprisingly, her stories deal with death over and over again; it is death that gives the best of them their emotional edge.

In "Pale Horse, Pale Rider" and "The Jilting of Granny Weatherall," Porter personifies and stares Death in the face. In "Pale Horse," she records a captivating life-after-death vision a young woman is forced to relinquish as she waves the pale rider on, stoically taking up life again in spite of a near-fatal blow. In "Granny

Weatherall," Porter creates with remarkable insight the old woman's passage to last breath. Weaving the reader in and out of the dying woman's conscious reality and her unconscious reprise of the most painful and significant experiences of her life, Porter suspends time while demonstrating how one *should* meet death: with fear at bay and with stoic acceptance when the inevitable comes. Granny Weatherall, seeing the reality of her last moment, blows out the flickering breath of life herself.

At 88, then 89, then 90, Porter knew what was coming, and she didn't take kindly to her decline. When I met her, she was already hobbled by stroke and bedridden, but her core personality seemed intact: she could be loving, funny, furious, intractable; on a good day, her mind probed and she held strong opinions, even if she couldn't always clearly say what she wished. She was vain of her appearance—and quite beautiful—even in the final days when she had become too fragile and fatigued to be conscious of whether or not her hair was curled and combed. And always, there was charisma in her wit and charm that ensured the attention from others that she so roundly craved. I first met her as a student, critic, and admirer of her work. As a sometime companion to her during her purgatory, I came to love her as many people did, for her spirit and her courage, for the feisty way she had of heading back into the ring after a bloody bad day.

Over the two weighted years it took age and illness to kill her, Porter raged against and yearned for this last lover, refusing and denying Death many days, and keening after him on others. Her death was not simply an event of September 18, 1980. She let go of life and breath in imperceptible increments over hundreds of days. There were times when she repeated and repeated that she wanted to die; there were others when she told me calmly that she had lived a good life, and did not mind that it was ending. On September 18, her life finished, and with it, the final struggle this tough, sensitive woman had endured.

The blessing of long life unfortunately means outliving most of one's friends; and Porter had also, in her stroke-induced paranoia, cut herself off from her much-loved niece and nephew and others like her attorney, E. Barrett Prettyman, and her secretary, Bill Wilkins, who were closest to her before the stroke. The stroke's first blow was the loss of the use of her writing hand; the second was the loss of language, her life's blood, whether written or spoken. Sometimes she could be patient with it, saying, "Now wait a minute, Honey," while she strove to give voice to a bit of information. At other times, it was bitter to her to be unable to retrieve and pronounce words her mind still knew. The easy contact, camaraderie, and comfort of friends so vital to her followed quickly on these thefts. Cut off from both work and love, she was also physically trapped, and it frustrated and enraged her.

She could be trying, and her fury venomous. The woman who nursed her daily caught the brunt of her frustration and anger. But she was neither cold nor a mean-spirited person defined only by her prejudices. She was gifted. She was flawed. She had demons; but when they fired on her, she hauled herself up to face them. Her last struggle was no different. "Look at me," she asked once. "I can't speak. I can't write. But no wrist-slitting—that's too easy."

In the year before her last decline, most often I would find her reading, books open on her lap or stacked on her bedside table: The poems of John Malcolm Brinnin, and of Stevie Smith, Pauline de Rothschild's memoir of her travels in Russia, Allen Tate's essays, and her own. She would hunch forward over a book in her big hospital bed, thick glasses perched on her nose. Her immobilized right eye was covered with a patch; her good eye magnified and vivid blue. She would hold the book on her knee with her left hand and slowly wade through the words as if giving a public reading.

In April she was still thinking about work, wanting me to write to Ned O'Gorman, who had requested an interview for his biography of Allen Tate. Porter thought it too soon after Tate's death, and spoke of some of her last conversation with Tate. When I showed her the letter of acceptance I had just gotten from a university press for a book on her work, she told me matter-of-factly, "They mean business. This is very good. I've seen dozens of these, and they mean it."

Preparing to move to a nursing home arranged for her by her nephew and guardian, Paul, she said she was getting out of the place she had lived in and was taking "only one or two things" and her clothes. "I'm leaving all the rest of it," she said, apparently unconcerned about the shelves and shelves of well-read books, the Victorian and Mexican furniture, the photos, the keepsakes. But of course, she had done this over and over all her life; it must have seemed like just one more move, to what she hoped would be a better situation.

Her move to a bright room at Carriage Hill Nursing Center was hardly the getaway I think she wished for. She adjusted as well as she was able, and on May 15 ended her ninetieth year. A few days later, she entered a real decline that showed itself in the journal I was keeping.

May 26. She is frail and more fatigued. My visits became a ritual and a tableau: I stand at her bedside so she can see me, she holding my hand tightly and then placing it in the hollow of her cheek, which seems to comfort her. "My darling, I'm so glad you're here," she says. I talk to her about "Pale Horse, Pale Rider," and her vision of a luminous fan of light behind all the people she had ever loved. I talk to her about the rich life she has had, that it is hard to let go of that, and hard for it to let her go. I begin to feel like an acolyte attending the mystery that is starting to unfold in earnest. I want to smooth her descent, and since I can't ease her pain, I want to soothe fear and stop the anxiety she can only express cloaked in anger.

The nurse tells me that Katherine Anne has given up; she is not eating, and I am afraid to ask how much longer she can go on in that state. She looks almost skeletal, the wonderful bones of her face honed to a fine essence, but there is still strength in her hand squeezing mine as it rests against her face. I remember Theodore Roethke's *Elegy for Jane* and feel myself, like the poet, standing by, "with no rights in the matter," neither daughter nor lover. I pick up her linen winding sheet from the laundry, and for the first time, I pray that she will die. Take her home, Lord. Let go, Katherine Anne.

May 30. She is alert again, and complaining in her stroke-stifled speech that she can't understand why her life has come to *this*. And why doesn't somebody do something to help her? I tell her no one *can* do anything about it, but that the good Lord will take care of her. She takes a very firm face with me, as if she is not about to be hoodwinked or cajoled. To distract her, I re-read birthday cards from Isabel Bayley and a group of students who have been studying her stories. Both messages please and settle her. When I tell her I'm going down the hall briefly to speak to the nurse, she tells me, "I'll be here," and laughs. I'm glad to see the humor in her and remind her that friends are coming the next day. "Can you fit that in your schedule?" I ask. She laughs again and says she isn't going anywhere. Later, as she drifts into sleep, she murmurs, "Don't leave me."

Summer comes in. On a given day, she may sit up, wearing a deep blue shawl that sharpens the color of her eyes and the whiteness of her hair, a little color on her lips. If her body is awesomely fragile, she still has piercing eyes and lovely cheekbones. It is possible to see the skull beneath the skin, but there is also the ancient beauty of her face, now wrinkled out of youth and prosperity, but still classically beautiful. Another day she may seem confused and then surprise me with the clarity of her focus. On one such morning, I answer a phone call from Monroe Wheeler, and explain to him that she will be able to understand him, but that she isn't speaking clearly. She takes the phone from me as I tell her who is calling, and she says to him in utterly clear tones, "Hello, my darling. I love you," and arranges a Saturday visit with him.

On the days when the process of giving up life seems painfully slow, she refuses to be comforted, refuses to accept what is happening to her, and lets me know she thinks I am naïve to believe that people are doing their best for her. She can screw up her face with all the old fury her scrappy personality is capable of and tell me I am crazy and heartless, and how can I stand there looking like a nice person and say something like that to her? And so it goes.

July 14. She wants to know why she has to be where she is and why nobody will do anything about it. It is impossible to distract or console her. I tell her I have to go and that I'll be back in a few days. "Here?" she asks, incredulous. Yes, I say. She is angry and I am traitorous.

September 16. The doctor checks her regularly and finds her still strong, vital signs OK. But her face seems cadaverous, and she looks as if she could snap like a twig. Her breath rattles her fragile body. On the bedside table a record of her fluid intake is taped: 8 a.m., 8 cc coffee. Beside the record sheet are three opened containers with the liquids still in them.

Huddled in a nest of pillows, she takes my hand and holds on, drifting in and out. Once she murmurs, "Isn't it strange?" I tell her I love her, and how her friend Bill [Wilkins] and I have talked two nights before about how she has always inspired such ardent affection in people. She smiles into her pillow and says distinctly, "That's true," with perfect acceptance. She opens her eyes, but looks past me, at something else. I remember what my mother always said when new babies smile—that they were seeing angels. I wonder if Katherine Anne is doing the same. I am rooted in the concrete, conscious of clothes on my body, hair hanging around my face, my solid weight. I feel stuck to the chair I lean from. Katherine Anne floats. Her hand holding mine, perhaps more lightly than usual, is the other tether between us.

An aide appears and announces firmly that she must turn Katherine Anne and I must leave the room. I stand outside the door and listen to Katherine Anne crying out and imagine the woman's hands pulling the sheets, structuring pillows, and hauling the thin body back into this rude world. When I return, bedsores have been prevented, but Katherine Anne no longer nestles. She lies stiffly propped against double pillows plumped and put in their proper place. She is upset, and nothing consoles her. I wish I had left earlier, when she was still content.

September 18. I go to see her at noon. She is alert, in pain, but unable to say what is wrong. The nurse and I try to get her to take some soup, eat a little ice cream, but nothing helps. I stay until 1:30. A little after three the director of the nursing home calls to say Katherine Anne has had "an episode," and that her pulse is very weak.

I run the two blocks to Carriage Hill and arrive to find her awake—eyes wide but out of touch. She is getting oxygen to keep her comfortable, but she consumes it like a crude commodity she no longer needs, in short, raspy breaths, slowly, slowly giving it up. Before leaving the room, the nurse tells me Katherine Anne can hear me, though she gives no sign of understanding. I take her hand and tell her she is not alone. I tell her I am with her, standing on one side holding her hand, and that the good Lord is on the other, with arms held out to her. All she has to do is reach. No sign of recognition.

I get up and set the bedside clock ticking—notches of sound to ground me during my last time with her. I sing what I can: "Pale horse, pale rider, done taken my love from me. . . . ." and tell her she will finally be with Alex, the lover she lost in 1918; that her mother, her sisters, Gay and Mary Alice, her grandmother and her father will all be there to welcome her with shining eyes. I tell her that she is leaving herself with us in her wonderful stories, that those stories have given her immortality and it is all right for her to go. She holds my hand lightly. Gradually, softly, finally, she lets the light die. Her color leaves her. Her lips begin to look mottled and her fingers blue. Her hand gets colder under mine, and once in a while she misses a breath, making my heart stop until she draws another. Finally, her eyelids drowse, and the lazy breath simply doesn't return. It is not quite 5 p.m., and Katherine Anne Porter is gone.

You know what I will miss?" she had asked one afternoon. "I will miss the sound of the wind when I am dead." As I still miss the sound of her voice.

52 / Lynn Darling

Lynn Darling (1952–), a freelance journalist, grew up in northern Virginia, received a B.A. from Radcliffe College, and in 1975 went to work for the *Washington Post*. In 1986 she married Lee Adrien Lescaze, White House correspondent at the *Post*. The story of that marriage, which ended with Lescaze's death in 1996, is the heart of Darling's 2007 book *Necessary Sins: A Memoir*. Her work has appeared in *Esquire, Harper's Bazaar, The Traveller*, and *Elle*, among other magazines.

Source: Lynn Darling, "The Life of the Party: Celebrating Katherine Anne Porter's 91st Birthday," *Washington Post* 18 May 1981: C1, C6.

Katherine Anne Porter, who died last September, was famous and honored and old, and she had crafted her life with care. "Look how long I have lived!" she once wrote. "Well, what an amiable sort of incurable trouble to have . . . I don't mind at all."

Last Friday, her friends gave Katherine Anne Porter a party on the day she would have been 91 years old. "She dreaded the idea of there not being any more parties for her after she died," said Deborah Toll, the wife of the president of the University of Maryland, to which she had donated her library. And so they threw the party, and hoped it was in a style she would have appreciated, good liquor and quick-witted company.

"She told people before she died that she believed she was going to Fiddler's Green," said her lawyer, Barrett Prettyman, who serves also as special counsel to the House Ethics Committee. "It's an Irish concept that is neither heaven or hell, but a place where you go and gambol among green pastures."

They came together, old friends and young writers, admirers of the woman and her work. They drank champagne, they ate an elegant meal, they toasted her memory. Katherine Anne, they called her and at times there was a gentle competition to paint her portrait in the truest colors. But memory could only play second fiddle to life.

Katherine Anne Porter was an exquisite and painstaking writer, whose short stories were diamond bright and whose novel *Ship of Fools* brought her wealth and fame in the autumn of her life. By then, she was a wanderer, she had lived in Mexico and Paris, she knew revolutionaries and literary giants and blithe skaters gliding on thin ice. "I don't like gloomy sinners," she once wrote, "but the merry ones charm me." Katherine Anne was a good cook and a good talker, she collected her friends and lovers with care, she liked champagne and she knew how to make a good entrance. And a good exit—she was married and divorced three [sic] times.

"The last four or five years were so tough," said her nephew, Paul Porter, a New York businessman. "I find that the memories of the other times are just coming back." The ones he proffered were gentle, the woman who emerged a pale shadow that played lightly on the wall. He talked of meeting her at 17 and being "dazzled, anyone would be," of the hours they spent talking about everything under the sun, of the way she had of scribbling in the margins of her books, arguing or commending. "I remember her quarreling with a recipe for glazed carrots," he said. He looked contemplatively at the food on his own plate. "I have no idea what this is," he said finally, "but it's easy to eat, so I like it."

They talked of her short stories, which she began writing in 1923 and which of them could be made into movies,[23] and Paul Porter mentioned how he once tried to get Dolores Del Rio interested in one,[24] but he never heard back. And so famous beauties of the day were discussed, the eyes of one the cheekbones of another, in the way that people have when they are grateful for a subject of conversation. "Cheekbones," huffed one guest with admirable loyalty. "Talking of cheekbones at a party for the queen of cheekbones."

It came time for toasts, and one by one they remembered her kindly. They remembered her delight at walking into Tiffany's to indulge her taste in emeralds with the money that *Ship of Fools* brought her. "She told me she walked in and told the clerk, 'Honey, don't show me anything small,' said Josephine Jacobsen. And you know, she never showed anyone anything small." It was not, said Prettyman, "a request but an order that we should all have some drink and some fun and to think of her with the very best of happy thoughts, not to despair of her passing, but to be happy we all knew her."

Paul Porter, however, made no toast to his aunt Friday night. No, he said, as his slim gold cigarette lighter caught the light from the single white candle in the middle of the table. Katherine Anne was too complicated a woman to sum up in just a few words. He had been her guardian the last few years and he is the executor of her will. Last month he took her ashes back to Indian Creek, Tex., where she was born, and there, as the wind howled in the mesquite trees, and the wheat fields waved in the distance, he buried them beside her mother's grave. On her tombstone he put the inscription she had said she wanted, the motto of Mary, queen of Scots: "In my end is my beginning."

"Would you please come over," Father Joseph Gallagher remembered her once asking him. "I know you can't say anything new, but I'd like to hear the old things again." It was the prayers for the dying she wanted to hear. "Some nuns who were friends of hers had called me once and asked me to come over and say the prayers and give her holy communion," said Father Gallagher. "But she kept not dying, so I kept coming to see her. She used to weep as I read them. But she wanted to die, she wasn't afraid of dying. She said, 'You learn something the day you die; you learn how to die.'" He smiled. "She used to call me 'honey.'"

The guests ate strawberries and cream and fell to musing about the nature of their absent honoree, about the kind of woman she was. Someone remembered her as a woman who would drop a long white glove on the stage before a reading, to make sure the audience was with her. Another recalled her as a woman who would say, "Yes, indeed, I love a pretty man and I love a party," and to whom every man she loved did a disservice by getting in the way of her creative life. A feminist, someone called her. Not so, said another. "She hated the word, incidentally," said her nephew.

Toward the end of the party, the guests moved out on the patio to watch a movie of her as the evening wind blew cold. Katherine Anne Porter was dressed in black and she wore pearls and her dark eyes were bright like the eyes of some little night creature, alert to the lessons the wind has to teach it. She talked about writing in her sharp quick voice that seemed to hurry over the words. "Writing can't be taught," she said. "It has to be learned." Read history, she advised, and "for the love of heaven don't pay any attention to Freud. Pay attention to human beings," she said, and "you'll learn all you have a right to know."

"Boy," said one of the guests, as they all filed back inside for brandy or more champagne. "The great ones can always come through with a good punch line."

Even in death, she was the life of the party.

List of Reminiscences

(See Works Cited for complete bibliographic information.)

Part 1. Texas and Colorado, 1890–1919

Crawford, Kitty Barry. Letter to George Hendrick, 13 November 1961.
Crume, Paul. Review of *Pale Horse, Pale Rider: Three Short Novels.*
Hendrick, Willene. "Indian Creek: A Sketch from Memory."
Holloway, Gay Porter. Letters to Katherine Anne Porter. 25 July 1954, 14 December 1955, 26 February 1956, 18 October 1961, 22 January 1962, 3 November 1962.
Johns, Erna Schlemmer. Letters to Katherine Anne Porter. 3 May 1939, 13 April 1978.
———. *To Whom It May Concern,* 1: 62–63.
Naylor, Pauline. "Early Porter Tales Written Here."
———. "Katherine Anne Porter's Ft. Worth Days Recalled."
Sexton, Kathryn Adams. "Katherine Anne Porter's Years in Denver," 14, 16–21, 24.
Stalling, Donald. "Katherine Anne Porter: Life and the Literary Mirror," 23, 28–29, 35, 36.

Part 2. New York, Connecticut, and Mexico, 1920–1931

Anderson, Elizabeth. *Miss Elizabeth: A Memoir,* 203–5.
Cowles, W. H. Report to W. J. Burns, 10 October 1921.
Herbst, Josephine. "A Year of Disgrace."
Hill, Winifred. Personal interview. 17 August 1981.
Hoover, J. Edgar. Memorandum, 2 August 1921.
Josephson, Matthew. *Life among the Surrealists,* 352–54.
Plunkett, Robert. Telephone interviews. 11 May 2006 and 13 October 2007.

Part 3. Europe, Texas, and Louisiana, 1932–1940

Brooks, Cleanth. "The Woman and Artist I Knew."
Hardy, John Edward. "Remembering KAP."
Porter, Breckenridge. Telephone interview. 12 April 1997.
Porter, Paul. "A Bouquet for Aunt Katherine."
———. "Remembering Aunt Katherine."
Welty, Eudora. "My Introduction to Katherine Anne Porter."

Wescott, Glenway. "Katherine Anne Porter: The Making of a Novel."
Willison, Toni. Personal interviews. 13–14 June 1996.

Part 4. New York, Washington, DC, and California, 1941–1951

Bayley, Isabel. "Forever May."
Brinnin, John Malcolm. *Dylan Thomas in America,* 18–20.
Clark, Eleanor. "The Friendships of a Lifetime."
Goyen, William. "Katherine Anne Porter: An Appreciation."
Scowcroft, Richard. Telephone interview. 9 July 1995.
Spencer, Elizabeth. *Landscapes of the Heart: A Memoir,* 236–37.
Winslow, Marcella. Letters to Anne Goodwin Winslow. In *Brushes with the Literary,* 42–45, 50–55, 56–57, 59–61, 63–64, 66–69, 71–76.

Part 5. New York, Europe, Michigan, Virginia, and Washington, DC, 1952–1961

Davis, Barbara Thompson. Untitled reminiscence.
Hardwick, Elizabeth. "Katherine Anne."
Johns, Rita. Personal interview. 29 October 1994.
Lawrence, Seymour. Letter to Darlene Harbour Unrue. 9 December 1992.
Locher, David. "Katherine Anne Porter."
———. "Summer Straw & Blue (Ann Arbor, July 1954)."
O'Connor, Flannery. Letters. In *Letters of Flannery O'Connor: The Habit of Being,* 260, 275, 276, 417.
Rockwell, Jeanne. "The Magic Cloak: On Meeting Katherine Anne Porter."
Ruoff, James. "Katherine Anne Porter Comes to Kansas."

Part 6. New York, Washington, DC, and Maryland, 1962–1973

Dobson, Clark. "An Unforgettable Decade."
Eichner, Maura. "Try It On."
———. "Visit to Katherine Anne Porter: after the stroke."
Feeley, Kathleen. "In My End Is My Beginning."
Liberman, M. M. "Meeting Miss Porter."
Lopez, Enrique Hank. *Conversations with Katherine Anne Porter: Refugee from Indian Creek,* xiii–xviii.
Prettyman, E. Barrett, Jr. "My Years with Katherine Anne—as Friend and Lawyer."
Prince, John. Untitled reminiscence.
Prokosch, Frederic. "The Nightmare of Literary Life."
Scott, Michael. "A Classic Manner."
Wilkins, William R. Personal interviews. 27 May 1995 and 13 August 1997.

Part 7. Texas and Maryland, 1974–1981

Darling, Lynn. "The Life of the Party: Celebrating Katherine Anne Porter's 91st Birthday."
DeMouy, Jane. "Elegy for Katherine Anne."
Gallagher, Joseph. "Katherine Anne Porter: The Last Candle Is Out."
Laughlin, Charlotte. "How I Accompanied Katherine Anne Porter on the Last Great Pilgrimage of Her Life."
Wojtasik, Ted. "The Final Year of Katherine Anne Porter."

Additional Reminiscences

Brooks, Cleanth. Personal interviews with Darlene Harbour Unrue. 18–22 December 1993.

Brooks, Roger. "Hosting Miss Porter." *Katherine Anne Porter and Texas: An Uneasy Relationship.* Ed. Clinton Machann and William Bedford Clark. College Station: Texas A&M UP, 1990. 110–21.

Bruccoli, Matthew J. Personal interview with Darlene Harbour Unrue. 31 March 1996.

Clark, Eleanor. Personal interviews with Darlene Harbour Unrue. 28–29 January 1994.

Clayton, Imogene. Letter to Katherine Anne Porter. 15 January 1957. Papers of Katherine Anne Porter, Special Collections, U of Maryland, College Park, Libraries.

Crawford, Kitty Barry. Letter to George Hendrick. 20 November 1961. Collection of Darlene Harbour Unrue.

Doherty, Mary Louis. Letters to Peggy Doherty. Papers of Mary Louis Doherty. Special Collections, U of Maryland, College Park.

———. Personal interview with Thomas F. Walsh. Ca. 1982. Papers of Thomas F. Walsh, Special Collections, U of Maryland, College Park.

Guzman, Soledad. Personal interview with Darlene Harbour Unrue. 15 August 1981.

McMillan, James B. "K.A.P. Was Here." *Alabama Alumni News* 45 (March/April 1964): 4–5, 11.

O'Gorman, Juan. Personal interview with Darlene Harbour Unrue. 12 August 1981.

O'Higgins, Pablo. Personal interview with Darlene Harbour Unrue. 12 August 1981.

Porter, Paul. "Katherine Anne Porter's Coffin: The Last Word?" *Newsletter of the Katherine Anne Porter Society* 5 (1998): 1.

———. Personal interview with Darlene Harbour Unrue. 29 October 1994.

———. "Remembered Laughter." *Newsletter of the Katherine Anne Porter Society* 14 (2008): 1–2.

Prince, John, and Catherine Prince. Personal interview with Darlene Harbour Unrue. 28 May 1995.

Rickards, George, and Mabel Rickards. Personal interview with Darlene Harbour Unrue. 11 August 1981.

Robinson, Lucille Clayton. Letter to Katherine Anne Porter, 12 December 1930. Papers of Katherine Anne Porter, Special Collections, U of Maryland, College Park, Libraries.

Rubin, Louis D., Jr. "'We Get Along Together Just Fine . . . .'" *Four Quarters* 12 (March 1963): 30–31.

Stegner, Wallace. Letter to Joan Givner, 8 January 1978, unsent. Papers of Wallace Stegner, Stanford U.

Steiner, Herbert. Letter to Darlene Harbour Unrue, 11 July 2000.

———. Telephone interview with Darlene Harbour Unrue, 10 July 2000.

Subramanian, Alexandra. "Katherine Anne Porter and Sam Lawrence: A View from Beacon Hill [A personal interview with Merloyd Lawrence]." *Newsletter of the Katherine Anne Porter Society* 14 (2008): 1–2, 7.

Tyson, A. Mervyn. Telephone interview with Darlene Harbour Unrue. 17 July 1995.

Warren, Rosanna. Personal interview with Darlene Harbour Unrue. 28 January 1994.

Welty, Eudora. Personal interview with Darlene Harbour Unrue. 28 February 1994.

Willison, Malcolm. "A Visit with Katherine Anne Porter." Unpublished reminiscence. Papers of Toni Willison, Special Collections, U of Maryland, College Park.

Winslow, Marcella Comès. Personal interview with Darlene Harbour Unrue. 16 April 1994.

Winters, Janet Lewis. Personal interview with Darlene Harbour Unrue. 15 July 1994.

Notes

Introduction

1. See Paul Crume (No. 5).

2. Revised entries appeared in the editions of 1942, in which Porter acknowledges her last two marriages (but not the first three), and 1955, in which she talks about her work in progress and her dislike of deadlines.

3. KAP to Porter Family, 31 December 1920, Papers of KAP, Special Collections, University of Maryland, College Park, Libraries.

4. KAP, "Reflections on Willa Cather," *Collected Essays* 34.

5. KAP to Kenneth Burke, 20 November 1954, Kenneth Burke Papers, Pennsylvania State University Libraries. Quoted with permission of Barbara Thompson Davis, trustee, the KAP Literary Estate, and Pennsylvania State University Libraries.

6. KAP to James Brown (of the James Brown and Associates Agency), 24 June 1952, copy in Papers of KAP, Special Collections, University of Maryland, College Park, Libraries.

7. See Elizabeth Hardwick (No. 30).

Part 1

1. Gay is referring to the trip to Indian Creek KAP made with her sister Baby and their father in 1936, when the Porter house had already been torn down. See Unrue, *Porter* 161.

2. Harry Ray (Harrison Paul) Porter.

3. Reverend David Porter, a cousin of KAP's grandfather Asbury Duval Porter, was pastor of the Mountain View Baptist Church from 1872 through KAP's childhood. He was a frequent visitor at her grandmother's house.

4. Catharine Ann Skaggs Porter, KAP's paternal grandmother.

5. Gay and KAP's sister Mary Alice, also known as "Baby."

6. Catharine Ann Skaggs Porter hired a series of live-in tutors for her grandchildren, some of whom KAP remembered as down-on-their-luck women her grandmother took in; others were distant relatives.

7. KAP tells a version of this anecdote in "Notes on the Texas I Remember."

8. A similar scene occurs in KAP's stories "The Fig Tree" and "The Witness."

9. A scene like this appears in KAP's story "He."

10. The house was not the same house. The Porters' log house had been replaced before

1936 with the house in which Mary McAden and Cora Posey lived. See Gay Porter Hollo-way to KAP, 14 December 1955 (No. 1).

11. Mary McAden is confused about the order of the Porter children. Johnny was born (and died) before Callie's birth.

12. Mary McAden's memory is faulty here; Callie was only a little past two when she left Indian Creek after her mother's death.

13. This anecdote was passed on to Stalling by Terrell Sledge in a letter dated 10 May 1951. After Alice Porter died in 1892, Harrison took his children to Kyle, in Hays County, to be largely reared by his widowed mother, Catharine Ann Skaggs Porter, widely known affectionately as "Aunt Cat" in the region where her nieces and nephews and grandnieces and grandnephews exceeded one hundred.

14. Anna Gay was living there with the family, too.

15. Cora Posey is confused about the year, which would have been 1904, not 1906. Callie, who was calling herself "Katherine" by then, was a student at the Thomas School and enthusiastically participating in dramatic productions there. She also took singing lessons at the nearby Lady of the Lake convent. It is true that she had ambitions to go on the stage, and in the summer of 1905 she and her sister Gay played summer stock at Electric Park in San Antonio. See Unrue, *Porter* 33–38.

16. Harrison Porter was Sunday school superintendent of the Oswalt Methodist Church between 1886 and 1892.

17. Stalling interviewed Cora Posey, the McAdens, and others who supplied information about the Porter family at Indian Creek. For an overview of the Porter family's years at Indian Creek, see Stalling 22–61.

18. The 1900 census taker recorded Anna Gay's name as "Annie."

19. Willene Hendrick concludes her essay with a list of some of the factual errors that KAP perpetuated about herself that have since been corrected in the published biographies.

20. Elise Weimer (1865–1942) was the Schlemmer family's beloved housekeeper.

21. Amy, Miranda's aunt, is a character in the short novel.

22. "Witch" was the nickname KAP gave herself; it was inspired by her fascination with Joan of Arc, who was accused of being a witch. KAP assigned Erna the nickname "Fairy."

23. KAP insisted she never worked for the *Dallas Morning News*, but Lon Tinkle, who worked for the paper, was certain she did, as was KAP's friend Kitty Barry Crawford. See Stalling 62–65.

24. These words can be attributed to Kitty Barry Crawford, who says something similar to George Hendrick but asks that she not be quoted.

25. This glove was one of the few items of clothing left that belonged to KAP's mother. KAP kept it all her life and thought it brought her good luck. It is among her possessions preserved in the Papers of KAP, Special Collections, University of Maryland, College Park, Libraries.

26. KAP's leftist sympathies show here. Eamon De Valera (1882–1973), a strenuous

supporter of Irish resistance to British control, was a leader in the Easter Monday uprising of 1916. He served as president of the political party Sinn Fein and later as president of the Republic of Ireland (1959–73).

27. Rose Wilder Lane (1887–1968), the daughter of Laura Ingalls Wilder, was a leftist writer whom KAP met in Greenwich Village in 1919–20.

28. In 1919–20 KAP became friends with Ernestine Evans (1889–1967), who as features editor for the *Christian Science Monitor* encouraged KAP to write articles from Mexico. Evans herself regularly participated in socialist causes.

29. Gertrude Emerson Sen (1890–1982), a descendant of Ralph Waldo Emerson, was an editor at *Asia* and at *Every-Land,* a children's magazine in which KAP published three retold fairy tales. Emerson made possible KAP's job ghostwriting *A Chinese Marriage,* which was published serially in *Asia* before appearing as a book.

30. KAP worked for the Arthur Kane Agency writing publicity releases for movies. She interviewed Charles Ray for *Motion Picture Magazine.* See KAP, "The Real Ray."

31. Tiam Franking (1889–1919) was expecting a government position but hardly an ambassadorship. He did not die on the boat but rather in San Francisco, of tuberculosis, at the age of twenty-nine.

32. This account is an exaggeration. KAP took months to finish the work, which began to appear serially when she was in Mexico. It went through several printings but was far from being a best-seller. She corrected the account, probably supplied by Kitty Barry Crawford, in a 23 March 1956 letter to Stalling. Copy in Papers of KAP, Special Collections, University of Maryland, College Park, Libraries.

33. Luis Morones and probably J. H. Retinger, a Polish expatriate who was affiliated with Morones and was for a time KAP's lover. See Unrue, *Porter* 81, 82, 83, 88, 91, 92, 95, 123, 125.

34. KAP was editor for the only two issues of *Magazine of Mexico:* March and April 1921.

35. "The Dove of Chapacalco" was never finished, but fragments were published posthumously in *Uncollected Early Prose.* Kitty Barry Crawford was the likely source of this information.

36. This observation was most likely made by Kitty Barry Crawford, at whose Fort Worth home KAP was working on "The Dove of Chapacalco" in 1921.

37. KAP used some of these experiences in "Pale Horse, Pale Rider."

38. KAP played Marie in *Poor Old Jim* opposite Roscoe Carnrike and Hunter Gardner, Rosalind's brother, and Columbine in *The Wonder Hat.* KAP wrote an article for the *Star-Telegram* praising the Little Theater's attempts "to free the artist from conventionalized forms, to weave color, music, movement, light [and] the faithful interpretation of human emotions into [. . .] a four-dimensional art far removed from the mere spectacle of a show" (9 November 1921, 2). See Jones 132–33.

39. Winold Reiss (1886–1953) was a German-born artist and art school teacher with whom KAP became friends in the fall of 1920 when he was in Mexico for a six-week visit.

40. KAP arrived in Colorado in the spring of 1918. She spent a short time in a tu-

berculosis sanatorium and the bigger part of the summer on Cheyenne Mountain, near Colorado Springs, in a rented cabin. She began work at the *Rocky Mountain News* in September.

41. KAP fell ill in October and was hospitalized for over a month.

42. Thomas Hornsby Ferril (1896–1988) later became a well-known regional poet.

43. KAP fictionalized this experience in "Pale Horse, Pale Rider."

44. See Hilt and Alvarez ix–x, 80–103.

45. KAP never aspired to be a journalist. She wanted to be a serious artist, and worked as a freelance journalist only to support herself. See KAP, "You Are What You Read."

46. KAP was a reporter for the *Rocky Mountain News.*

47. Kitty Barry Crawford's husband sent her to Denver for recuperation, and KAP's brother, Paul, paid her expenses.

48. Both KAP and Kitty Barry Crawford were patients at the Oaks, the tuberculosis sanatorium at Adams Memorial Hospital in Denver. Crawford later was a patient at Agnes Memorial Hospital.

49. A. D. Stone was a reporter for the *Denver Post.*

50. G. William Holden was a co-founder with Lawrence Phipps of Agnes Memorial Sanatorium, in Montclair, a suburb of Denver.

51. Fola La Follette (1882–1970), the daughter of Wisconsin governor and senator Robert M. La Follette and the suffragette Bella Case La Follette, was an actress, the wife of playwright George Middleton, and one of the leftist reformers with whom KAP socialized in Greenwich Village in 1919 and 1920.

52. See Unrue, *Porter* 91–93, for an account of the exhibit.

53. KAP went to Mexico in the spring of 1923 on an assignment for *Survey Graphic* to gather pieces for a special issue on Mexico.

54. KAP's pet monkey was named J. Alfred Prufrock.

55. "The Future Is Now" is the title of an essay KAP published in *Mademoiselle* in 1950 in which she stressed the importance of living for each moment because we don't know when the atom bomb might blow us all up.

Part 2

1. Miss Mikowitz is most likely Natasha Michaelova, who was deported in May 1921 with Charles Francis Phillips. KAP knew both of them well, and according to her diary notes, their deportation made her fearful of a similar fate.

2. Luis Napoleón Morones (1890–1946) was head of the Confederación Regional Obrera Mexicana (CROM; Regional Confederation of Mexican Workers) and helped ensure Álvaro Obregón's victory in the 1920 Mexican presidential election. KAP was friendly with him in 1920 and 1921, and even danced with him at the inaugural ball, but later considered him only one among many corrupt Mexican politicians.

3. The description of the contents of the April issue of *Magazine of Mexico* has provided all that is known about it, since no extant copy has been located. The March issue,

which KAP also put together, is available in the Papers of KAP, Special Collections, University of Maryland, College Park, Libraries.

4. See KAP, *Uncollected Early Prose* 62–72.

5. Grendel A. Hole (1903–72) was a naive eighteen-year-old single man with a little family money at the time he met W. D. Outman (see note 6), who convinced him to invest in the *Magazine of Mexico*.

6. William D. Outman (b. 1877), former president of a Montana savings bank, had pled guilty in 1912 for accepting a deposit in an insolvent bank. He had been an oil operator and broker in Washington, Oregon, Montana, and Texas before he met the young Grendel Hole (see note 5) and convinced him to invest in the short-lived *Magazine of Mexico*. Although the magazine was highly regarded for its literary quality, it folded for lack of money after the Mexican government declined an appeal for support.

7. On Haberman, see "Roberto Haberman Dead at 79" and Andrews, "Robert Haberman."

8. If Haberman was the betrayer he is portrayed as being, KAP's close friend Mary Louis Doherty (1896–1995) was deceived as well. In a letter to her sister Peggy Doherty dated 1 June 1921, the month before Haberman was in Washington, DC, being interviewed by Hoover, Mary Doherty mentioned that "all our crowd," including KAP, was on the Mexican government's deportation list and that "Bob [Haberman]," a "hindrance to American money interests" who had done "splendid work" in Mexico setting up schools and writing articles in favor of Mexico, was "in hiding" (Papers of Mary Louis Doherty, Special Collections, University of Maryland, College Park). Doherty, a graduate of the Rand School of Economics in New York, lived and worked in Mexico most of her life. She and KAP lived together (with Eugene Dove Pressly) for six months in 1931 and again, briefly, in Washington, DC, in 1944. She was the primary model for Laura in KAP's story "Flowering Judas."

9. See Retinger; "Joseph Retinger" (obituary); and Unrue, *Porter* 81, 82, 83, 84, 88, 91, 92, 95, 123, and 125.

10. Sen Katayama (Yabuki Sugataro [1859–1933]) was a founding member of both the American and Japanese Communist parties. As an officer for the Comintern, he was sent to Mexico in 1921 and later that year to Moscow, where he remained until his death.

11. Louis Frayna (1894–1953), also known as Luigi Carlo, Louis C. Fraina, and Lewis Corey, among other aliases, was an organizer for the Socialist Labor Party until he embraced communism, which he eventually renounced. He was sent with Katayama to Mexico to organize for the party, but along with Katayama he was considered an interloper by the Mexican revolutionaries.

12. The FBI's extensive files on KAP and her circle of revolutionary friends reveal how closely they all were watched by U.S. officials. See Andrews.

13. See KAP, "Gertrude Stein: Three Views," *Collected Essays* 251–70, and Herbst, "Miss Porter and Miss Stein."

14. Herbst is referring to the house that she and Herrmann rented for the summer.

15. Ernest Stock, an Englishman, former member of the Royal Air Force, and a painter

who frequented the Art Students League in New York City, lived with KAP in the summer of 1926. Joan Givner, in *Porter: A Life,* wrongly identifies him as one of KAP's husbands.

16. The quote is from the anonymous poem "Trust in Women."

17. Nathan Asch (1902–64) was a member of the expatriate colony in Paris that included Ernest Hemingway. In 1926 he and his wife, Liesl, had a farmhouse in New Preston, Connecticut, near the property of Herbst and her husband, John Herrmann.

18. Ted Paramore, an advertising copywriter, and Florence O'Neill, a showgirl from *George White's Scandals,* were among the guests who arrived at the Herbst and Herrmann farm that summer. O'Neill was the model for Daisy in Edmund (Bunny) Wilson's *I Thought of Daisy* (1929). See Meyers 121.

19. Asch's novel *Love in Chartres* was published in 1927.

20. An allusion to the 1920 horror film *The Cabinet of Dr. Caligari.*

21. Dorothy Day (1897–1980), writer, social activist, and founder of the Catholic Worker Movement in 1933, became KAP's friend in 1927, and KAP stayed with her for several weeks in Mexico in 1930. Her daughter was Tamar.

22. The book was *The Profane Earth,* Holger Cahill's first novel.

23. Matthew Josephson, diary, Matthew Josephson Papers, Beinecke Library, Yale U.

24. Josephson summarizes KAP's life inaccurately, especially the time she had spent in New York and Mexico. In notes she made in 1964 after the publication of his *Life among the Surrealists* (1962), she contradicted his account of how she was hired at Macaulay and his labeling her work as "routine copy editing." She did not work at home, she said, but had her own desk in the publisher's offices and was paid a salary (Notes, KAP to Paul Porter, Collection of Darlene Harbour Unrue). Despite its inaccuracies, Josephson's recollection provides a snapshot of KAP in 1927.

25. KAP would not have said this in 1927, when her grandmother would have been one hundred.

26. If this was indeed KAP's characterization of her grandmother, it is counter to everything she said about her elsewhere. See, e.g., "Portrait: Old South," *Collected Essays* 160–65.

27. Josephson gives himself too much credit for KAP's writing. In the 1964 notes she said that Josephson's assertion that she gave him stories in progress to review was "not only a downright lie, but comes pretty close to slander" (Notes, KAP to Paul Porter, Collection of Darlene Harbour Unrue). She said that Josephson never saw any of her stories until they were published, but one of her letters suggests that she showed him a draft of at least one of her stories (KAP to Matthew Josephson, 19 March 1929, Matthew Josephson Papers, Beinecke Library, Yale U). Being less sure of herself in writing poetry, she sent him poems she had written and asked him to criticize them freely. See, e.g., KAP to Matthew Josephson, 29 January 1929, Matthew Josephson Papers, Beinecke Library, Yale U.

28. Helen Rebecca Edelman Crawford (1892–1972) was born in Russia and immigrated to the United States with her parents when she was two years old. Business manager of the Playwrights' Theatre in Greenwich Village in the early 1920s, when she met KAP, she married John Crawford (1895–1974) in 1925. He was a southerner and would-be nov-

elist who aspired to an acting career, worked as a copyreader for the *New York Times,* and eventually became chairman of the newspaper guild at the *Times.* The Crawfords were leftists whose hospitality included opening their Brooklyn home to politically like-minded persons, especially writers and artists. In 1929 Becky Crawford collected money to send KAP to Bermuda for a six-month sojourn (she stayed only five) to work on her biography of Cotton Mather, which was to be dedicated to Becky, and to recuperate from both a bout of pneumonia and her broken relationship with Matthew Josephson. KAP's story "Flowering Judas" was completed at the Crawfords' house in the winter of 1929–30.

29. The Palmer Raids, named for the U.S. attorney general under President Woodrow Wilson, Alexander Mitchell Palmer (1872–1936), were part of a campaign against left-wing political groups. By 1919, when KAP arrived in New York City, J. Edgar Hoover was named head of the General Intelligence Division of the Bureau of Intelligence with the charge of collecting names of suspected anarchists and radical leftists.

30. Emma Goldman (1869–1940), who had been imprisoned many times for radical activities, was deported to Russia at the end of 1919, herself the victim of Hoover and Palmer. After two years she went to England, and she didn't return to the United States until 1934, when Robert Plunkett was likely to have seen her at his mother's house. KAP saw Goldman in Greenwich Village shortly before her deportation and again in Paris in 1932.

31. Caroline Ferguson Gordon (1895–1981), Kentucky-born writer, graduate of Bethany College in West Virginia, and first wife of Allen Tate, was among KAP's best friends in Greenwich Village in the mid-1920s, when they were sympathetic to one another's struggles to support themselves by their writing, a struggle apparent in their extensive correspondence. Although Gordon and KAP occasionally had fallings-out, they were friends for most of the rest of their lives.

32. John Orley Allen Tate (1899–1979), poet, essayist, and biographer, was born in Kentucky and studied at the Cincinnati Conservatory of Music before entering Vanderbilt University, where he joined a group of young poets known as the Fugitives and later the Southern Agrarians. He and KAP were close friends until their last years. There is some evidence that they had an affair in the late 1920s or the early 1930s.

33. Marguerite (Peggy) Guggenheim (1898–1979), a wealthy American art collector, associated with members of the bohemian artistic communities in New York and Paris.

34. Eva Le Gallienne (1899–1991), a successful English-born actress and director, arrived in New York in 1920 and became popular in theatrical circles. Although she was considered apolitical, her lesbianism placed her among radicals and leftists.

35. Harold Hart Crane (1899–1932), influential American poet inspired by T. S. Eliot and Ezra Pound, met KAP, Gordon, Tate, and other bohemian writers and artists in Greenwich Village in the mid-1920s. He and KAP considered themselves good friends until Crane visited her in Mexico in 1931, when their friendship disintegrated, largely because of his drinking. Until the end of her life, however, she retained ambivalent feelings for him. See Unrue, *Porter* 108, 130, 260.

36. Malcolm Cowley (1898–1989), novelist, literary critic, journalist, editor, and poet, earned a B.A. from Harvard after serving in World War I in the American Field Service.

He married the artist Peggy Baird, whom he divorced to marry Muriel Maurer. After her divorce, Baird formed an intimate relationship with Hart Crane, with whom she was traveling in 1932 from Mexico to the United States when he jumped overboard to his death. KAP, who considered Baird a good friend throughout the 1920s, distanced herself after the Crane alliance. Although Cowley was supportive of KAP by giving her books to review for the *New Republic,* where he was the book review editor, KAP argued with him over the relationship between politics and art and the way he portrayed her time in Mexico in *Exile's Return.*

37. KAP and Becky Crawford met Eugene Gladstone O'Neill (1888–1953), Nobel Prize–winning dramatist, in Greenwich Village in the early 1920s, when his plays *Beyond the Horizon* and *"Anna Christie"* won the Pulitzer Prize for Drama in 1920 and 1922, respectively.

38. Richard Wright (1908–60), writer of novels, short stories, and essays, was the grandson of Mississippi slaves. He was active in the Communist Party and in the 1930s became Harlem editor of the *Daily Worker.* KAP is unlikely to have met him at the Crawfords'.

39. William Rollins Jr., *The Shadow Before* (1934). Rollins, Robert Plunkett, and KAP were all listed as residents at the Crawford house in the census of 1930.

40. For the political circumstances in Mexico in 1930 and 1931, see Walsh 136–64 and Unrue, *Porter* 125–31.

41. According to KAP, when Elizabeth Anderson called on her she was in bed suffering from tonsillitis.

42. KAP met Eugene Pressly about this time, but they did not live together until they rented a house in Mixcoac with Mary Doherty in 1931.

43. Mary Louis Doherty to Peggy Doherty, 1 June 1921, Mary Louis Doherty Papers, Special Collections, University of Maryland, College Park.

44. Mrs. Hill was unclear about the year in which she met KAP. It is unlikely that she met her in 1920 or 1921, but she might have met her in 1922 or 1923.

45. Carlton Beals (1894–1979) was an American journalist and teacher who spent considerable time in Mexico. A friend of KAP's, he went with Porter to see Diego Rivera's frescoes at the Preparatory School. He was the model for the poet/journalist in "That Tree" and contributed to the character Carlos in "Virgin Violeta." See his *Glass Houses.* See also Britton.

46. Tina Modotti (1896–1942), Italian photographer, silent-film actress, and leftist, arrived in Mexico in 1922, when she met KAP among Mexican expatriate writers, artists, and revolutionaries. See Hooks.

47. William Spratling (1900–1967), American silversmith and professor of architecture, moved to Mexico in 1929 and became a friend of Diego Rivera. At his home in Taxco, where Elizabeth Anderson lived for a while, Spratling designed works in silver based on pre-Columbian designs. KAP visited him there at least once.

48. Dr. Atl [Gerardo Murillo, 1875–1964], Mexican artist who participated in the renaissance led by Diego Rivera, was KAP's friend from 1922 until his death.

49. Diego Rivera (1886–1957), painter, muralist, communist activist, and de facto

leader of the Mexican artistic renaissance in the 1920s, became acquainted with KAP in 1922. She based the character Rubén in her story "The Martyr" on him and planned several others inspired by him. See, e.g., the unfinished story "The Lovely Legend" in KAP, *Uncollected Early Prose.*

50. Natalie Vivian Scott (1890–1957), war heroine, newspaperwoman, playwright, teacher, and social worker, became acquainted with William Spratling at Tulane University and eventually joined his Mexican circle of friends in Taxco that included KAP and Elizabeth Anderson.

51. Adolfo Best-Maugard (1892–1964), Mexican artist, lecturer, and theorist, has been given credit, along with Dr. Atl, for launching the Contemporary Mexican Art Movement. He encouraged KAP to go to Mexico in 1920, and she based the character Betancourt in her short novel "Hacienda" on him.

52. KAP and Tina Modotti could not have attended Mrs. Hill's parties together in 1931, since Modotti was not in Mexico. KAP and Modotti are likely to have met in 1923, when they moved in the same social circles for a few months, and during this period they possibly attended the Hills' Sunday parties together.

53. Pablo (Paul) O'Higgins (1904–82), painter, pianist, communist, and assistant to Diego Rivera from 1924 to 1928, met KAP in 1930 or 1931, when he gave her piano lessons. She saw him again in 1931 in Berlin when he was on his way to the Soviet Union for a year of study.

54. She sold it to Chole's, where it remained for many years.

Part 3

1. KAP admired French writer Sidonie-Gabrielle Colette, known simply as Colette (1873–1954), and cited her as a woman who was able to write because she, unlike KAP, had men who took care of her.

2. KAP was twenty-five at the time of her first diagnosis of tuberculosis, but because she was vague or deceptive about her age, she might well have implied that she was younger when she first was hospitalized. The following account is consistent with her descriptions to other friends of that frightening period of her life.

3. Mack Sennett (1880–1960), innovator of slapstick comedy and founder of Keystone Studios; his films often included a group of bathing beauties.

4. Gloria Swanson (1899–1983), silent screen star who returned to acclaim with *Sunset Boulevard* (1950); Mabel Ethelreid Normand (1895–1930), a popular comedy star of the silent screen.

5. See the account in Unrue, *Porter* 51–52.

6. Wescott or KAP may have conflated KAP's experiences with Hollywood directors and producers. If Wescott is referring to Sidney Franklin (1893–1972), he was very much alive at the time Wescott wrote the article. He was, however, the first producer for whom KAP worked in Hollywood. After leaving Franklin and MGM, KAP worked with dramatist Jacques Théry for Paramount Pictures and producer Charles Brackett (1892–1969). See Unrue, *Porter* 202–3.

7. *Young Bess* (1953), produced by Sidney Franklin.

8. KAP was paid well ($1,500 a week by MGM and $2,000 a week by Paramount) but was notoriously unable to manage money effectively.

9. Paramount Pictures did not complete the movie, a remake of the 1924 film that starred Gloria Swanson. In 1962 it was produced as a French/Italian/Spanish film that starred Sophia Loren.

10. Monroe Wheeler (1899–1988), publisher and key figure in the Museum of Modern Art in New York, became KAP's friend in the early 1930s in Paris when he and Barbara Harrison, a wealthy heiress, published KAP's *French Song-Book* and her long story *Hacienda* as a small book under the imprint Harrison of Paris. Wescott's lover for many years, he remained KAP's friend until her death.

11. Charles Shannon. See Unrue, *Porter* 196–99.

12. KAP probably is referring to her long novel, *No Safe Harbor,* "Erasmus of Basel," "The French Murder Mystery," and an anthology of her favorite stories. She had put out of her mind for the moment her unfinished biography of Cotton Mather, "The Devil and Cotton Mather."

13. Janice Biala (1903–2000), Polish-born American painter, lived with the British novelist Ford Madox Ford in Paris and the United States in the 1930s. Her brother was the painter Jack Tworkov, to whom Toni Willison was briefly married in the 1920s. KAP was friends with Ford from the 1920s and became friends with Biala in Paris in 1932.

14. Ford Madox Ford [Ford Hermann Hueffer, 1873–1939], influential British novelist, critic, editor, biographer, and poet, whose *English Review* and *Transatlantic Review* were important modernist journals. He was mentor to Caroline Gordon, among others, and both a friend and supporter of KAP and Eudora Welty. KAP met him through Gordon and Tate in Greenwich Village in the 1920s and became close friends with him in Paris in the 1930s.

15. KAP's review is titled "Pull Dick, Pull Devil" and is reprinted in *Collected Essays* 141–44.

16. At the time the property was in Ballston Spa, later part of Malta.

17. See Unrue, *Porter* 183–92; and KAP, "A House of My Own," *Collected Essays* 174–79.

18. When KAP was at Skidmore, George Willison was already deceased. Toni Willison probably meant that she went to see KAP with her son, Malcolm, and that KAP visited her at South Hill.

19. Willison and Malcolm went to see KAP in 1975. An account of that visit, written by Malcolm, is in Toni Willison's Papers at the University of Maryland, College Park.

20. Ann Holloway Hemmerly Heintze (1921–87), the daughter of KAP's sister Gay Porter Holloway, became close to KAP in the 1930s. In 1945 she stayed in Hollywood with her aunt, and KAP lived briefly with her in New York when Ann was divorcing Walter Hemmerly and marrying Walter Heintze. KAP planned and carried out an elaborate wedding for Ann and "Walter II."

21. Elsa Schiaparelli (1890–1973), a prominent Parisian designer of the 1920s and 1930s, was a favorite of KAP's.

22. See "Letters to a Nephew," *Collected Essays* 109–22; and KAP to Paul Porter in Porter, *Letters* 203–16, 251–53, 260–65, 273–76, 405–6, 413–16, and 462–67.

23. Claudio Monteverdi (1567–1643), Italian composer whose late Renaissance and Baroque music KAP especially liked.

24. Maggie Teyte (1888–1976), British soprano; Isobel Baillie (1895–1983), Scottish soprano; Kathleen Ferrier (1912–53), British contralto; Fortunato (Ezio) Pinza (1892–1957), famous basso of the Metropolitan Opera.

25. Richard Hoffman (1831–1909), English-born American composer and pianist; Constantin (Dinu) Lipatti (1917–50), Romanian pianist.

26. A comic opera by Richard Strauss (1864–1949), first performed in 1911; the Marschallin is a beautiful, aging noblewoman betrayed by men who prefer younger women.

27. KAP saw Lehmann in the opera in Salzburg in 1934 with Barbara Harrison and Barbara's father and stepmother.

28. A song made famous by Ella Fitzgerald and Louie Jordan.

29. The vaudeville comedy team Bert Williams (1874–1922) and George Walker (1873–1911) made this song popular.

30. Edith Piaf (1915–63), popular French singer; Mahalia Jackson (1911–72), world-famous gospel singer; Charles Trenet (1913–2001), French singer and songwriter; Marlene Dietrich (1901–92), German-born American actress and singer.

31. A group of twelfth- and thirteenth-century clergymen who wrote satirical poems in Latin.

32. Hart Crane (1899–1932), not Stephen Crane (1899–1932); see Unrue, *Porter* 108, 130, 260.

33. Robert Penn Warren (1905–89), poet, novelist, critic, and one of the founders of the New Criticism, was KAP's friend from the 1920s until her death.

34. KAP was a longtime friend of poet Marianne Moore (1887–1972), who was editor of the *Dial* from 1925 to 1929.

35. The poem is "Then the Ermine," which includes these lines: "So let the *palisandre* settee express it, / 'ebony violet,' / Master Corbo in full dress, / and shepherdess. . . ." The poem first appeared in Moore's *Like a Bulwark* (1956). See Moore 160–61.

36. See Elizabeth Anderson (No. 14).

37. Frank O'Connor (1903–66), Irish writer with whom KAP became acquainted in the 1930s.

38. Maud Powell (1867–1920), widely considered the first great American violinist.

39. Sidney Kingsley (1906–95), a Pulitzer Prize–winning dramatist.

40. This event took place when KAP was writer-in-residence at Washington and Lee University, in Lexington, Virginia. At that time she was sixty-nine.

41. Caroline Gordon and Allen Tate's estate, Benfolly, in Clarksville, Tennessee.

42. In the deleted section, Brooks refers to the "artistic gifts" apparent in KAP's letters and describes the importance of the correspondence between KAP and Brooks's wife.

43. Brooks concludes his essay by quoting substantial portions of six letters from KAP to him and/or his wife.

44. Henry Allen Moe (1894–1975) was secretary of the John Simon Guggenheim Foun-

dation at the time. Later he was that foundation's president and the first chairman of the National Endowment for the Humanities.

45. "Season of Fear" was never published. "The Leaning Tower" was published in the autumn 1941 issue of the *Southern Review* and was the title story of KAP's 1944 collection.

46. This short novel was later published separately by Doubleday.

47. Albert Russel Erskine Jr. (1912–93) was KAP's fifth husband. In 1941 they were separated, and they divorced in 1942. At the time KAP wrote the letter, Erskine was an editor with New Directions. Later he was with Doubleday, Doran and then Random House. He became Welty's editor as well as Robert Penn Warren's. KAP's reference to his being delighted indicates either his admiration for Welty's work or his friendship with Diarmuid Russell.

48. Colin McPhee (1900–1964), Canadian composer, critic, and UCLA professor best know for avant-garde compositions inspired by Balinese music. Karnig Nalbandian (1916–89), Romanian-born American visual artist.

49. Porlock, a town in southwest England, the origin of an unwelcome intruder mentioned by Samuel Taylor Coleridge in a "Note" with the first publication of his poem "Kubla Khan" (in *Cristabel*). Coleridge claimed that "Kubla Khan," a fifty-four-line fragment, would have been completed had he not been interrupted by the Porlock visitor.

50. KAP's joking reference to Welty's editor, John Woodburn.

51. The anecdote appears in "The Journey," first published as "The Old Order" in the winter 1936 issue of the *Southern Review,* and again in the essay "Portrait: Old South," published in *Mademoiselle* in February 1944.

52. Elliott Coleman (1906–80) founded the Department of Writing, Speech, and Drama at Johns Hopkins University, where many prominent writers came as guest teachers. In addition to KAP, E. E. Cummings, Dylan Thomas, W. H. Auden, and Robert Frost made appearances at Coleman's seminars.

53. Susanne Katherina Knauth Langer (1895–1985), an American philosopher of art and a follower of the cultural philosopher and Kantian idealist Ernst Cassirer, is best known for her *Philosophy in a New Key* (1942).

54. Royal Earle Thompson is the protagonist of KAP's "Noon Wine."

Part 4

1. John Peale Bishop (1892–1944), West Virginia–born writer of poems, novels, short stories, and essays, was KAP's friend for many years. Although, according to Liberman (see No. 47), KAP once said that Bishop was the only man she ever loved, there is no evidence that they ever had an affair.

2. When KAP arrived in Washington, DC, to begin her appointment at the Library of Congress, she became an additional boarder in a house rented by Allen Tate and Caroline Gordon and Brainerd (Lon) and Frances (Fanny) Cheney, longtime Tennessee friends of the Tates.

3. Bracketed information here supplied by Winslow.

4. Johnny Winslow, Marcella Winslow's young son, was ill with scarlet fever.

5. Allen Tate and Caroline Gordon's daughter, Nancy, who was born in 1926. In 1944 she married Percy Hoxie Wood. She died in Mexico on 28 March 2007.

6. Marcella Winslow provided this paragraph of explanation after the previous letter.

7. Marcella Winslow's young daughter.

8. Federico Castellón (1914–71), a Spanish-American painter KAP met at Yaddo, who with his wife was KAP's guest the last winter she lived at South Hill; Charles Shannon (1915–86), an Alabama painter with whom KAP had an affair in 1944; Lincoln Edward Kirstein (1907–96), influential art critic, writer, and one of the founders of both the School of American Ballet and the New York City Ballet, who became acquainted with KAP in Paris in the 1930s.

9. Francisco Aguilera: see Unrue, *Porter* 99–101, 191, 196.

10. While Marcella Winslow and her children went to a Delaware beach for a summer vacation, KAP rented their house to share with Mary Doherty and Mary's sister, Peggy.

11. Clark is referring to the 1982 edition of Givner's *Porter: A Life*.

12. KAP's first marriage, to John Henry Koontz, lasted from 1906 to 1915. According to the divorce decree, Koontz was physically abusive. See Unrue, *Porter* 38–46, 51, 102–3, 116, 128–29.

13. KAP apparently had a miscarriage around 1911, but she had a stillborn child in 1924.

14. Clark is referring to *The Itching Parrot* (*El periquillo sarniento*, by José Joaquin Fernández de Lizardi). Although KAP is credited with the translation, it was roughly translated from the Spanish by KAP's fourth husband, Eugene Pressly. She rewrote it for style and added an introduction. See "Notes on the Life and Death of a Hero," *Collected Essays* 357–84.

15. Willard and Mary Trask were engaged by Barbara Harrison and Monroe Wheeler, co-owners of Harrison of Paris, who published the *Song-Book,* to translate the Old French songs that KAP could rewrite for style.

16. "The Wooden Umbrella" was first published as "Gertrude Stein: A Self Portrait" in the December 1947 issue of *Harper's*. KAP changed the title to "The Wooden Umbrella" for *The Days Before* (1952).

17. George Platt Lynes (1907–55), American fashion and commercial photographer, met Gertrude Stein, Glenway Wescott, and Monroe Wheeler in Paris. Through Wescott and Wheeler he met KAP, whom he photographed for years, as he did Katharine Hepburn, Gloria Swanson, and other members of the film and art industries. He was the chief photographer for the Vogue studios in Hollywood in the 1940s, when KAP lived with him and his friends for a while.

18. Goyen met KAP in the summer of 1947 in Santa Monica, California, when she was working as a scriptwriter for Hollywood studios and he was traveling in California with his friend Walter Berns. Robert Phillips, the editor of Goyen's *Selected Letters from a Writer's Life,* raises the question of why Goyen in his eulogy to KAP misdated his meeting with her. Phillips suggests that Goyen might have wanted to obscure the fact that he already knew her when she wrote what Joan Givner called "a highly laudatory review" of

Goyen's *The House of Breath* for the *New York Times Book Review*. A careful examination of the review, however, reveals that it was hardly laudatory, that, in fact, KAP warned Goyen about his failures in "the objective method" and took her young friend to task for "absurd recklessness of revealment" (see "This Strange, Old World" in KAP, *"This Strange, Old World" and Other Book Reviews by Katherine Anne Porter* 128–32). It is more likely that Goyen simply misremembered the dates of the meetings, placing the Santa Monica meeting later than the New York meeting, which occurred when he was on his way to Yaddo, where KAP had recommended him for a residency. Shortly after the 1950 meeting he and KAP began a two-year affair that Stephen Spender described in an afterword to the *Selected Letters* as an "elusive game" they both played. Goyen was one among several bisexual or homosexual men with whom KAP engaged in fantasy love affairs in the 1940s and 1950s.

19. KAP owned the house and property she called South Hill in Ballston Spa, New York. She owned two pieces of land, one in Louisiana and one in California, on both of which she planned to build houses but sold before beginning construction. See Unrue, *Porter* 170, 176, 183–93, 205–6.

20. Goyen called on KAP several times in Santa Monica in the summer of 1947.

21. Whether this is Goyen's impression or KAP's characterization of her Hollywood work, it is inaccurate. See Unrue, *Porter* 201–15.

22. By 1947 KAP had been struggling for more than a decade with her long novel, *Ship of Fools,* titled at that point *No Safe Harbor.* She had published four segments of it as excerpts from a work-in-progress.

23. Sarah Orne Jewett (1849–1909), American novelist and short-story writer, was known for the realistic local color of her fiction.

24. Anaïs Nin (1903–77), French-born writer who became famous for her published journals and erotica.

25. KAP was referring to *Ship of Fools.*

26. KAP received a Litt.D. (Doctor of Literature) degree (her first) from the Woman's College of the University of North Carolina, Greensboro, on 30 May 1949.

27. *Katherine Anne Porter: The Eye of Memory* first aired on the *American Masters* series of the Public Broadcasting Corporation on 7 July 1986.

28. Daniyal Mueenuddin.

29. David Heintze, son of Ann Holloway Heintze.

30. Josephine Baker (1906–75), celebrated African-American singer and dancer who, although American-born, became a French citizen in 1937.

31. Lady Mary Wortley Montagu (1689–1762), an English writer best known for the eloquence and wit of her letters.

32. See "Opening Speech at Paris Conference, 1952," *Collected Essays* 216; it is incorrectly identified as a speech given at the International Exposition of the Arts.

33. Wanda Landowska (1879–1959), Polish-born French harpsichordist and teacher who toured extensively and is best known for her interpretations of the music of Johann Sebastian Bach.

34. Joseph Russell Lynes Jr. (1910–91), art historian, editor at *Harper's Magazine,* and KAP's friend from the 1940s on; Oscar Williams (Oscar Kaplan, 1900–1964), poet and

compiler of anthologies such as *The Pocket Book of Modern Verse* (1954); Frances Steloff (1887–1989), founder of the Gotham Book Mart in 1920, a magnet for writers and artists, including KAP, in New York City; Cyrilly Abels (1903–75), managing editor of *Mademoiselle* from 1945 to 1960 and later literary agent whose clients included KAP.

35. Peter Hillsman Taylor (1917–94), Pulitzer Prize–winning writer and teacher, was KAP's friend and one of her protégés. See McAlexander, *Peter Taylor*. William Humphrey (1924–97), teacher and writer of short stories and novels, including *Home from the Hill* (1957), considered KAP his mentor and friend. William Jay Smith (1918–), poet, translator, and poetry consultant to the Library of Congress from 1968 to 1970, was KAP's close friend in the last several decades of her life.

36. Geraldine Sue Page (1924–87), American stage and screen actress who won an Oscar, an Emmy, and a Golden Globe; Alexander Schneider (1908–93), Russian-born violinist, conductor, and promoter of chamber music.

37. Welty appeared on ABC's *The Dick Cavett Show* (1969–74) several times in the early 1970s.

38. *The Fable of the Bees; or, Private Vices, Publick Benefits* (1714) was an infamous satire by Kenneth Mandeville or Bernard de Mandeville (1670–1733); *In Praise of Folly* (1511), by Desiderius Erasmus (1466–1536), was one of KAP's favorite satires and one that inspired her *Ship of Fools,* as did *Das Narrenschiff* (1494), by Sebastian Brant (1457–1521), whose title KAP translated and took for her novel.

39. Harvey Breit (1909–68) was a reviewer for the *New York Times Book Review* from 1940 to 1965. His essays about famous writers he had interviewed are collected in *The Writer Observed* (1956).

40. Wysten Hugh Auden (1907–73), British poet with whom KAP became friends in 1938 when Auden and his companion, the poet and librettist Chester Kallman (1921–75), visited KAP and her fifth husband, Albert Russel Erskine Jr., in Baton Rouge. James Rufus Agee (1909–55) was an influential film critic at the time of the party. His autobiographical novel, *A Death in the Family* (1957), was awarded the Pulitzer Prize posthumously. Louis Kronenberger (1904–80), an editor at Boni and Liveright from 1926 to 1933, encouraged Horace Liveright to give KAP an advance contract for a biography of Cotton Mather. Irish writer James Stern (1904–93) and his wife, Tania, were friends of KAP's for many years. Charles J. Rolo (1916–82) was a longtime reviewer for the *Atlantic Monthly.*

41. Karl Shapiro, who was at the party, wrote a poem about the event ("Emily Dickinson and Katherine Anne Porter," *Collected Poems, 1940–1978* [New York: Random House, 1978], 257), and Sydney Michaels reconstructed it as a scene in his 1964 play *Dylan.*

Part 5

1. Only five of KAP's twenty-eight stories and short novels appeared first in the *Southern Review:* "The Circus, "The Old Order" (later titled "The Journey"), "Old Mortality," "Pale Horse, Pale Rider," and "The Leaning Tower."

2. KAP was married five times, but she shared that fact with very few persons. Hardwick was obviously not one of them.

3. Natalie Clifford Barney (1876–1972), whose Paris literary salon was famous for more than a half century.

4. Tate apparently was the only person outside KAP's family to whom she confided the actual number of her marriages.

5. Lawrence was responding to questions I had posed to him about KAP's composition of *Ship of Fools.* I have omitted the questions that he answered in the letter.

6. Lawrence is referring to a segment of KAP's novel-in-progress, titled then *No Safe Harbor,* which focused on a troupe of dancers that were de facto pimps and prostitutes as well as practitioners of a confidence game. The excerpt was published in March 1956 as "Ship of Fools" in the *Atlantic Monthly.*

7. Abels, a friend, acted only informally as KAP's agent until she left *Mademoiselle,* where she was managing editor, and established her own literary agency.

8. Pigeon Cove, on Cape Ann in Rockport, Massachusetts, was the final hideaway Lawrence arranged and the place KAP finally finished *Ship of Fools.*

9. According to other accounts, it was not a drunken professor who kept pestering KAP but Mark Schorer, who had written the influential review of *Ship of Fools* that appeared in the *New York Times* on 1 April 1962 ("We're All on the Passenger List"). See William Maxwell to Frank O'Connor, 2 April 1962, in O'Connor and Maxwell 172–73.

10. Mrs. Treadwell, one of several autobiographical characters in *Ship of Fools,* is a sexually repressed woman who violently attacks the predatory William Denny.

11. Foreword to Régine Pernoud's *The Retrial of Joan of Arc: The Evidence at the Trial for Her Rehabilitation, 1450–1465,* trans. J. M. Cohen (New York: Harcourt, Brace, 1955), v–viii.

12. The album was *The Writer as Reader* (1953), part of the Columbia Records Literary Series. Others who read were W. Somerset Maugham, Aldous Huxley, John Collier, Sacheverell Sitwell, Osbert Sitwell, Edith Sitwell, John Steinbeck, Christopher Isherwood, Truman Capote, Edna Ferber, and William Saroyan. A copy of the album is among the recordings in the Papers of KAP, Special Collections, University of Maryland, College Park, Libraries.

13. Barbara Thompson, "Katherine Anne Porter: Mistress of the Grand Gesture," *Washington Post and Times Herald* 25 November 1956: F7.

14. See Barbara Thompson, "Katherine Anne Porter: An Interview," *Paris Review* 8 (Winter–Spring 1963): 87–114.

15. Characters in the novels of Julian Green (1900–1998) are said to be Poe-like in their extreme behavior and psychological complexity.

16. KAP's marginalia in Virginia Woolf, *A Writer's Diary: Being Extracts from the Diary of Virginia Woolf,* ed. Leonard Woolf (London: Hogarth, 1953), illustrates the point Davis is making. Personal collection of Barbara Thompson Davis.

17. Ghulam Mueenuddin, informally called Mueen.

18. Jean Stafford (1915–79), short-story writer and novelist, was married successively to poet Robert Lowell, photographer Oliver Jensen, and *New Yorker* writer A. J. Liebling. KAP knew her during her marriage to Lowell, whose mental instability inspired one of Stafford's best-known stories, "The Interior Castle." Her first novel, *Boston Adventure* (1944), earned wide praise.

19. Quoted in Makowsky 167.

20. Robert A. Beach Jr. was assistant to the president for university relations at the University of Maryland.

21. The phrase is drawn from Yeats's poem "The Coming of Wisdom with Time": "Though leaves are many the root is one; / Through all the lying days of my youth / I swayed my leaves and flowers in the sun; / Now I may wither into the truth." Yeats, *Responsibilities and Other Poems* 102.

22. KAP's affair with Jordan Pecile was widely known. She met him at Cornell in 1952 when he was a student assigned to escort her to events on campus. See Unrue, *Porter* 244.

23. Thomas F. Gossett (1916–2005), professor of English at Wake Forest University, and his wife, Louise, who became friends with many American writers, including O'Connor.

24. Ellipsis by Sally Fitzgerald.

25. Ellipsis by Sally Fitzgerald.

26. O'Connor's last novel, *The Violent Bear It Away* (1955), was published in 1960.

27. In the fall of 1960, O'Connor gave a talk at the College of St. Teresa in Winona, Minnesota.

28. Ellipsis by Sally Fitzgerald.

29. Mary Therese McCarthy (1912–89), American writer with a liberal political bent. With the exception of McCarthy's memoir, KAP disliked her writing but liked some of her political stands.

30. William Saroyan (1908–81), an Armenian-American writer who grew up in Fresno, California, and wrote plays and short stories about impoverished immigrant life.

31. Ellipsis by Ruoff.

32. Laurence Sterne (1713–68), English novelist best known for *The Life and Opinions of Tristram Shandy, Gentleman* (9 vols., 1759–69), which KAP often claimed was her earliest model of good writing.

33. Ellipsis by Ruoff.

34. KAP's estimate of five unfinished novels is accurate, but forty short stories is an exaggeration.

35. There are mistakes in the text, but perhaps not so many as KAP suggests.

36. Because *Flowering Judas* was published in 1930 in a limited edition of six hundred copies, it indeed has become "a collector's item."

37. This is a faulty transcription of KAP's words. The purse does not contain gold pieces; it was made of gold lamé and is the image of one given KAP by her friend Delafield Day Spier. KAP would have said "janitress," as it is in the story. Ruoff made an audio recording of KAP's session at Wichita State University; this accounts both for his verbatim quotes from her and also errors that resulted from garbled sound.

38. Ellipsis by Ruoff.

39. KAP considered Salinger's story "A Perfect Day for Bananafish" (1948) a nearly perfect example of the genre.

40. Ellipsis by Ruoff.

41. KAP was objecting to the political element in the fiction of these African-American writers. Baldwin, on the other hand, greatly admired her work and nominated her for the Prix Formentor in 1965.

42. Although the novel had been announced for the fall of 1961, it was not published until April 1962.

43. Ellipsis by Ruoff.

44. Ellipsis by Ruoff.

45. Ellipsis by Ruoff.

46. KAP to Caroline Gordon, 28 August–24 September 1931, in Porter, *Letters* 46–60.

47. "After a Long Journey," *Collected Essays* 491–94.

48. Ellipsis by Ruoff.

49. Huey Pierce Long Jr. (1893–1935), Democratic governor of Louisiana from 1928 to 1932, was the primary model for Willie Stark in *All the King's Men* (1946), the Pulitzer Prize–winning novel by Robert Penn Warren to which KAP was referring in her earlier remark that Warren was not really a novelist.

50. George Palmer Garrett Jr. (1929–2008), American poet and novelist, taught for many years at the University of Virginia and the University of South Carolina. KAP consistently praised his fiction. Walter Clemons (1929–94), journalist, editor, critic, and short-story writer, was one of the younger generation of writers KAP especially encouraged. He was the first recipient of a grant through the Katherine Anne Porter Foundation, which KAP established in 1966.

51. KAP had misunderstood the intentions of the University of Texas administrators. Her "library" was to be only a room in the Harry Ransom Humanities Research Center. While waiting for her library to be built, she temporarily deposited her papers in the Library of Congress. When she became aware of her mistake about the intentions of the University of Texas, she gave her papers to the University of Maryland. See Unrue, *Porter* 242–43, 264.

Part 6

1. The Sitwells—Edith (1887–1964), Osbert (1892–1969), and Sacheverell (1897–1988)—committed their lives to art. Edith was a prolific and much honored poet, and her brothers were poets, fiction writers, and art critics. KAP was acquainted with them all, but she reserved most of her praise for Edith's poetry. See "The Laughing Heat of the Sun" (*Collected Essays* 58–62), KAP's laudatory review of Edith's *The Canticle of the Rose* (1949); and "The Fair-Haired Man" (*"This Strange, Old World" and Other Book Reviews* 88–92), KAP's mixed review of Sacheverell's *The Gothick North: A Study of Medieval Life, Art and Thought* (1929).

2. KAP's remark about Steinbeck dates the party to 1962, but the standard biographies of the Sitwells indicate that they were not in New York in 1962. By then Edith, who died in 1964, was in a wheelchair. The Sitwells' visits to New York took place in the late 1940s and early 1950s. More than likely Prokosch conflated parties, one in 1948 or 1949 given for the Sitwells by Monroe Wheeler, and one or more later, including one in 1962

at which both he and KAP were present (but not the Sitwells) and she made the remark about Steinbeck. See Glendinning 278 and Pearson 402.

3. *The Unquiet Grave: A Word Cycle by Palinurus,* by Cyril Connolly (1903–74), published in New York in 1945 by Harper and Brothers, is a miscellany of epigrams, impressions, and cynical remarks in the spirit of Pascal's *Pensées.*

4. Paul Hindemith (1895–1963), German composer and conductor.

5. Buck won the Nobel Prize in 1938, Faulkner in 1949, Hemingway in 1954, and Steinbeck in 1962.

6. Prettyman is referring to Givner's *Porter: A Life* (1982).

7. Keir Dullea played Adam in the television production of an adaptation of KAP's *Pale Horse, Pale Rider* shown 11 November 1964, in the first season of *The Wednesday Play,* a drama anthology that ran on BBC from 1964 to 1970. Miranda, KAP's autobiographical character, was played by Joan Hackett.

8. Givner, *Porter: A Life* 479–80.

9. John Cheever (1912–82), novelist and short-story writer who set his fiction primarily in New York suburbs, won numerous awards, including the Pulitzer Prize for Fiction in 1979 and the National Book Critics Circle Award in 1982. He was a member of the American Academy of Arts and Letters with KAP. Tillie Lerner Olsen (1912–2007), the daughter of Russian Jewish immigrants, dropped out of high school, worked as a waitress, housekeeper, meat trimmer, and union organizer before beginning to write stories and essays that focused on the special struggle of women writers. In *Silences* (1978) she held up KAP as an example of a woman who achieved artistic significance despite obstacles. She credited KAP with advancing her career and reputation and helping her get published. Although she had been a social activist all her life, in her last years she regretted that she had been adopted by feminist critics at the expense of a more inclusive artistic reputation. KAP especially admired Olsen's stories "Tell Me a Riddle" and "I Stand Here Ironing." Like Welty and others, Olsen was passionately devoted to the defense of KAP against detractors. Kay Boyle (1902–92), fiction writer, essayist, and social activist, became acquainted with KAP in the 1930s and corresponded with her for many years. KAP favorably reviewed her *Wedding Day and Other Stories* and *Plagued by the Nightingale* ("Example to the Young") and admired *Being Geniuses Together, 1920–1930,* a book about expatriates in Paris that Boyle coauthored with Robert McAlmon (1896–1956), a friend of KAP's from the 1930s until his death.

10. John Simmons Barth (1930–), fiction writer, musician, and college professor, whose works are considered representative of postmodernism.

11. The documentary, to be called *Death Row, USA,* although completed by Capote and Prettyman, was dropped by ABC, and according to Prettyman in an April/May 1997 interview in *Bar Report,* was claimed by ABC to be lost. See "Legends in the Law."

12. KAP had an assignment from *Playboy* to write an article about the launch of the last Apollo moon shot of the twentieth century. See Unrue, *Porter* 279–80.

13. Mina Kirstein Curtiss (1896–1985), teacher and writer, was a graduate of Smith College and Columbia University. She taught English at Smith and worked with Orson Welles and John Houseman on scripts for the Mercury Theatre of the Air. In 1964, the year

of her conflict with KAP, she founded Chapelbrook Foundation, the purpose of which was to provide funding to writers past the age of forty to encourage them to complete works that might otherwise remain unfinished, the kind of foundation that KAP might have turned to during the years she was trying to support herself and finish *Ship of Fools*.

14. KAP's contract with Atlantic–Little, Brown for *Ship of Fools* put a limitation on her monthly income. At the time of the signing of the contract, Lawrence explained to KAP that it protected her income from the "tax-man," but he probably also had in mind protecting her from herself. Future works by her, such as an anthology of her favorite short stories, would have their separate contracts and produce income above the $3,000 limit.

15. *Ship of Fools* the movie was in production at the time.

16. The poet Katherine Garrison Chapin Biddle (1890–1977) and U.S. attorney general Francis Biddle (1886–1968).

17. KAP is referring to the anthology of stories she had compiled, hoping it could be marketed as a college textbook. She never finished the preface, and the anthology was never published.

18. See Unrue, *Porter* 266–67.

19. Although KAP said more than once that she had purchased the coffin from a shop in Arizona, statements and correspondence in her papers show that the shop was in Montana.

20. See Paul Porter's recollection of the coffin purchase in "Katherine Anne Porter's Coffin: The Last Word?"

21. The coffin was eventually painted "Mexican style" by Joseph Mayhew, a retired Library of Congress employee and an artist interested in cartooning and science fiction. See "Joseph Mayhew, Painted KAP's Wooden Coffin."

22. Jeanne Bécu, Comtesse du Barry (1743–93), French courtesan, mistress of Louis XV of France, and a victim of the so-called Reign of Terror, a period from September 1793 to July 1794 marked by massive guillotine executions. See Allen, "Katherine Anne Porter: The Vanity of Excellence." KAP's humorous linking of herself with Mme du Barry is similar to her serious appropriation of Mary Queen of Scots's declaration ("In my end is my beginning") embroidered on her cloth of state while awaiting her own execution by beheading. The latter is KAP's epitaph.

23. See Unrue, *Porter* 84–87, 90, 92, 95, 97, 101, 102, 191, and 260.

24. See Unrue, *Porter* 91, 92, 94, 96, 126–27, 138, 260.

25. KAP admitted to an early and brief marriage, implying that it had not been consummated, and to her last two marriages. No one outside her family knew the full truth, although she divulged the number (without details) to Allen Tate.

26. Lopez, "A Country and Some People I Love."

27. Norbert Schlei (1929–2003) was an assistant attorney general in the Kennedy administration and a senior lawyer in the Johnson administration; he was the primary drafter of the Civil Rights Act of 1964 and the Voting Rights Act of 1965.

28. To date, these tapes have not been located. They are neither with Lopez's papers at UCLA nor with KAP's papers at the University of Maryland.

29. The essay continues with Lopez's account of the writing of his book. He says he dis-

covered contradictions in the taped interviews, but it is clear also that he misunderstood KAP's words, which were sometimes garbled in the tapes.

30. KAP, *The Never-Ending Wrong* (1977).

31. KAP, *Collected Essays* 313–51.

32. George Corley Wallace Jr. (1919–98), four-time governor of Alabama, was known for his pro-segregation attitude during the desegregation period, a position he altered after the 1964 Civil Rights Act. The 15 May 1972 assassination attempt, by Arthur Bremer, left Wallace paralyzed.

33. Norman Mailer (1923–2007), one of those associated with New Journalism and the author of well-known novels such as *The Naked and the Dead* (1948), was often the object of KAP's derision.

34. This story is no doubt fictionalized.

35. The quotation, which Mary Queen of Scots embroidered on her cloth of state, was one of KAP's favorites, and KAP chose it for her epitaph. The quotation has sometimes been credited to T. S. Eliot, whose poem "East Coker," the second of the *Four Quartets,* begins with the line, "In my beginning is my end."

36. This is the mass that KAP several times recalled attending as an adolescent and evoking her father's anti-papist bias. According to autobiographical notes in the Papers of KAP, Special Collections, University of Maryland, College Park, Libraries, Harrison Porter had asked her to explain the virgin birth. When she did, he told her that there was only one way for babies to be conceived and born and that any other explanation was irrational. This conversation is likely to have taken place when KAP and her sisters were placed temporarily in convent schools in San Antonio between 1902 and 1903.

37. James Farl Powers (1917–99), novelist and short-story writer who, like Flannery O'Connor, drew inspiration from his Roman Catholic faith, was one of KAP's friends and a writer she supported. See Unrue, *Porter* 220; Powers; and KAP to J. F. Powers, letters, in Porter, *Letters* 349–54, 494–97, 510–12, 520–22, 530, 545–46, 557, 572–73, 610–11, 621–22.

38. North Carolina poet Eleanor Ross Taylor (1920–) married Peter Taylor in 1943. Her published books of poetry include *Wilderness of Ladies* (1960), *Welcome Eumenides* (1972), and *New and Selected Poems* (1983).

39. To please her hostesses she is remembering some of her Roman Catholic friends.

40. Sister Maura Eichner, "Katherine Anne Porter (1890–1980)," *Baltimore Sun* 30 September 1980: A15.

41. KAP's response is an interesting equivocation. Not wanting to lie to these Catholic students or to the nuns, she gave an answer that could be interpreted to mean that the original of Adam Barclay in "Pale Horse, Pale Rider" was no more real than a ghost. She had often led others to believe that Adam was based on a real lover who had died during World War I. She told Barbara Wescott in a December 1962 letter that her lover's name had been Alexander and that she had changed his name to Adam in the story. As Jewel Brooker pointed out to me, however, Alexander Barclay is the name of the translator of Brant's *Das Narrenschiff,* which KAP read in Basel in 1932. Whether she deliberately chose the name as a private joke or pulled his name out of her subconscious memory is not clear. See KAP, *Letters,* 601–6.

42. The event was covered by a reporter for the *Baltimore Sun*. See Schoettler.

43. Pierre Teilhard de Chardin, S.J. (1881–1955), a French Jesuit priest, paleontologist, and philosopher, whose book *Le phénomène humain* (*The Phenomenon of Man*), written in 1938–40 and published in French in 1955 and in English in 1959, was denied publication in his lifetime by church superiors who disliked his liberal position on evolution. It was published posthumously after Pope John XXIII lifted the sanctions against it.

44. Father Joseph Gallagher.

45. Brackets by Sister Kathleen.

46. John David Horner (1924–93) was a graduate of Carnegie Mellon with a degree in engineering. He served in the Pacific during World War II, as a military attaché in Saigon in the 1950s, and later as a military aide in the White House. He was introduced to KAP by Bob Beach. Her friends were not surprised that she was drawn to the tall, handsome army major, who became a dependable friend to her in the last decade of her life.

47. Jennie Tourel Davidovich (1900–73), Russian-born mezzo soprano who made her debut in Paris in 1931 and at the Metropolitan Opera in New York in 1937. Denise Duval (1921–), French soprano known especially for her roles in operas by Francis Poulenc, one of KAP's favorite composers.

48. A comic operetta by Johann Strauss II (1825–99) with libretto by Carl Haffner and Richard Genée.

49. Although Capote and KAP were initially friendly, each became the object of the other's ridicule. Capote pilloried KAP in his unfinished *Answered Prayers* (1987), in which he based a fictional pair of lovers on KAP and William Goyen.

50. Barbara Harrison married Glenway Wescott's brother Lloyd. She provided sporadic financial support to KAP, who dedicated *Ship of Fools* to her.

51. See Blotner 457–58.

52. Kevin Foley, a local telephone company employee, was introduced by Dobson to KAP, who enjoyed the young Irishman's wit and humor.

53. See Kreiter-Foronda.

54. In the 1940s KAP had asked Glenway Wescott to be literary executor, but she withdrew the designation after their friendship collapsed. She had approached friends such as Robert Penn Warren and Eudora Welty, but each of them recognized the burden of functioning in that capacity in addition to commitments to their own writing and had suggested she look for younger persons. She wanted Peter Taylor, but he declined for reasons of time, too. She then looked at young academics who had written pieces about her fiction of which she approved. George Core had turned down the offer before she decided on Liberman. By that time, however, the designation was "literary trustee." Her attorney, E. Barrett Prettyman Jr., was to be executor.

55. Liberman curiously confuses KAP's marginalia in his book with that in George Hendrick's *Katherine Anne Porter* (1965). KAP made only factual corrections in Liberman's book, but her comments in Hendrick's were indeed vitriolic. Her rage at Hendrick, who had investigated her past and interviewed persons who had known her, revealed her fear that segments of her past life that she preferred to keep hidden would be exposed.

56. Liberman was asked to be KAP's literary trustee, not literary executor. See note 54.

57. The label given by journalists and commentators for President Richard Nixon's 20 October 1973 dismissal of Watergate special prosecutor Archibald Cox and the resignations of Attorney General Elliot Richardson and Deputy Attorney General William Ruckleshaus.

58. Warren's first wife, Emma Cinina Brescia Warren Gardner (1906–69).

59. Isabel Bayley (1911–93). Barbara Thompson Davis accepted the trusteeship after Bayley's death.

Part 7

1. Brooks's chronology of developing and executing the five-day itinerary is included in his essay "Hosting Miss Porter," a transcription of a talk Brooks gave at Southwestern Texas State University in April 1999 at the opening of an exhibit of his KAP archive.

2. KAP was familiar with Augustine's *City of God,* but his *Confessions* remained one of her favorite and most often reread works.

3. The verses explain that the Levitical law, the ceremonial law, was within the city (tabernacle or tent), but the sacrifice offered by Christ took place literally outside the walls of the city of Jerusalem and spiritually outside the realm of "law" so that it was by grace alone, free to anyone and everyone, not just to the Hebrews, but for the whole world to have a bright future of love, joy, and light (information supplied by Laughlin).

4. See *Collected Essays* 489.

5. The visit KAP made in 1936.

6. Bill Crider's mystery novel *Dying Voices,* set at a small four-year college during a seminar honoring a visiting author, echoes some of the HPU faculty's experiences at the 1976 KAP seminar.

7. KAP had accumulated more than a dozen Litt.D.'s by then.

8. The woman friend was Jane DeMouy, whose dissertation was revised and published as *Katherine Anne Porter's Women: The Eye of Her Fiction* (1983).

9. This story was a conflation of several similar stories KAP told dating from the 1920s through the 1940s. One encounter was with Carson McCullers at Yaddo. See Unrue, *Porter* 185.

10. KAP was a descendant of Daniel Boone's brother Jonathan and a several-times-removed cousin of William Sydney Porter, but a relationship to Cole Porter has not been established.

11. The lines "Life remains a blessing / Although you cannot bless" are from Auden's "As I Walked Out One Evening" (1940).

12. The Adam/Alexander story is a fabrication and one KAP encouraged.

13. Father Gallagher's comments omitted here are repeated in Lynn Darling's article (No. 52).

14. KAP's nephew Paul Porter.

15. Core and Hartley, eds., *Katherine Anne Porter: A Critical Symposium.*

16. Johnson, "Another Look at Katherine Anne Porter."

17. Rhea Johnson (1926–95) was born in Texas and received a degree in music from

Baylor University. He spent time in Hollywood with his friend Fess Parker and eventually worked for the Agency for International Development. As the boarder already in residence in the basement of the house KAP rented on Q Street in Georgetown, he became KAP's good friend and one of the few persons she allowed to peruse her baskets of manuscripts. It was he who found "Holiday" and "The Fig Tree," both of which had been written long before and forgotten by KAP. See Unrue, *Porter* 245, 262, 273.

18. In retrospect, Wojtasik thought Paul Porter and Barrett Prettyman allowed him to proceed with the letters edition only as a temporary amusement to KAP. Eventually, the McKeldin librarians denied him access to the letters.

19. KAP went to Mexico twice as an emissary of the U.S. Department of State to give lectures and readings. The first trip was made in 1960. The second was made in 1964, when she became very ill and asked that a priest come to her room in the Hotel Prado and administer last rites.

20. Ed Horner is John David Horner, also known as Jack Horner.

21. Katherine Mansfield (1888–1923) and John Middleton Murry (1889–1957) were husband and wife. In her 1937 review of *The Short Stories of Katherine Mansfield,* KAP praised Mansfield's "hard-won craftsmanship, a triumph of discipline over the unruly circumstances and confusions of her personal life and over certain destructive elements in her own nature" (*Collected Essays* 49–50).

22. KAP habitually referred to persons, especially biographers, who feasted off the renown of others as "hyenas."

23. KAP had been writing for many years; her earliest pieces were children's stories, journalistic pieces, and retold fairy tales. Her first original published story for adults was "María Concepción," which appeared in 1922.

24. Dolores del Rio (1904–83), Mexican film star in Hollywood during the silent era and later. Paul Porter was thinking of "María Concepción" for possible adaptation to film.

Works Cited

"Aguilera, Francisco." *National Directory of Latin Americanists.* 2nd ed. Hispanic Foundation Bibliographical Series 12. Washington, DC: Library of Congress, 1966: 13.

Allen, Henry. "Present at the Destruction." *Washington Post* 31 March 1974; *Potomac Magazine,* 12–14. Rpt. as "Katherine Anne Porter: The Vanity of Excellence" in Givner, *Conversations* 162–72.

Anderson, Elizabeth, with Gerald R. Kelly. *Miss Elizabeth: A Memoir.* Boston: Little, Brown, 1969.

Andrews, Gregg. "Robert Haberman, Socialist Ideology, and the Politics of National Reconstruction in Mexico, 1920–25." *Mexican Studies/Estudios Mexicanos* 6 (Summer 1990): 189–211.

Asch, Nathan. *Love in Chartres.* New York: A. & C. Boni, 1927.

Augustine of Hippo, Saint. *The Confessions.* Trans. E. B. Pusey. London: J. M. Dent, 1932. New York: Harcourt Brace, 1956.

Bayley, Isabel. "Forever May." Unpublished fragments of reminiscence. Papers of Isabel Bayley, Special Collections, U of Maryland, College Park.

Beals, Carleton. *Glass Houses: Ten Years of Freelancing.* Philadelphia: Lippincott, 1938.

"Bessie Beatty, 61, Commentator Dies." *New York Times* 7 April 1947: 23.

Blotner, Joseph. *Robert Penn Warren.* New York: Random House, 1997.

Brinnin, John Malcolm. *Dylan Thomas in America: An Intimate Journal.* Boston: Atlantic–Little, Brown, 1955.

Britton, John A. *Carleton Beals: A Radical Journalist in Latin America.* Albuquerque: U of New Mexico P, 1987.

Brooks, Cleanth. "The Woman and Artist I Knew." Machann and Clark 13–24.

Brooks, Roger. "Hosting Miss Porter." Machann and Clark 110–21.

Busby, Mark, and Dick Heaberlin, eds. *From Texas to the World and Back: Essays on the Journeys of Katherine Ann Porter.* Fort Worth: Texas Christian UP, 2001.

Cahill, Holger. *The Profane Earth.* New York: Macaulay, 1927.

Capote, Truman. *Answered Prayers: The Unfinished Novel.* London: Plume, 1987.

"Charles Shannon, an Art Instructor and Painter, 81." Obituary. *New York Times* 20 April 1996: 50.

Clark, Eleanor. "The Friendships of a Lifetime." *Washington Post Book World* 26 July 1981: 1–2, 9–10.

Coleridge, Samuel Taylor. *Cristabel.* 2nd ed. London: William Bulmer, 1816.

Connolly, Cyril. *The Unquiet Grave: A Word Cycle by Palinurus.* New York: Harper and Brothers, 1945.

Core, George, and Lodwick Hartley, eds. *Katherine Anne Porter: A Critical Symposium.* Athens: U of Georgia P, 1969.

Cowles, W. H. Report to W. J. Burns, Chief of the U.S. Bureau of Investigation (Department of Justice), 10 October 1921, Record of the U.S. Embassy in Mexico, vol. 12, National Archives, Washington, DC.

Cowley, Malcolm. *Exile's Return: A Narrative of Ideas.* New York: Norton, 1934. Rpt. as *Exile's Return: A Literary Odyssey of the 1920s.* New York: Viking, 1951.

Crawford, Kitty Barry. Letter to Donald Stalling, 23 March 1956. Papers of KAP, Special Collections, U of Maryland, College Park, Libraries.

———. Letter to George Hendrick, 13 November 1961. Collection of Darlene Harbour Unrue.

Crider, Bill. *Dying Voices.* New York: St. Martin's, 1989.

Crume, Paul. "*Pale Horse, Pale Rider: Three Short Novels,* by Katherine Anne Porter." *Southwest Review* 25.2 (1940): 213–18.

"Cyrilly Abels." Obituary. *New York Times* 9 November 1975: C9.

Darling, Lynn. "The Life of the Party: Celebrating Katherine Anne Porter's 91st Birthday." *Washington Post* 18 May 1981: C1, C6.

Davis, Barbara Thompson. Untitled and unpublished reminiscence. Written especially for this volume.

DeMouy, Jane Krause. "Elegy for Katherine Anne." *Virginia Quarterly Review* 75 (1999): 504–10.

———. *Katherine Anne Porter's Women: The Eye of Her Fiction.* Austin: U of Texas P, 1983.

Dobson, Clark. "An Unforgettable Decade." Reminiscence written especially for this volume.

Eichner, Sister Maura, S.S.N.D. "Katherine Anne Porter (1890–1980)," *Baltimore Sun* 30 September 1980: A15.

———. "Try It On." *Four Quarters* 21.1 (1971): 39.

———. "Visit to Katherine Anne Porter: after the stroke." *America* 15 November 1980: 302.

"Ernestine Evans, Editor-Critic 77." Obituary. *New York Times* 4 July 1967: 19.

Feeley, Kathleen, S.S.N.D. "In My End Is My Beginning." Reminiscence written especially for this volume.

"Francisco Aguilera Dies: LC Hispanic Specialist from 1944 to 1969." *Library of Congress Information Bulletin* 19 June 1981: 216.

"Francisco Aguilera: Specialist in Hispanic Culture." Obituary. *Washington Post* 14 June 1981: B4.

Gallagher, Joseph. "Katherine Anne Porter: The Last Candle Is Out." *Baltimore Evening Sun* 30 September 1980: A11.

Givner, Joan. *Katherine Anne Porter: A Life.* New York: Simon and Schuster, 1982. Rev. ed. Athens: U of Georgia P, 1991.

———, ed. *Katherine Anne Porter: Conversations.* Jackson: UP of Mississippi, 1987.

Glendinning, Victoria. *Edith Sitwell: A Unicorn Among Lions*. New York: Knopf, 1981.

Goyen, William. "Katherine Anne Porter: An Appreciation." *Dallas Morning News* 28 September 1980: G1.

———. *Selected Letters from a Writer's Life*. Ed. Robert Phillips. Austin: U of Texas P, 1995.

Hardwick, Elizabeth. "Katherine Anne." *Vanity Fair* March 1984: 81–85.

Hardy, John Edward. "Remembering KAP." Unpublished reminiscence. Collection of Darlene Harbour Unrue.

Hendrick, George. *Katherine Anne Porter*. New York: Twayne, 1965.

Hendrick, George, and Willene Hendrick. *Katherine Anne Porter*. Rev. ed. Boston: Twayne/G. K. Hall, 1988.

Hendrick, Willene. "Indian Creek: A Sketch from Memory." Machann and Clark 3–12.

Herbst, Josephine. "Miss Porter and Miss Stein." *Partisan Review* 15 (1948): 568–72.

———. *The Starched Blue Sky of Spain and Other Memoirs*. New York: HarperCollins, 1992.

———. "A Year of Disgrace." *Noble Savage* 3 (1961): 128–60. Rpt. in *The Starched Blue Sky of Spain and Other Memoirs* 53–98.

Hill, Winifred. Personal interview with Darlene Harbour Unrue. 17 August 1981.

Hilt, Kathryn, and Ruth M. Alvarez. *Katherine Anne Porter: An Annotated Bibliography*. New York: Garland, 1990.

Holloway, Gay Porter. Letters to Katherine Anne Porter, 25 July 1954, 14 December 1955, 25 February 1956, 18 October 1961, 22 January 1962, and 3 November 1962. Papers of Katherine Anne Porter, Special Collections, U of Maryland, College Park, Libraries.

Hooks, Margaret. *Tina Modotti: Photographer and Revolutionary*. New York: Pandora, 1993.

Hoover, J. Edgar. Memorandum. 2 August 1921. U.S. Department of Justice, Bureau of Investigation, File number 25-230.

Humphrey, William. *Home from the Hill*. New York: Knopf, 1958.

Jaeger, Art. "Celebrated Writer Assigned Guardian." *Prince Georges County Journal* 5 October 1977: 1, 7.

Jewell, Edward Allen. "Three Phases of a Hardy Perennial [Ernest Stock]." *New York Times* 14 April 1935: X7.

Johns, Erna Schlemmer. Letters to Katherine Anne Porter, 3 May 1939 and 13 April 1978. Papers of Katherine Anne Porter, Special Collections, U of Maryland, College Park, Libraries.

———. *To Whom It May Concern*. 2 vols. Austin: Privately printed, 1977.

Johns, Glover S., Jr. *The Clay Pigeons of St Lô*. Harrisburg, PA: Military Publishing, 1958.

Johns, Rita. Personal interview with Darlene Harbour Unrue. 29 October 1994.

Johnson, James William. "Another Look at Katherine Anne Porter." *Virginia Quarterly Review* 36 (1960): 598–613. Rpt. in Core and Hartley 83–96.

Jones, Lan J. *Renegades, Showmen, and Angels: A Theatrical History of Fort Worth from 1873–2001*. Fort Worth: Texas Christian UP, 2006.

"Joseph Mayhew, Painted KAP's Wooden Coffin." *Newsletter of the Katherine Anne Porter Society* 8 (2001): 11.

"Joseph Retinger, Polish Diplomat." Obituary. *New York Times* 24 June 1970: 27.

"Josephine Herbst, Novelist and Social-Political Reporter, Dead." *New York Times* 29 January 1969: L38.

Josephson, Matthew. *Life among the Surrealists.* New York: Holt, Rinehart and Winston, 1962.

"Katherine A. Porter Gives Books, Grant to Md. U. Library." *Washington Post* 21 December 1966: C3.

Katherine Anne Porter: The Eye of Memory. A film produced by Calvin Skaggs. Lumiere Productions, 1988.

Kempf, James Michael. *The Early Career of Malcolm Cowley: A Humanist among the Moderns.* Baton Rouge: Louisiana State UP, 1981.

Kreiter-Foronda, Carolyn. "On 'Katherine Anne Porter's Secret.'" *Newsletter of the Katherine Anne Porter Society* 12 (2005): 5.

Kunitz, Stanley, ed. *Authors Today and Yesterday.* New York: H. W. Wilson, 1933.

Kunitz, Stanley, and Veneta Colby, eds. *Twentieth Century Authors—First Supplement—A Biographical Dictionary of Modern Literature.* New York: H. W. Wilson, 1955.

Kunitz, Stanley, and Howard Haycraft, eds. *Twentieth Century Authors—A Biographical Dictionary of Modern Literature.* New York: H. W. Wilson, 1942.

Langer, Elinor. *Josephine Herbst.* Boston: Little, Brown, 1984. Rpt. Boston: Northeastern UP, 1994.

Langer, Susanne K. *Philosophy in a New Key: A Study in the Symbolism of Reason, Rite, and Art.* Cambridge: Harvard UP, 1942.

Laughlin, Charlotte. "How I Accompanied Katherine Anne Porter on the Last Great Pilgrimage of Her Life." Reminiscence written especially for this volume.

Lawrence, D. H. *Mornings in Mexico.* New York: Knopf, 1927.

Lawrence, Seymour. Letter to Darlene Harbour Unrue, 9 December 1992. Collection of Darlene Harbour Unrue.

"Legends in the Law: A Conversation with E. Barrett Prettyman." http://www.dcbar.org/for_lawyers/resources/legends_in_the_law/prettyman.cfm.

Letters of Flannery O'Connor: The Habit of Being. Ed. Sally Fitzgerald. New York: Farrar, Straus and Giroux, 1979.

Liberman, M. M. *Katherine Anne Porter's Fiction.* Detroit: Wayne State UP, 1971.

———. "Meeting Miss Porter." *Georgia Review* 41 (1987): 299–303.

———. "The Responsibility of the Novelist: The Critical Reception of *Ship of Fools.*" *Criticism* 8 (1966): 377–88.

Locher, David. "Katherine Anne Porter." Unpublished reminiscence. Collection of Darlene Harbour Unrue.

———. "Summer Straw & Blue (Ann Arbor, July 1954)." *America* 16–23 July 1977: 23.

Lopez, Enrique Hank. *Conversations with Katherine Anne Porter: Refugee from Indian Creek.* Boston: Little, Brown, 1981.

————. "A Country and Some People I Love." *Harper's Magazine* September 1965: 58–68. Rpt. in Givner, *Conversations* 120–34.

Machann, Clinton, and William Bedford Clark, eds. *Katherine Anne Porter and Texas: An Uneasy Relationship.* College Station: Texas A&M UP, 1990.

MacKinnon, Janice R., and Stephen R. MacKinnon. *Agnes Smedley: The Life and Times of an American Radical.* Berkeley: U of California P, 1988.

Makowsky, Veronica A. *Caroline Gordon: A Biography.* New York: Oxford UP, 1989.

Mallett, Daniel Trowbridge. "Ernest Stock." *Mallett's Index of Artists: International— Biographical.* New York: Peter Smith, 1948. 811.

Marlor, Clark S. "Ernest Stock." *The Society of Independent Artists: The Exhibition Record, 1917–1944.* Park Ridge, NJ: Noyes P, 1984. 600.

McAlexander, Hubert H. *Peter Taylor: A Writer's Life.* Baton Rouge: Louisiana State UP, 2001.

Meyers, Jeffrey. *Edmund Wilson: A Biography.* Boston: Houghton Mifflin, 1995.

Miller, William D. *Dorothy Day: A Biography.* New York: Harper and Row, 1982.

Moore, Marianne. *The Complete Poems of Marianne Moore.* New York: Viking, 1967.

Naylor, Pauline. "Early Porter Tales Written Here." *Fort Worth Star-Telegram* 17 April 1966, sec. 5: 16.

————. "Katherine Anne Porter's Ft. Worth Days Recalled." *Fort Worth Star-Telegram* 10 April 1966, sec. 5: 16.

O'Brien, Edward J., ed. *The Best Short Stories of 1923 and The Yearbook of the American Short Story.* Boston: Small, Maynard, 1924.

O'Connor, Frank, and William Maxwell. *The Happiness of Getting It Right: Letters of Frank O'Connor and William Maxwell, 1945–1966.* Ed. Michael Steinman. New York: Knopf, 1996.

Olsen, Tillie. *Silences.* New York: Delacorte/Seymour Lawrence, 1978.

Pearson, John. *The Sitwells: A Family Biography.* New York: Harcourt Brace, 1978.

Plunkett, Robert. Telephone interviews with Darlene Harbour Unrue. 11 May 2006 and 13 October 2007.

Porter, Breckenridge. Telephone interview with Darlene Harbour Unrue. 12 April 1997.

Porter, Katherine Anne. "A Christmas Story." *Mademoiselle,* December 1946: 155, 277–79. Rpt. as separate publication by Seymour Lawrence/Delacorte, 1967.

————. "The Circus." *Southern Review* 1 (1935): 36–41. Rpt. in *Collected Stories* 343–48.

————. *The Collected Essays and Occasional Writings of Katherine Anne Porter.* New York: Seymour Lawrence/Delacorte, 1970. Rpt. Boston: Houghton Mifflin/Seymour Lawrence, 1990.

————. *The Collected Stories of Katherine Anne Porter.* New York: Harcourt Brace, 1965.

————. "The Cracked Looking-Glass." *Scribner's Magazine* May 1932: 271–76, 313–20. Rpt. in *Collected Stories* 103–34.

————. "A Day's Work." *The Nation,* 10 February 1940: 205–7, 226–34. Rpt. in *Collected Stories* 388–406.

————. *The Days Before.* New York: Harcourt Brace, 1952.

———. "A Defense of Circe." *Mademoiselle*, June 1954: 46, 48, 96–97. Rpt. as book *A Defense of Circe*. New York: Harcourt Brace, 1955.

———. "The Downward Path to Wisdom." *Harper's Bazaar*, December 1939: 72–73, 140, 142, 144–45, 147. Rpt. in *Collected Stories* 369–87.

———. "Example to the Young." *The New Republic* 22 April 1931: 279–80. Rpt. in *"This Strange, Old World"* 101–5.

———. "The Fig Tree." *Harper's* June 1960: 55–59. Rpt. in *Collected Stories* 352–61.

———. "Flowering Judas." *Hound & Horn* 3 (1930): 316–31. Rpt. in *Collected Stories* 90–102.

———. *Flowering Judas*. Limited edition. New York: Harcourt Brace, 1930.

———. *Flowering Judas and Other Stories*. New York: Harcourt Brace, 1935.

———. "The Future Is Now." *Mademoiselle* November 1950: 75, 130–32.

———. "The Grave." *Virginia Quarterly Review* 11 (1935): 177–83. Rpt. in *Collected Stories* 362–68.

———. "Hacienda." *Virginia Quarterly Review* 8 (1932): 556–69.

———. *Hacienda*. New York: Harrison of Paris, 1934. Rpt. in *Collected Stories* 135–70.

———. "He." *New Masses* 3 (1927): 13–15. Rpt. in *Collected Stories* 49–58.

———. "Holiday." *Atlantic Monthly* December 1960: 44–56. Rpt. in *Collected Stories* 407–35.

———. "The Jilting of Granny Weatherall." *transition* 15 (1929): 139–46. Rpt. in *Collected Stories* 80–89.

———. *Katherine Anne Porter's French Song-Book*. New York: Harrison of Paris, 1933. Rpt. in *Katherine Anne Porter's Poetry* 95–149.

———. *Katherine Anne Porter's Poetry*. Ed. Darlene Harbour Unrue. Columbia: U of South Carolina P, 1996.

———. "The Leaning Tower." *Southern Review* 7 (1941): 219–79. Rpt. in *Collected Stories* 436–95.

———. *The Leaning Tower and Other Stories*. New York: Harcourt Brace, 1944.

———. *Letters of Katherine Anne Porter*. Ed. Isabel Bayley. New York: Atlantic Monthly, 1990.

———. "Magic." *transition* 13 (1928): 229–31. Rpt. in *Collected Stories* 39–41.

———. "María Concepción." *Century* 105 (1922): 224–39. Rpt. in *Collected Stories* 3–21.

———. "The Martyr." *Century* 106 (1923): 410–13. Rpt. in *Collected Stories* 33–38.

———. *My Chinese Marriage*, by M. T. F. New York: Duffield, 1921. Rpt. as *Mae Franking's My Chinese Marriage*. Ed. Holly Franking. Austin: U of Texas P, 1991.

———. *The Never-Ending Wrong*. Boston: Atlantic–Little, Brown, 1977.

———. "Noon Wine." *Story* 10 (1937): 71–103. Rpt. in *Collected Stories* 222–68.

———. "Notes on the Texas I Remember." *Atlantic Monthly* March 1975: 102–6.

———. "Old Mortality." *Southern Review* 2 (1937): 686–735. Rpt. in *Collected Stories* 173–221.

———. "The Old Order." *Southern Review* 1 (1936): 495–509. Rpt. as "The Journey," *Collected Stories* 326–40.

———. *Outline of Mexican Popular Arts and Crafts.* Los Angeles: Young and McCallister, 1922. Rpt. in *Uncollected Early Prose* 136–87.

———. "Pale Horse, Pale Rider." *Southern Review* 3 (1938): 417–66. Rpt. in *Collected Stories* 269–317.

———. *Pale Horse, Pale Rider: Three Short Novels.* New York: Harcourt Brace, 1939.

———. "Portrait: Old South." *Mademoiselle* February 1944: 89, 151–54.

———. "The Real Ray." *Motion Picture Magazine* October 1920: 36–37, 102.

———. "Rope." *The Second American Caravan.* Ed. Alfred Kreymborg. New York: Macaulay, 1928. 362–68. Rpt. in *Collected Stories* 42–48.

——— "Ship of Fools." *Atlantic Monthly* March 1956: 33–38.

———. *Ship of Fools.* Boston: Atlantic–Little, Brown, 1962.

———. "The Source." *Accent* Spring 1941: 144–47. Rpt. in *Collected Stories* 321–25.

———. "The Spivvleton Mystery." *Ladies' Home Journal* August 1971: 74–75, 101.

———. "That Tree." *Virginia Quarterly Review* 10 (1934): 351–61. Rpt. in *Collected Stories* 66–79.

———. "Theft." *Gyroscope* November 1929: 21–25. Rpt. in *Collected Stories* 59–65.

———. *"This Strange, Old World" and Other Books Reviews by Katherine Anne Porter.* Ed. Darlene Harbour Unrue. Athens: U of Georgia P, 1991.

———. "Two Plantation Portraits" ("The Witness" and "The Last Leaf"). *Virginia Quarterly Review* 11 (1935): 85–92.

———. *Uncollected Early Prose of Katherine Anne Porter.* Ed. Ruth M. Alvarez and Thomas F. Walsh. Austin: U of Texas P, 1993.

———. "Virgin Violeta." *Century* 109 (1924): 261–68. Rpt. in *Collected Stories* 22–32.

———. "You Are What You Read." *Vogue* October 1974: 248, 250, 252.

Porter, Paul. "A Bouquet for Aunt Katherine." *Newsletter of the Katherine Anne Porter Society* 12 (2005): 1, 2, 4.

———. "Katherine Anne Porter's Coffin: The Last Word?" *Newsletter of the Katherine Anne Porter Society* 5 (1998): 1, 8.

———. "Remembering Aunt Katherine." Machann and Clark 25–37.

Powers, Katherine A. "Katherine Anne Porter, J. F. Powers, and Katherine A. Powers." *Newsletter of the Katherine Anne Porter Society* 9 (2007): 1, 2.

Prettyman, E. Barrett, Jr. "My Years with Katherine Anne—as Friend and Lawyer." Reminiscence written especially for this volume.

Prince, John. Untitled and unpublished reminiscence. Papers of John and Catherine Prince, Special Collections, U of Maryland, College Park.

Prokosch, Frederic. "The Nightmare of Literary Life." *Harper's* March 1983: 58–59.

Retinger, Jerome Joseph. *Memoirs of an Eminence Grise.* Ed. John Pomian. Foreword by H. R. H. Prince Bernhard of the Netherlands. Sussex, UK: The UP, 1972.

"Roberto Haberman Dead at 79: Founder of Mexican Labor Unit." *New York Times* 5 March 1962: 23.

Rockwell, Jeanne. "The Magic Cloak: On Meeting Katherine Anne Porter." *Michigan Quarterly Review* 5 (1966): 283–84.

Rollins, William, Jr. *The Shadow Before*. New York: Robert McBride, 1934.

Rueckert, William H. *Glenway Wescott*. New York: Twayne, 1965.

Ruoff, James. "Katherine Anne Porter Comes to Kansas." *Midwest Quarterly* 4 (1963): 305–14.

Schoettler, Carl. "Katherine Anne Porter Reigns for Students." *Baltimore Evening Sun*, 15 April 1974: B1. Rpt. in Givner, *Conversations* 173–76.

Schorer, Mark. "We're All on the Passenger List." *New York Time Book Review* 1 April 1962: 1, 5.

Scott, Michael. "A Classic Manner." *The Spokesman* 63 (Spring 1965–66): 19–22.

Scowcroft, Richard. Telephone interview with Darlene Harbour Unrue. 9 July 1995.

Sexton, Kathryn Adams. "Katherine Anne Porter's Years in Denver." Unpublished M.A. thesis, U of Colorado, 1961.

Shapiro, Karl. *Collected Poems, 1940–1978*. New York: Random House, 1978.

Shi, David E. *Matthew Josephson, Bourgeois Bohemian*. New Haven: Yale UP, 1981.

Spencer, Elizabeth. *Landscapes of the Heart: A Memoir*. New York: Random House, 1998.

Spender, Stephen. Afterword. *William Goyen: Selected Letters from a Writer's Life*. Ed. Robert Phillips. Austin: U of Texas P, 1998. 411–13.

Stalling, Donald. "Katherine Anne Porter: Life and the Literary Mirror." Unpublished M.A. thesis, Texas Christian U, 1951.

Thompson, Barbara. "Katherine Anne Porter: An Interview." *Paris Review* 29.1 (1963): 87–114. Rpt. in Givner, *Conversations* 78–98.

———. "Katherine Anne Porter: Mistress of the Grand Gesture." *Washington Post and Times Herald* 25 November 1956: F7.

Unrue, Darlene Harbour. "The Game Players: Katherine Anne Porter and William Goyen." *Mississippi Quarterly* 49.1 (1995–96): 119–26.

———. *Katherine Anne Porter: The Life of an Artist*. Jackson: UP of Mississippi, 2005.

Ureña, Pedro Henriquez. *Honenaje a Salomón de la Selva: 1959–1969*. León, Nicaragua: Cuadeemos Universitarios, 1969.

Vann, William H. *The Texas Institute of Letters, 1936–1966*. Austin: Encino, 1967.

"Von Pless." Obituary. *Buffalo Evening News* 29 March 1954: 23.

Walsh, Thomas F. *Katherine Anne Porter and Mexico: The Illusion of Eden*. Austin: U of Texas P, 1992.

Warren, Robert Penn. *All the King's Men*. New York: Harcourt Brace, 1946.

Welty, Eudora. *A Curtain of Green and Other Stories*. New York: Doubleday Doran, 1941.

———. "My Introduction to Katherine Anne Porter." *Georgia Review* 44.1–2 (1990): 13–27.

Wescott, Glenway. "Katherine Anne Porter: The Making of a Novel." *Atlantic Monthly* April 1962: 43–49.

Wilkins, William R. Personal interviews with Darlene Harbour Unrue. 27 May 1955, Baltimore, and 13 August 1997, College Park, Maryland.

Willison, Florence (Toni). Personal interviews with Darlene Harbour Unrue. 13–14 June 1996, South Hill, Malta, NY.

Wilson, Edmund. *I Thought of Daisy*. New York: Scribner's, 1929.

Winslow, Marcella Comès. *Brushes with the Literary: Letters of a Washington Artist, 1943–1959*. Baton Rouge: Louisiana State UP, 1993.

Wojtasik, Ted. "The Final Year of Katherine Anne Porter." Reminiscence written especially for this volume.

Wolfe, Bertram D. *The Fabulous Life of Diego Rivera*. New York: Stein and Day, 1963.

Wood, Sally, ed. *The Southern Mandarins: Letters of Caroline Gordon to Sally Wood, 1924–1937*. Baton Rouge: Louisiana State UP, 1984.

Woolf, Virginia. *A Writer's Diary: Being Extracts from the Diary of Virginia Woolf*. Ed. Leonard Woolf. London: Hogarth, 1953.

Yeats, William Butler. *Responsibilities and Other Poems*. New York: MacMillan, 1916.

Index

Porter, Katherine Anne (*continued*)
honesty of, 135; honorary degrees received by, 67, 122, 206, 212, 237, 280n26; house owned by, 67, 88, 103; humility of, 199; idols of, 73, 147; illnesses of, 2, 7, 29, 32–33, 58–59, 63, 77, 96, 106–7, 113, 118, 129, 141, 166, 187, 209, 253, 269n40, 270n41, 270n48, 275n2; imaginary life of, 188, 190; impertinence of, 225; impressions stored up by, 219–20; impromptu performances of, 100; income earned by, 192; influences on, 90, 179; and isolation, 67, 115; jewelry owned by, 118, 119, 128, 141, 157, 194, 199, 203, 212, 219, 237, 243, 260; and Joan of Arc, 147; jokes told by, 75; journalism career of, 22, 23, 25, 29–31, 268n23, 269n40; Katherine Anne Porter Foundation established by, 185; kindness of, 185, 222; knowledge of, 107; as lady, 110; legal problems of, 186; letter writing of, 62, 81; library of, 70; as Library of Congress fellow, 103, 109–10, 155, 278n2; literary reputation of, 142; literary standards of, 120; literature important to, 119; Little Theater career of, 28, 269n38; loneliness of, 113, 129, 160, 181, 202; love affairs of, 35, 38, 46, 103, 109, 111, 140, 141, 161, 166–67, 283n22; loving spirit of, 220; loyalty of, 116; magazine subscriptions of, 70; make-believe love affairs of, 141, 188; malicious spirit of, 63; marginalia by, 226, 250, 288n55; marriages of, 2, 7, 9, 55, 69, 82, 103, 114–15, 116, 140, 141, 165, 202, 278n47, 279n12, 282n2, 286n25; meals served by, 73, 92, 108, 128, 143, 159–60, 162, 187, 203, 205, 208, 212, 226; as mentor, 220; mesmerizing ability of, 4, 46; monkey owned by, 34, 270n54; music preferred by, 69–70, 116, 218; mystical experience of, 59; as mythic figure, 152; names known by, 4–5, 7, 21, 139, 165, 268n22; narrative art of, 62; near-death experiences of, 248; as nest builder, 141; operas attended by, 218–19; overdressed fluffiness of, 140; papers placed by, 179; paralysis of, 130, 163, 188, 209,

213, 221, 241; paranoia of, 4, 188, 248, 254; perfumes preferred by, 76, 124; petite size of, 218; phonograph recordings by, 58; photographers disapproved by, 57; pilgrimage to Lourdes desired by, 168; and Pindar, 199–200; pleasantness of, 169; poetry loved by, 71, 116; political activities of, 103; posing for photographs, 117, 155, 159; possessions of, 33, 34, 119, 128, 130, 141, 148, 159, 162, 192, 198; poverty of, 7, 118; as prima donna, 106, 107, 112; prize money lost by, 51; property owned by, 280n19; publishers of, 137, 139, 143, 144; pure, organic language defended by, 120; quotations favored by, 213, 214; as raconteur, 183, 204, 212; on radio programs, 106, 109, 250; reading and speaking career of, 99, 169; recipes of, 72, 73, 81, 108, 109, 238, 260; recklessness of, 75; reconciliation with Roman Catholic Church, 211–12; as recondite writer, 174; religious ancestry of, 232; residences of, 33, 34, 42, 44–45, 48, 50, 53, 55, 63, 65, 67, 69, 76, 77, 81, 82, 83, 86, 89, 90, 91, 92, 94, 96–97, 98, 105, 106, 110, 112, 115, 119, 121–22, 125, 128, 143, 147, 154, 155, 156, 157–58, 159, 161, 165, 184, 191, 192, 194, 197–98, 208, 211, 212, 226, 237, 241, 244–45, 250, 255, 260; resilience of, 132, 142; restlessness of, 110, 202; revolutionary friends of, 37; as role model, 212; Roman Catholicism of, 60, 110, 114, 171, 179, 211; romantic inclinations of, 83, 141; as rounder, 79; Russian works introduced to, 20; sadness of, 93, 181, 190, 202; seizure suffered by, 210; self-destructive mood of, 185; sense of humor of, 49, 74, 209, 256; sense of joy of, 213; sensitivity of, 110, 254; serenity of, 171, 247; sharp tongue of, 4; shuttle take-off viewed by, 187; sincerity of, 199; singing of, 20; smile of, 190, 242; smoking by, 140; and *Snow White*, 207; as sob-sister, 31; social grace of, 170; social life of, 109; social talent of, 3; socializing of, 49; sophistication of, 141; speaking career of, 55, 58, 73, 98, 103, 124, 126, 135, 137, 187, 202, 212;

Tourel, Jennie, 218, 288n47
Townsend, Herbert, 79
Trenet, Charles, 70, 277n30
Trilling, Diana, 134
Trilling, Lionel, 134
Tworkov, Jack, 66

Ulysses (Joyce), 172
"Under Milkwood" (Thomas), 127
University of California, Los Angeles: archives at, 2
University of Kansas: writers' workshop, 124
University of Maryland, College Park, 189; archives at, 2; Katherine Anne Porter Room in McKeldin Library, 128; papers donated to, 179
University of Michigan, Ann Arbor, 124, 126, 137, 145–46, 151
University of Texas at Austin: archives at, 2; confusion about library to be named for KAP, 284n51; intended as repository of KAP papers, 177
University of Virginia, 137, 155
University of Wichita, 137, 171
Unquiet Grave, The (Connolly), 181
Unrue, Darlene Harbour: *Katherine Anne Porter: The Life of an Artist* (Unrue), 2, 3

Vagabond Players, 26
"Virgin Violeta" (Porter), 274n45
Virginia Quarterly Review, 139
Volckman, Nancy, 194, 195
Vonnegut, Kurt, 143

Wallace, George, 207, 287n32
Waller, Fats, 70
Walsh, Thomas F., 2; *Katherine Anne Porter and Mexico: The Illusion of Eden*, 2
War and Peace (Prokofiev), 219
Warren, Cinina Brescia, 226, 289n58
Warren, Eleanor Clark. *See* Clark, Eleanor.
Warren, Gabriel, 113, 117
Warren, Robert Penn, 71, 81, 98, 105, 113, 128, 129, 172, 187, 207, 212, 220, 226, 229, 245, 277n33
Warren, Rosanna, 113, 117, 220
Washington and Lee University, 137, 165

Washington, DC, 34, 77, 105, 106, 128, 147, 154, 156, 159, 167, 184, 191, 194, 197–98, 244–45
Weeks, Edward, 143
Welty, Eudora, 55, 74, 84, 105, 130, 135, 172, 185, 191, 208, 214–15, 220; *Curtain of Green, A*, 87, 94, 95; "Death of a Traveling Salesman," 84; "Memory, A," 94; "Old Mr. Marblehall," 94; *The Robber Bridegroom*, 87
Wescott, Barbara Harrison, 55, 70, 124, 127, 220, 288n50
Wescott, Glenway, 4, 55, 57, 74, 88, 127, 185, 187, 188, 191, 192, 195, 206, 220, 226, 248, 251
Wheeler, Monroe, 55, 74, 108, 124, 127, 181, 187, 191, 207, 220, 221, 229, 248–49, 250, 251, 256, 276n10
Wilkins, David, 206
Wilkins, Fern Stahl, 206, 207
Wilkins, Robin, 206, 207
Wilkins, William R. (Bill), 206, 237, 238, 254, 257
Williams, Oscar, 127
Willison, Florence (Toni) Hauser, 55, 66, 97, 210
Willison, George Findlay, 66, 67, 97; *Saints and Strangers*, 67, 97
Willison, Malcolm, 66, 67, 276n19
Wilson, Desmond, 157
Wilson, Edmund, 46, 181, 182, 203; *I Thought of Daisy*, 272n18
Winslow, Harriet, 107
Winslow, John (Johnny), 108, 110
Winslow, Marcella Comès, 3, 105, 106
Winslow, Mary, 108, 110
Winslow, William Randolph, 103
Winters, Janet Lewis, 5, 122
Winters, Yvor, 122
Wolf Trap Farm Park, 219
Woodburn, John, 87, 89, 92
"Wooden Umbrella, The" (Porter), 115
Woolf, Leonard, 157
Woolf, Virginia, 62, 140, 157, 245
Wojtasik, Ted, 131, 229, 244; as KAP's last beloved, 251–52
Wright, Richard, 49, 174, 274n38